Reflections on Life

LIVING ONE WORD AT A TIME

Paul Goeller

I dedicate this book to my loving wife of over 50 years.

May, it is to you that I owe so very much.

PROLOGUE

Some years ago—perhaps about 20—I was browsing in a bookstore when I happened to pick up a daily devotional. I was impressed by the simple design of a scripture for each day and a page of encouraging words. I thought to myself that I would like to do that someday.

Over two years ago—July of 2023, actually—I came across a "One Word a Day" devotional published by Guideposts. My wife and I thought this would be good to add to our nightly reading along with our other evening devotions. Shortly after starting, I got to thinking that perhaps it was time for me to do the same.

For the first week or so, I used the same one word as the devotional but added my own thoughts. It was not long before I was "finding" my own words to write about.

It just seemed like one word led to another. In the course of the year that followed, I was never without a "word" to write about— actually, I had a rather long list of words. I discovered something about myself (that I probably knew already): I seem to have something to say about just about everything.

Not sure that is a good characteristic, but I must say I have enjoyed putting "pen to paper."

There were times when I knew pretty much what I wanted to say about a subject, but often what I actually wrote was very different. At other times I was clueless as to what to write but just went with the first thought that came to my head. So it really was a sort of adventure for me—never sure of what I would actually write, and often surprised. Some of the things I wrote were not typically mainstream, and I myself was convicted of some wrong thinking along the way. I have concluded that much of what I have written is directed toward me and my own personal spiritual maturity.

I shared each devotion with a small group of friends via text. I know some got bored or otherwise stopped reading, while others encouraged me. It seemed like what I wrote was often useful to others besides myself.

I am pretty sure that some of these devotions have been inspired by God. I wish I could say they all were, but I know my flesh can get in the middle of things. Regardless, I am confident that God can use these devotions to help draw all of us closer to Him.

And that is my prayer and my hope: that everyone who might come across these devotions would be drawn into a deeper, more intimate relationship with God.

AUTHOR

Paul Goeller - Born. In 1942, married to May since 1973. Devoted believer since 1977 - served as deacon and elder multiple times and has been a small group leader for many years.

TABLE OF CONTENTS

1.BOW

Psalms 5:7 (NIV)

But I, by your great love, can come into your house; in reverence I bow down toward your holy temple.

Square dancing begins with a bow—perhaps it would be useful for us to also begin our days with a bow? A bow indicates that we are approaching a person, a situation, or anything else with reverence, respect, and honor. No grumbling or complaining or even a low growl. Just a simple awareness that today is the day that the Lord has made, and a choice to receive that day and every person or situation in it as sent by the Lord.

How would our days be if we began with a quick moment of reverent pause—a bow of respect, humility, deference, and submission to our Lord and His provisions?

So let us begin this "one word" journey together by bowing before our Creator God. Let us acknowledge that without Him we are in trouble. Let us stay mindful that life can be a great adventure—but the greatest adventure, and the richest rewards, come when we reverently bow before the Lord of the universe.

When we bow, we are not just lowering our heads, we are lifting our hearts. We are choosing humility over pride, trust over fear, and dependence over self-reliance. A bow is more than a gesture—it is a posture of the soul that says, Lord, I belong to You, and I want to follow Your lead today.

Lord, please lead us to begin every day with a bow. Let it be so, Lord.

2.START

Psalms 110:7 (NIV)

He will drink from a brook along the way, and so he will lift his head high.

I read that a glass of water right after waking is good for the body. How should we, as Christians, start our days? Perhaps the point the Psalmist was making is that our bodies need nourishment to be refreshed. The point I want to make is that followers of Jesus would be wise to start the day with spiritual nourishment.

It makes sense to start the day with intention—placing ourselves in the presence of the Almighty so that we can receive the spiritual nourishment needed for the day. There are many ways to do this, but praying through the Scriptures is an especially good way.

Simply select a book (perhaps the Psalms or one of the Gospels), read a few verses, and then pray about what you have just read. Ask God to give you insight into how those words can be applied in your life.

Lord, please lead us to start our days in Your presence.

3.PLANT

Exodus 15:17 (NIV)

You will bring them in and plant them on the mountain of your inheritance— the place, LORD, you made for your dwelling, the sanctuary, Lord, your hands established.

My wife, May, and I love flowers and plants. Watching things grow has always brought us great joy. Over the years, we have learned that where a plant is placed, and how it is nurtured, makes all the difference in the world.

For a plant to yield good fruit with great abundance it must be planted in good soil and placed where it will receive the proper amount of nourishment. As its roots grow deep it has all it needs to produce an abundant harvest.

The same truth applies to us as individuals. You may have heard the expression, "bloom where you are planted." It sounds good, but it cannot work if the soil of your soul is lacking in nutrients and is not being nurtured by God's Word.

When a poorly rooted plant is buffeted by wind and rain it often fails to produce good fruit, and sometimes even dies prematurely. The same applies to us—to bear good fruit for God we need to be planted deeply in good soil and rooted in the Word of God.

Lord, please plant us deeply in the good soil of Your word— use us, Lord, to bear fruit for Your kingdom.

4.SOAR

Isaiah 40:30-31 (NIV)

Even youths grow tired and weary, and young men stumble and fall; but those who hope (wait) in the LORD will renew their strength. They will soar on wings like eagles; they will run and not grow weary; they will walk and not be faint.

These are a couple of my very favorite verses. I quoted them often over the years, which is really kind of strange. I am an impatient person. I do not like waiting. I would rather be "doing" than sitting around waiting and hoping in the Lord.

So, I live in this conflicted state a lot. I want to be "doing," and yet I know it is more important to be "being." After all, we are called human "beings," not human "doings."

If I really want to SOAR, I must wait on God. Put all of my trust in Him and totally surrender. Otherwise, instead of soaring I end up more like a "flying" squirrel than an eagle.

Lord, it is all about You. I contribute nothing except to surrender. In You is the only way I can soar above the troubles of life and dwell in Your presence. Thank You.

5.BOND

Ephesians 4:2-3 (NIV)

Be completely humble and gentle; be patient, bearing with one another in love. Make every effort to keep the unity of the Spirit through the bond of peace.

There is a principle in "Small Group Theory" that once a group has been together for a while, and seems to be operating successfully, a crisis will almost always arise. That crisis usually does one of two things: it either moves the group forward in their relationships and effectiveness, or it tears them apart. Sometimes the individuals cannot get past the crisis, and the group breaks up.

The same thing can be seen in marriages. All seems well until a financial, relational, health, or even a death-related crisis arises. Couples are seldom the same after such a moment. They either bond together, supporting one another through the storm, or they turn against each other—becoming angry and argumentative, or sullen and withdrawn, often blaming one another.

As followers of Jesus, we too are "in a group"—the Body of Christ. Paul urges us to be humble, patient, and gentle with one another. He reminds us to bear with one another—because after all, who among us is perfect?

We are called to do everything we possibly can to keep the bond of peace between us. When we maintain peace and show love for one another, even in the midst of circumstances, trials, or difficulties, we become living examples to a watching world.

Lord, please forgive us when we pursue our own interests instead of the bond of peace. Lead us to bond and unite with our brothers and sisters in Christ. Thank You.

6.KNIT

Psalms 139:13-14 (NIV)

For you created my inmost being; you knit me together in my mother's womb. I praise you because I am fearfully and wonderfully made; your works are wonderful, I know that full well.

In a broad sense, the word *knit* means to unite. Consider the miracle of every human being—marvelously and wonderfully made: 60 trillion cells, 100 thousand miles of nerve fiber, 60 thousand miles of vessels carrying blood around the body, 250 bones, to say nothing of joints, ligaments, and muscles (Bible Believer's Commentary (BBC)). All knitted together to work wonderfully well. No chance this was an accident. Just miracle after miracle in front of our eyes for those who can "see."

God has a vision for the church—the Body of Christ. It is a vision of people knitted firmly together in Christ: encouraging one another, helping one another, praying for one another, serving one another— all in love.

Lord, You are the Master Knitter. Unite us together into the fully functioning Body of Christ You envision.

7.HAIR

Matthew 10:29-32 (NIV)

Are not two sparrows sold for a penny? Yet not one of them will fall to the ground outside your Father's care. And even the very hairs of your head are all numbered. So don't be afraid; you are worth more than many sparrows. "Whoever acknowledges me before others, I will also acknowledge before my Father in heaven."

There are about 100,000 hairs on a person's head (probably means younger persons?). That is a lot of hair to keep track of. Yet even something so small and detailed is known and counted by God. But that is nothing compared to the stars in the universe. Medium-sized galaxies like our Milky Way have around 100 billion to 400 billion stars. Then multiply that by the number of galaxies in the universe (100 billion to 200 billion), and you have an absolutely astounding number of stars. The sheer immensity is almost impossible for us to imagine.

We are like a speck of dust; very insignificant indeed—except for one overwhelming fact. We are the children of the Creator of the universe. The same God who set the stars in place, who knows their number and their names, also knows us by name. He loves and cares for us in ways that go far beyond our understanding. That truth changes everything.

Dear God, let us not be afraid or weary, but let us find rest in You. Thank You for reminding us that even in the vastness of creation, we are seen, we are known, and we are loved.

8.TASTE

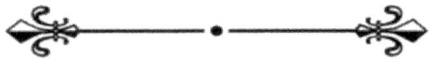

Psalms 34:8 (NIV)

Taste and see that the LORD is good; blessed is the one who takes refuge in him.

Ah, what a wonder the sensory gift of taste truly is! How bland and dull life would be if everything tasted the same, don't you agree?

Have you ever tried to explain to someone how good something tastes? It's almost impossible. It is only in the actual act of tasting that we come to understand flavor. And so it is with God. Unless we ourselves have tasted the goodness of God, how can we truly know what we are talking about?

"We may argue about God, His existence, and the external evidences which the universe and providence provide. However only when His love and presence touch our hearts can we really know Him in His unspeakable goodness." (BBC)

We must share Christ by our example. As we taste of the goodness of God, people can see we have dined with the Creator of the universe. They in turn will become hungry to taste of the Lord. space

Matthew 5:6 (NASB)

Blessed are those who hunger and thirst for righteousness, for they shall be satisfied.

Lord, please give us a deep hunger and an unquenchable thirst for the righteousness that comes only from You. Let us continually taste of Your great goodness, find our satisfaction in

You alone, and give thanks for the joy of Your presence. Thank You.

9.REMODEL

Ezekiel 11:19-20 (NASB)

And I will give them one heart and put a new spirit within them. And I will take the heart of stone out of their flesh and give them a heart of flesh, that they may walk in My statutes and keep My ordinances and do them. Then they will be My people, and I shall be their God.

Philippians 1:6 (NASB)

For I am confident of this very thing, that He who began a good work in you will perfect it until the day of Christ Jesus.

Ever watch a "Do It Yourself" program and say to yourself, *"I can do that"*? Sometimes I think I can, but I know better. I am not a handy person, and it is best to leave real work to a professional.

Unfortunately, in a spiritual sense, I am not always so wise. The heart remodel that I need (you also, by the way) is definitely a job for a Professional—it is not something you or I can do. Jeremiah knew what he was talking about when he said our hearts were so deceitful we cannot even know it (Jeremiah 17:9).

Lord, sometimes we think we can "fix" ourselves, but if we are paying attention to Your Word it will be obvious that it is Your work to do and not ours. Lead us to walk in humble submission to Your most perfect work in us. Thank You.

10.CAROUSEL

Philippians 4:4 (NIV)

Rejoice in the Lord always. I will say it again: Rejoice!

The word *rejoice* reminds me of the "carousel seasons" of our lives. Times when fun, joy, and happiness are easy to find—especially with a loved one or a good friend. I hope you can remember such seasons in your life.

As the years go by, sometimes the fun of the "merry-go-round" is not so much fun anymore. Life can become tedious, busy, and often frustrating. Sometimes it feels like we're just going around and around without getting anywhere.

Maybe it's simply that we are getting older, perhaps a little worn or jaded by life. Yet what do we do with this verse that commands us to rejoice always—and then repeats it for emphasis? Are we really to rejoice even when life feels stagnant, when it seems as though we are going in circles? **Yes, absolutely.** We rejoice because we are God's children, and we already know how the story ends. This life is not the final ride. A brand-new carousel season—one filled with joy that never fades—awaits us for all eternity.

So let us not be discouraged about the here and now. A time will come when all things are made new and God completes His work in you and in me. *"Oh, what a day that will be—when Jesus we shall see, and He takes us by the hand and leads us through the Promised Land."*

Lord, thank You for the carousel of seasons, for the ones we have already lived and for the ones that are still to come. Teach

us to walk each day with joy and with the hopeful expectation of eternity in Your presence.

11.VESSEL

2 Timothy 2:20-21 (NASB)

Now in a large house there are not only gold and silver vessels, but also vessels of wood and of earthenware, and some to honor and some to dishonor. Therefore, if anyone cleanses himself from these things, he will be a vessel (instrument NIV) for honor, sanctified, useful to the Master, prepared for every good work.

Vessels are meant to hold something. Each vessel has a specific purpose. A glass is made to hold something to drink, while a gas can is meant to carry something very different. A vessel is only useful when it serves its intended purpose. Gas in a glass is not a good thing.

We too are like vessels. God has designed us with a specific purpose. To be truly useful to Him, our vessel, our very lives, must be guided by His Spirit. Too often we decide what our vessel will contain instead of allowing God to choose. When we do this, we miss out on God's highest calling for our lives.

One of the major problems today is that we fill our lives with so many things that end up being nothing more than distractions from God's true purpose. The result is that our vessels, our lives, remain unfulfilled in God's eyes.

Lord, please reveal everything in our lives that keeps us from being the most useful vessel in Your hands. Thank You.

12.BLEMISH

1 Samuel 16:7 (NIV)

But the LORD said to Samuel, "Do not consider his appearance or his height, for I have rejected him. The LORD does not look at the things people look at. People look at the outward appearance, but the LORD looks at the heart."

Hebrews 9:14 (NIV)

How much more, then, will the blood of Christ, who through the eternal Spirit offered himself unblemished to God, cleanse our consciences from acts that lead to death, so that we may serve the living God!

Looking at outward appearances is what people did in the time of Samuel, and to a large extent continue to do today. It is so easy for us to form opinions about people by "first impressions."

The other day an elderly couple and their daughter entered a restaurant and took a table near May and me. Immediately I was impressed by their outward appearances. They were well dressed, held themselves tall, with perfectly styled hair and clothes. In my mind these people were "high caliber."

However, I knew nothing about them, and my opinion was based solely on what I observed on the outside. I made these observations and formed my opinion almost at my first glance, totally unconsciously.

Even though I know I should not judge others by their outward appearances, good or otherwise, the "old man" from Romans 7 shows up again.

I am so thankful God is still doing His work in me. Although I will not find perfection from my many blemishes, inside and out, on this side of heaven, I rejoice in the unblemished work of Jesus Christ my Savior who loves me, blemishes and all.

Dear Lord, thank You for loving me the way I am and for loving me enough to change me. What a wonder it is to be part of Your Ohana (family). Teach me Your ways, Lord, in all things.

13. TILL

Hosea 10:12 (NIV)

Sow righteousness for yourselves, reap the fruit of unfailing love, and break up your unplowed ground; for it is time to seek the LORD, until he comes and showers his righteousness on you.

As a young Catholic altar boy in the Bronx, I didn't know what it meant to "till the soil" or to "break up unplowed ground." Someone had planted roses in the church's garden long before I was even thought of. The roses were dark red, abundant, climbing on a wall, and I can almost smell them to this day.

Up to that point in my life I had not planted anything, but for some reason I wanted to grow flowers. Living in a five-story apartment building I had no yard to garden in, so I asked one of the priests if I could grow flowers in their garden near the roses. As a "favored" person I was given the OK.

Of course, I knew nothing about growing flowers. But I had my seeds and I was ready to go. I don't remember how I planted them, but I do remember being told, *"What you are doing will not work."* I guess my dislike of authority had already kicked in, and I did not listen. Instead, I "did what I thought was best in my own eyes" (if that sounds familiar, check out the book of Judges).

Needless to say, my efforts were wasted, and my seeds could not survive where and how they were planted. To my memory, not even one seed grew.

What is the moral of the story? Simply this: if the soil of our hearts and minds and spirits is unplowed, then all our outward good works will be fruitless in the eyes of God. How do we get hearts and minds and spirits that have been tilled by God? Simply ask and surrender!

Lord God, please till the soil of my heart. Let there be no unplowed ground in me. Thank You.

P.S. My next "adventure" in growing things was some 20 years later in Hawaii. That is another story for another time.

14. TRUTH

Psalms 25:5-6 (NIV)

Guide me in your truth and teach me, for you are God my Savior, and my hope is in you all day long. Remember, LORD, your great mercy and love, for they are from of old.

Pilate asked, *"What is truth?"* (John 18:38). Our culture says that truth is "whatever you want it to be," that there is no absolute truth. As Christians, we know better. Yet sometimes I wonder if we too deny truth even while acknowledging it. Double-minded, you say? Yes, it is—but consider the following:

- **Life is short** – yet we waste much of our lives on things that are inconsequential. We leave the important things for later, which often never comes.

- **Our resources are limited** – yet we take for granted God's provisions for us and are often wasteful because we live in a society of plenty.

- **Comparison is a thief of joy** – yet we often compare ourselves to what other people have or what others have achieved.

- **Happiness can't be bought** – yet we keep trying to win the lottery, or we become workaholics, or we spend excessively, looking for something to make us happy.

- **Possessions do not define us** – yet we accumulate more and more stuff, believing that others will think better of us or that our things prove we have "arrived."

- **We can't take it with us** – yet we are reluctant to give away what we have.

- **Experiences inside of relationships matter more than things** – yet we consistently forfeit meaningful experiences with others, working harder to buy more and striving for a "better" lifestyle.

- **Your life is too valuable to waste** – yet we spend our time frivolously on social media, playing games, watching TV, or doing meaningless work. We seldom reflect on what really matters in life.

- **Giving is better than receiving** – yet we often give only from our surplus rather than from our sufficiency.

Do you see what I mean? Do you see yourself in one or more of these scenarios? I know I do. Perhaps we are partially oblivious, living with our heads in the sand.

Dear Lord, please awaken Your slumbering people. Keep us from double-mindedness. Help us live the truths we say we believe. Above all, let us live in the truth that You are our Savior, that we are Your children, and that Your love for us is what truly matters. Thank You.

15.PIVOT

2 Chronicles 7:14 (NIV)

If my people, who are called by my name, will humble themselves and pray and seek my face and turn from their wicked ways, then I will hear from heaven, and I will forgive their sin and will heal their land.

The word *pivot* means to change direction or to completely change the way you do something. In a spiritual sense, to pivot sounds like repentance—in other words, to stop what you are doing and change direction.

Today's verse is a promise made to the Jews when they left their first love, God, and decided to do things their own way. God wanted them to pivot back to Him. Not too different from our culture today.

Even we Christians tend to want to do things our way. However, Jesus has His way, and His way is usually not our way.

This scripture called the Jews of that time, as well as us today, to wake up. It is time to pivot. It is time to humble ourselves and earnestly pray and seek the face of God. It is time to move away from the things that distract us and keep us from an intimate relationship with our Savior.

The challenge is this: are we willing to pivot? Perhaps we don't think we need to pivot. We should know better. We are called by God to a more perfect union with Him.

Lord, as "mature" believers we might think we know all we need to know about living the Christian life. I am pretty sure we

are often only following ourselves. Please give us a willingness to pivot in whatever way pleases You.

16.TRANSPLANT

Ezekiel 17:22-23 (NIV)

This is what the Sovereign LORD says: I myself will take a shoot from the very top of a cedar and plant it; I will break off a tender sprig from its topmost shoots and plant it on a high and lofty mountain. On the mountain heights of Israel I will plant it; it will produce branches and bear fruit and become a splendid cedar. Birds of every kind will nest in it; they will find shelter in the shade of its branches.

To transplant means to move or transfer something or someone to another place or situation, typically with some effort or upheaval. Even when intended for good, it may not seem that way to the one being transplanted.

If you have ever worked with plants, you know that sooner or later they need to be transplanted. With time and experience, you learn how to do it, and the process becomes familiar.

People often ask me how to transplant a plant, and I am always glad to offer advice. Most of the time, transplants result in a stronger, healthier plant. But sometimes serious damage—even death—can occur. This usually happens when the plant becomes stuck in its old pot, stubbornly unwilling to leave what it has grown used to.

In much the same way, God sometimes wants, even needs, to transplant us. There are many reasons He may choose to move us into a new situation or environment. Often it is to take us out of our comfort zone so that we can know Him more deeply and experience more of His presence.

We are like those plants. If we cooperate with His transplanting work, the process goes smoothly, and the result is a more mature and vibrant life. But if we resist, clinging to the familiar, we miss out on the very experiences God has prepared for us.

God's transplanting can happen in many ways. At times He may ask for a small but important change, such as showing kindness in a difficult situation. Other times, the change may be major—something as radical as selling everything and giving to the poor. Whether large or small, the wisest response is quick surrender. For obedience is the true hallmark of a disciple.

Lord, we grow comfortable with what is familiar, and we often resist leaving our comfort zones. Yet when we hear Your call to be transplanted, help us bow quickly in obedience to You. Thank You.

17.CHALLENGE

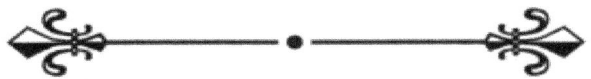

Isaiah 41:10 (NIV)

So do not fear, for I am with you; do not be dismayed, for I am your God. I will strengthen you and help you; I will uphold you with my righteous right hand.

Today's word reminds me that my perspective about challenges has changed over the years. As far back as I can remember, I really enjoyed challenging positions. I had an innate belief that I could figure things out.

As the years have passed, that confidence seems to have slipped away. These days I find myself preferring smooth and easy sailing, with as few challenges as possible. Yet, as you and I both know, life is filled with challenges of every kind.

Although I have lost my love of challenges, I have gained something far more wonderful and useful. I now know that when I am weak, God is strong. I do not need the assurance that I can master all of life's challenges. What I need is the assurance that God can and will take me through every one of life's ups and downs as long as I keep my eyes on Him.

You and I can choose to live in the flesh, which prefers the easy way with no bumps in the road. Or we can live in the Spirit, with the confidence that all challenges will work together for good.

Lord, I thank You for taking away my strength in the flesh and replacing it with Your strength.

18.DIGNITY

Genesis 2:7 (NIV)

Then the LORD God formed a man from the dust of the ground and breathed into his nostrils the breath of life, and the man became a living being.

Proverbs 31:25 (NIV)

She is clothed with strength and dignity; she can laugh at the days to come.

"Do I know you?" "How long have I known you?" Such simple questions can provoke such deep sorrow when asked by a parent to his or her child.

When a person loses their memory, countless connections to this world slip away. Some might think that such a person is no longer worthy of dignity and honor. But nothing could be further from the truth. Each one of us has been designed by God in His perfect image, and that image remains—even when it is tested to its very limits here on earth.

Why must we endure such heart-wrenching sorrow? Who can truly explain it? Many have tried to give answers, yet none can fully ease the pain of a heart broken by a loved one who no longer remembers.

We must show dignity and honor to our loved ones who have forgotten us. Hold them tight, spend time with them, even when they are not "there." Hold their hands, listen to their ramblings, patiently answer their questions (for the hundredth time). Listen to their music with them. Be fully present, just you and them.

Living with a loved one who has forgotten is often considered a burden, but I see it differently. It is a time of complete reliance on our Lord God—trusting Him even when all feels hopeless and the future promises only more loss.

It is not a burden. It is a time to walk with your loved one and watch what the Lord God will do. Look for Him to reveal Himself even in the greatest losses we could ever imagine.

Dear Father, I pray today for all who live with those who are no longer remembering. Please give them an extra measure of grace—to love unconditionally, to give honor and dignity each day, and to remain faithful until their loved one's journey is complete.

19.PURE

Psalms 24:3-5 (NIV)

Who may ascend the mountain of the LORD? Who may stand in his holy place? The one who has clean hands and a pure heart, who does not trust in an idol or swear by a false god. They will receive blessing from the LORD and vindication from God their Savior.

Matthew 5:8 (NIV)

Blessed are the pure in heart, for they will see God.

There you have it. If you want to be on the mountaintop with God and experience Him, all you must do is have a pure heart. Piece of cake, right?

But what does it really mean to be pure? Think about it. Have you ever encountered something that was truly pure—completely uncontaminated by any foreign element? Or have you ever met a person who was completely pure, untouched by this world and the desires it promotes?

As I reflect on this word, and on God's requirement of purity for those who dwell in His presence, I see more clearly how wretched I am without the Lord Jesus. As Paul tells us in Romans 7:24-25: *"What a wretched man I am! Who will rescue me from this body that is subject to death? Thanks be to God, who delivers me through Jesus Christ our Lord!"*

And so, our only rightful posture in this life is with head and heart bowed in thankfulness for Jesus Christ and His atoning sacrifice.

Dear God, I am a fallen man with many faults, and yet I come. Through the blood of Your Son, Jesus Christ, I long for Your presence. Thank You.

20.FAITHFUL

Hebrews 10:23-25 (NIV)

Let us hold unswervingly to the hope we profess, for he who promised is faithful. And let us consider how we may spur one another on toward love and good deeds, not giving up meeting together, as some are in the habit of doing, but encouraging one another—and all the more as you see the Day approaching.

Ever get discouraged and want to give up? With my melancholy nature, that has happened multiple times in my life. Sometimes I would have preferred to hide in a cave to escape my problems. If not for May, I probably would have ended up in a cave of some sort.

Over these 50-plus years with May, she has been my constant encourager. I wish I could say, "I needed no help." That, however, would be a bold-faced lie.

It took me a long time to learn (and I am still learning) that my weaknesses become most useful in the hands of God. There is no personality quirk, disorder, or dysfunction that He cannot use for His glory and for our growth, if only we surrender ourselves to Him.

We all need someone to encourage us. If we are married, our spouse should be our foremost encourager. Often, we also need others. Who is God placing in your life that needs encouragement? Will you reach out? Will you call? Will you be a friend? Will you encourage them?

Lord, thank You for the many people You bring into my life to encourage me. Thank You most of all for May, who knows me

better than anyone and yet remains faithful. Lead all of us to be Your faithful servants. Thank You.

21.FORGET

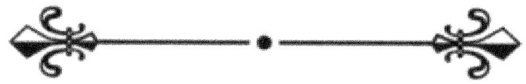

Isaiah 43:25 (NIV)

"I, even I, am he who blots out your transgressions, for my own sake, and remembers your sins no more."

Psalms 103:11-12 (NIV)

For as high as the heavens are above the earth, so great is his love for those who fear him; as far as the east is from the west, so far has he removed our transgressions from us.

Our brains are an extraordinary creation of God. They hold billions upon billions of pieces of information that can often be recalled in an instant. The Psalmist spoke truth when he declared that we are "fearfully and wonderfully made" (see Psalm 139).

One of the most remarkable features of the brain, I believe, is its ability to forget. To let go of a hurt, an insult, or the pain of being taken advantage of. Yes, the memory may still be tucked away somewhere in our minds, but in Christ we are given the grace to "forget" the sting and instead choose love. That is exactly what God does for us when He removes our sins. Should we do any less?

Oh Lord, how easy it is to keep a hurt alive in our minds. Please teach us to forget and to love instead. Thank You for the gift of forgetfulness.

22.CLIMB

Luke 19:4 (NASB)

So he ran on ahead and climbed up into a sycamore tree in order to see Him, for He was about to pass through that way.

Philippians 3:14 (NASB)

I press on toward the goal for the prize of the upward call of God in Christ Jesus.

Personally, I prefer to be on the ground rather than climbing. It is not that I am afraid of heights (though I once was). It is just that climbing is hard work—really hard work.

I remember running the Honolulu Marathon in 1982. The last couple of miles were a steady climb up and over Diamond Head before descending to the finish line on the other side of the ancient volcano. I had "hit the wall" somewhere around mile 20 to 22, and I was exhausted. Everything in me cried, "Stop!"—except for one thing: I wanted the prize of finishing.

The Christian life can often feel like running a marathon, long and exhausting. There are moments when we feel like giving up, especially as we look at the struggles in our culture, our families, and even our churches. Yet the promise remains sure—the prize is reserved for those who endure and finish the race.

Dear Lord, as we grow older, the temptation may be to finish our Christian walk on the sidelines. Please keep us in the race. Help us not to give up, but to keep climbing, and to finish well as You call us home. Thank You.

23.TEACHABLE

Proverbs 9:9 (NASB)

Give instruction to a wise man and he will be still wiser, teach a righteous man and he will increase his learning.

Acts 17:11 (NASB)

Now these (Bereans) were more noble-minded than those in Thessalonica, for they received the word with great eagerness, examining the Scriptures daily to see whether these things were so.

Are you more like the Thessalonians or more like the Bereans? What is your evidence?

The vast majority of us are like the Thessalonians. The human tendency to disregard any evidence that contradicts what we already believe to be true is well documented. We see it played out in the Scriptures between the established Jewish hierarchy and Jesus and Paul.

For example, how do you feel about this statement? *"Saturated fats are good for you, and there is no need to exclude them from your diet."* Many of us, after years of hearing how bad saturated fats are, have trouble accepting such a claim. Yet recent studies indicate that those "in the know" did not really know.

So let me ask the question another way: are you teachable? What evidence can you point to for your answer?

Father, You tell us to come to You if we need wisdom (James 1:5). Please help us to put aside our predisposed tendencies as we seek wisdom and understanding from You.

24.ANTICIPATION

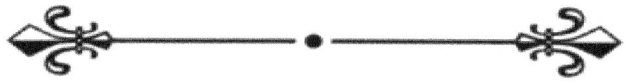

Hebrews 11:1 (NASB)

Now faith is the assurance of things hoped for, the conviction of things not seen.

Sometimes I find life a little upside down. Take the word *anticipation,* for example. Have you ever noticed that our anticipation of something can be more exciting and enjoyable—or more scary and dreadful—than the actual event?

I remember my anticipation for a trip May and I were planning. I was excited, like a young person going on a first date. Not sure what would happen, maybe a little nervous, but definitely looking forward to it. Years later, I remember my anticipation vividly, but I have almost no memory of the actual trip. Somehow my anticipation created a stronger memory than the event itself. Have you ever experienced anything like this?

As followers of Jesus Christ, we should always live in anticipation of two things. First, Jesus could return at any moment. Second, when the number of our days is over, He will call us into His presence. It is good to keep in mind that we are simply aliens and foreigners upon this earth.

Our anticipation can sometimes be more fulfilling—or more dreadful—than the event itself. But I am absolutely certain that our anticipation of what it will be like to be in the presence of God will be completely eclipsed by the reality.

Dear Lord, I anticipate that the number of my days is soon to play out. I cannot even begin to imagine what it will be like to be in Your presence. Thank You.

25.MESSAGE

John 17:20-22 (NIV)

My prayer is not for them alone. I pray also for those who will believe in me through their message, that all of them may be one, Father, just as you are in me and I am in you. May they also be in us so that the world may believe that you have sent me. I have given them the glory that you gave me, that they may be one as we are one.

God has used His messengers of the past to reveal the great mystery of reconciliation between God and man. He still uses His messengers today—you and I—as we live lives that reflect this message of reconciliation.

How do we live this message? By striving to be peacemakers and modeling Christ's love in our relationships: marriage and family, racial and ethnic, management and workers, landlord and tenant, wait staff and customers, government authorities and citizens, church leaders and parishioners, and so on. Not by living on the sidelines or ignoring difficulties, but by actively engaging and striving for peace, seeking unity as followers of Jesus Christ.

John 13:35 (NIV)

By this everyone will know that you are my disciples, if you love one another.

People are always watching to see what kind of message we are sending as professing believers. Is it a message of love, peace, forgiveness, unity, and reconciliation? Or is it something else?

Lord, every relationship we have is an opportunity to send the message of reconciliation and unity. Help us to send no other message. Thank You.

26. INNOCENT

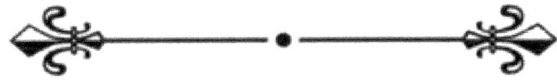

1 John 1:9-10 (NIV)

If we confess our sins, he is faithful and just and will forgive us our sins and purify us from all unrighteousness. If we claim we have not sinned, we make him out to be a liar and his word is not in us.

1 Corinthians 4:4 (NIV)

My conscience is clear, but that does not make me innocent. It is the Lord who judges me.

The American justice system is based on the principle that we are innocent until proven guilty. We have not lived this out perfectly, but most will agree it is far better than being considered guilty until proven innocent, which is how it works in many totalitarian nations.

As I considered the word *innocent,* I was struck by God's perspective: "we are all guilty—no one is innocent."

Romans 3:23 (NIV)

For all have sinned and fall short of the glory of God.

And yet, through the redeeming sacrifice of Jesus Christ, we are declared "justified," "not guilty," and "innocent" by His blood.

Romans 3:24 (NIV)

And all are justified freely by his grace through the redemption that came by Christ Jesus.

Lord God, lead us to humbly bow before You, remembering that although we are guilty, through Christ You declare us innocent. Thank You so much.

27.WEARY

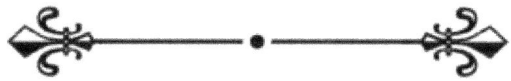

Hebrews 12:1-3 (NIV)

Therefore, since we are surrounded by such a great cloud of witnesses, let us throw off everything that hinders and the sin that so easily entangles. And let us run with perseverance the race marked out for us, fixing our eyes on Jesus, the pioneer and perfecter of faith. For the joy set before him he endured the cross, scorning its shame, and sat down at the right hand of the throne of God. Consider him who endured such opposition from sinners, so that you will not grow weary and lose heart.

In my experience, weariness is one of the hardest seasons to endure. When I am weary, even the simplest tasks feel overwhelming. I love working with orchids and flowers, yet when weariness settles in, even caring for them feels like a heavy burden.

The good news is that Scripture gives us clear guidance for overcoming weariness:

1. **Remember that we are not alone.** We are surrounded by a great cloud of witnesses cheering us on.

2. **Guard against the small things that hinder us.** Lack of rest, saying "yes" too often, or wasting time can drain us more than we realize.

3. **Recognize the weight of sin.** Sin will always trip us up. Living double-minded consumes our energy and leads to spiritual exhaustion.

4. **Run with intention.** Life is not a race to be run carelessly; it requires perseverance and focus.

5. **Keep your eyes on Jesus.** Weariness grows when our focus shifts away from Him.

6. **Run your own race.** God has marked out a unique path for each of us. Trying to live someone else's calling only leads to exhaustion.

7. **Seek true joy in intimacy with Jesus.** Accomplishments and possessions will never sustain us, but His presence will.

8. **Consider all that Jesus endured.** Compared to His suffering, our struggles are light and temporary.

9. **Fix your eyes on the prize.** Eternal life in the presence of God is the joy that awaits us.

Dear Lord, my prayer is that weariness will no longer overwhelm us. But if it comes, help us to remember the truths You have given us in Your Word. Thank You.

28.CERTAIN

Hebrews 4:6-7 (NIV)

Therefore since it still remains for some to enter that rest, and since those who formerly had the good news proclaimed to them did not go in because of their disobedience, God again set a certain day, calling it "Today." This he did when a long time later he spoke through David, as in the passage already quoted: "Today, if you hear his voice, do not harden your hearts."

To be *certain* is to know for sure, beyond a shadow of a doubt. I once heard it described as "knowing that I know." It is not just knowledge about something but a deeply rooted confidence.

Proverbs 24:3-4 gives us an example: *"By wisdom a house is built, and through understanding it is established; through knowledge its rooms are filled with rare and beautiful treasures."* This shows the progression from knowing about something to knowing with certainty.

"Today" is the day to know with certainty that you are in Christ. It is not a matter of wishing or hoping. It is living a life that reflects the Holy Spirit because you are certain beyond doubt that you are redeemed by the blood of Jesus and destined to dwell in the presence of God.

Lord, lead us to live lives that show the certainty of our relationship with You. Thank You.

29.SMILE

Psalms 42:11 (NIV)

Why, my soul, are you downcast? Why so disturbed within me? Put your hope in God, for I will yet praise him, my Savior and my God.

Sometimes even CNN gets it right:

"Adults who regularly say hello to their neighbors have higher well-being than those who are antisocial, a new Gallup poll found. However, if you loathe the idea of striking up a conversation, data shows even the slightest greeting—like a nod, a wave, or a fist bump—can boost your personal and community health."

When May and I first moved into this community (over 22 years ago), we were struck by the friendliness of the residents. Just about everybody waved at one another as they passed in their cars or golf carts. Yes, complete strangers greeting one another. It was one of the things that immediately enticed us to live here.

More and more, May and I are making it a habit to smile and talk with strangers whenever we are out and about. It is quite amazing what a smile and friendly word can do. Many people are surprised by an unexpected greeting from a stranger. Their surprise often gives way to a smile and a greeting in return. Sometimes those smiles turn into conversations, and every now and then into friendships.

The Psalmist wondered why his soul was downcast. I wonder even more why a follower of Jesus would be downcast. Even on our deathbeds, we have great reason to rejoice—as May and I have witnessed many times. May our faces and our actions reflect the reality of our relationship with the Messiah.

I often encourage followers of Jesus to "always be on mission." Sometimes that mission is as simple as a smile.

Oh Lord, may our countenance be so filled with Your joy that it brings joy to the people You place in our lives. Thank You.

30.FOLLOW

John 10:27-28 (NASB)

My sheep hear My voice, and I know them, and they follow Me; and I give eternal life to them, and they will never perish; and no one will snatch them out of My hand.

In our culture there are many voices calling out to us. Some are merely distractions, but others can become serious obstacles to hearing God's voice.

The voices come from all directions: the media, social platforms, our friends, families, and—sadly—sometimes even our churches. The real problem is not only the voices but our willingness to listen to them and let them shape our devotion to Jesus. Despite Paul's warning in Romans 12:1-2, many of us have become experts at being conformed to the world while failing at being transformed.

Romans 12:1-2 (NASB)

Therefore I urge you, brethren, by the mercies of God, to present your bodies a living and holy sacrifice, acceptable to God, which is your spiritual service of worship. And do not be conformed to this world, but be transformed by the renewing of your mind, so that you may prove what the will of God is, that which is good and acceptable and perfect.

If your immediate reaction is, "That's not me," be cautious. We can easily be blind to our own compromise. Ask yourself: is the church influencing our culture, or is the culture influencing the church?

Dear Lord, how sad it is when we allow the world to conform us—especially when we are unaware of it. Please reveal Yourself to us and plant deeply in our hearts, minds, and souls the desire to be transformed by the renewal of our minds through Your Word.

31.KNOCK

Matthew 7:7 (NASB)

"Ask, and it will be given to you; seek, and you will find; knock, and it will be opened to you."

Anyone who reads through the Sermon on the Mount (Matthew 5–7) is struck by how impossible it seems to live out the principles Jesus lays out. Perhaps that is why He included this verse.

Jesus knew, and I hope we have learned, that it is impossible to live the Christian life in our own strength. Only the Spirit of God can reshape our lives so that His commands not only seem desirable but become part of who we are in Christ.

Jesus tells us to ask, seek, and knock—and to keep on asking, keep on seeking, and keep on knocking. This is not a one-time event but a lifelong pursuit of God.

Jeremiah 29:13 (NASB)

You will seek Me and find Me when you search for Me with all your heart.

Nothing has changed since Jeremiah's day. To draw close to God, we must desire Him above everything else.

Oh dear God, quiet the many distractions that so often pull us away from You. Teach us to seek You with undivided hearts, longing for Your presence above all else. Thank You for always being near when we turn to You.

32.STREAMS

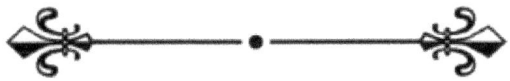

Psalms 1:3 (NASB)

He will be like a tree firmly planted by streams of water, which yields its fruit in its season, and its leaf does not wither; and in whatever he does, he prospers.

One of the challenges in growing "difficult" plants is finding the right environment. In the right place, a plant can thrive even with minimal care. In the wrong place, it may wither and die despite the best efforts.

The same is true for us. We are all "difficult" in our own ways. We are complex, and we often flounder when we are not in the right environment.

So what is the secret to being planted by streams of living water, yielding fruit in season, and not withering when life grows hard? The Psalmist gives us the answer:

Psalms 1:2 (NASB)

But his delight is in the law of the LORD, and in His law he meditates day and night.

It may sound too simple, but it is true. Those who delight in God's Word and meditate on it daily will find themselves rooted in a life that is fruitful, prosperous, and at peace.

Lord, Your ways are clear and true. Teach us to seek You earnestly and to delight in Your Word, trusting that everything else will align according to Your perfect will.

33. THINK

Philippians 4:8 (NIV)

Finally, brothers and sisters, whatever is true, whatever is noble, whatever is right, whatever is pure, whatever is lovely, whatever is admirable—if anything is excellent or praiseworthy—think about such things.

Romans 15:5-6 (NIV)

May the God who gives endurance and encouragement give you the same attitude of mind toward each other that Christ Jesus had, so that with one mind and one voice you may glorify the God and Father of our Lord Jesus Christ.

The Psalmist tells us that we are "wonderfully made" (Psalm 139). Could there be any part of us more wonderful than our minds? Our minds store vast amounts of information and shape nearly every moment of our lives.

My mind seems to never shut off. Sometimes it collects random thoughts that make no sense. At other times, I feel as though I receive bits of revelation from above. And still at other times, my mind runs negative, dwelling on things that are not helpful.

It may be natural for our minds to wander, but there is a better way. We are called to pursue the mind of Christ. This means training our thoughts—redirecting them, when necessary—toward what is noble, right, pure, lovely, admirable, excellent, and praiseworthy.

As Christians, we also have a responsibility to direct our thoughts toward the needs of others in the Body of Christ. Reflecting, praying, and seeking ways to love and serve them is part of glorifying our Savior.

Dear Father, please transform all of me, especially my mind. Teach me to think on the things that bring honor to You. Thank You.

34.PRIZE

Philippians 3:14 (NIV)

I press on toward the goal to win the prize for which God has called me heavenward in Christ Jesus.

A prize is something given as a reward for effort or accomplishment. As children, we often experienced it in small ways: *"Make your bed and you can have dessert,"* or later, *"Cut the grass and I'll cook your favorite meal."*

Prizes can be powerful motivators, but only when they are seen as valuable. If a prize seems trivial, it carries little weight and inspires little effort. But when a prize is viewed as truly precious, it has the power to stir deep commitment and wholehearted pursuit.

Paul clearly saw his prize as precious. He pressed on, making it his life's goal to win it. And what was this prize? Not simply salvation—Paul already knew Christ. His prize was the fullness of life with Christ, the eternal reward of knowing Him completely.

It is worth asking ourselves: What do I consider precious? What is worth reordering my entire life to attain?

Lord, what an incredible work You did in the life of Paul. Please do the same in us. Teach us to see the true prize and to live in pursuit of it. Thank You.

35.WALK

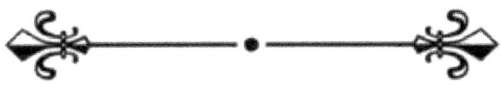

1 John 1:7 (NIV)

But if we walk in the light, as he is in the light, we have fellowship with one another, and the blood of Jesus, his Son, purifies us from all sin.

Do you remember the hymn that says, "And He walks with me, and He talks with me"? I once heard a story about someone singing it in church. A new believer was listening with great excitement. After the service, he rushed to the singer and asked, "What did He say? What did He tell you?"

The singer, bewildered, explained, "I didn't actually talk with God—I was just singing the words." The new believer left disappointed, wondering why anyone would sing something untrue.

I have often thought about that. Too many times I have sung songs of worship that, if I'm honest, never reached the ears of God—because I was only singing words, not offering my heart.

What about you? Do you sing with your mind elsewhere? Do you worship without truly engaging your heart? To "walk" with God means to live aware of His presence. Worship should never be empty words but the overflow of a heart alive in Him.

Lord, reveal any hypocrisy within us and draw our hearts wholly to You. Guard us from worship that is only words, and let our praise be genuine fellowship with You. Thank You.

36.MOVE

Luke 5:4 (NIV)

When he had finished speaking, he said to Simon, "Put out into deep water, and let down the nets for a catch."

Over the years, I have often emphasized the importance of "being" over "doing." After all, we are human beings, not human doings. Who we are matters more than what we do.

But that does not mean there is no place for movement. This verse shows us that there is a time to listen and a time to act. We must learn to balance being still in God's presence with being ready to move when He calls.

In my own life, I find it easier to move than to wait. Sometimes I act impulsively or feel driven by circumstances. The greater challenge is to listen carefully to the Spirit and know when it is truly time to move.

Our fulfillment comes when we find the balance: waiting quietly in His presence and then stepping out to do the work He has prepared for us (Ephesians 2:10).

Dear Lord, sometimes it is easier to keep moving than to wait on You. Help us to find that quiet place where we can hear Your voice, and give us the courage to move when You say, "Go." Thank You.

37.CHASE

Matthew 6:31-33 (NIV)

So do not worry, saying, 'What shall we eat?' or 'What shall we drink?' or 'What shall we wear?' For the pagans run after all these things, and your heavenly Father knows that you need them. But seek first his kingdom and his righteousness, and all these things will be given to you as well.

Matthew 6:20-21 (NIV)

But store up for yourselves treasures in heaven, where moths and vermin do not destroy, and where thieves do not break in and steal. For where your treasure is, there your heart will be also.

"We become what we love." (unknown)

"What we chase matters more than what we have." (Joshua Becker)

My dear friends, before you read another word, grab a pencil and paper and jot down what you have that is valuable to you.

Pencil and paper ready? What is missing? What are you chasing? Why are you chasing after it?

One of the great paradoxes of life is this: no matter how hard we chase after the next thing, whether it's closer relationships, better finances, a nicer home, a newer car, greater success, or just a little extra income, it never seems to satisfy for long. The thrill fades, and before we know it, the chase begins again.

Too often, our hearts grow restless, forgetting the sufficiency of God's provision. Instead of resting in His care, we conform to the loud expectations of our culture, running after what it tells us we need. Yet in the endless striving, we leave little space for the treasures that truly matter, the things of lasting value, the things that draw us closer to Him.

How foolish we are to not be content. It does not matter how much we have or do not have. Contentment comes with thankfulness and appreciation of the goodness of GOD.

1 Timothy 6:6-8 (NIV)

But godliness with contentment is great gain. For we brought nothing into the world, and we can take nothing out of it. But if we have food and clothing, we will be content with that.

Lord, open our eyes when we are blinded by the things we chase after. Teach us to rest in the deep contentment of being Your beloved children. Remind us that Your love for us is greater than we could ever understand, steadying our hearts in every season. Thank You for never failing us with Your perfect love.

38 RISK

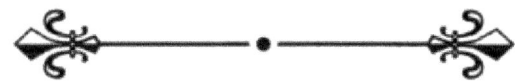

Lamentations 5:9 (NIV)

We get our bread at the risk of our lives because of the sword in the desert.

Mark 10:28-30 (NIV)

Then Peter spoke up, "We have left everything to follow you!" "Truly I tell you," Jesus replied, "no one who has left home or brothers or sisters or mother or father or children or fields for me and the gospel will fail to receive a hundred times as much in this present age: homes, brothers, sisters, mothers, children and fields— along with persecutions—and in the age to come eternal life.

"Nothing ventured, nothing gained" (Unknown)

"If you are not willing to risk the unusual, you will have to settle for the ordinary" Jim Rohn

What is your true propensity for risk? When it comes to finances, do you tend to hold back cautiously, or are you drawn to bold risks that promise greater reward? At the dinner table, do you find comfort in the familiar, or does your curiosity push you to taste new flavors and experiment with recipes? In your daily choices, do you lean on the "tried-and-true" methods, or do you feel a pull toward fresh, untested paths that might open new possibilities?

Do you play the same kind of games on your phone, or do you venture out and try something new? Do you eat at basically the same kind of restaurants? Are most of your friends mostly just like you?

Have you learned something new lately? Do you read materials beyond your natural preferences and interests?

Although the risks may seem minimal they are always there. We can be sorely disappointed or wonderfully surprised.

When we do not step out and take the risk we will never know. When we settle for the ordinary, we will not taste the potential rewards of the unusual.

Consider for a moment Peter's bold declaration to Jesus. He and the apostles were unwilling to settle for the ordinary; instead, they staked everything on the incomparable reward of a life wholly surrendered to the Lord. Each of us approaches risk in different ways, but I pray that you and I would learn to lay aside fear, embrace courage, and be willing to give all that we are in wholehearted devotion to Christ. May our lives echo the same resolve that Peter and the apostles displayed.

Father, we tend to cling to a lot of stuff. Help us to risk letting go of anything that hinders our walk with You.

39.WISH

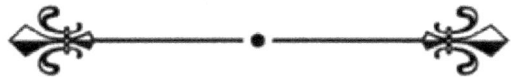

Revelation 3:15 (NIV)

I know your deeds, that you are neither cold nor hot. I wish you were either one or the other!

Over the years May and I have had multiple opportunities to be with people who were nearing the end of their days. It has, for the most part, been times of blessings for both them and us. Even in the midst of pain and suffering, there is something very special about knowing that your end is close at hand and that you have fully devoted yourself to the Lord, with no regrets.

Sadly it is not always that way. Many have told us, with broken hearts and tears in their eyes, "I wish I had." It is a most troubling place to be when you realize it is too late, and you can no longer do what you should have done.

Some of these regrets seem small in the grand scheme of things, wishing they had traveled more, learned to play an instrument, or taken the time to develop a new skill. Yet the deepest longings cut far more deeply: *I wish I had forgiven. I wish I had not squandered years on what never truly mattered. I wish I had cherished the fleeting moments with loved ones. I wish I had devoted myself more fully to knowing and pleasing God.*

I have trouble comprehending why this is. When we have the opportunity to do what is right, why do we still so often choose not to do it?

I write these words with a heavy heart. As I look around, I see many who profess to be followers of Jesus and yet their outward lives show little reflection of the reality of their profession. I fear many will approach the end of their days "wishing they had."

Oh Lord, what a heavy burden to bear as we approach the end of our days here on this earth. Let the words "I wish I had" be far, far from our consciousness as we purpose to live in the reality of being In Christ every moment of every day. Thank You.

40.LIGHT

Psalms 119:105 (NIV)

Your word is a lamp for my feet, a light on my path.

James 1:5-8 (NIV)

If any of you lacks wisdom, you should ask God, who gives generously to all without finding fault, and it will be given to you. But when you ask, you must believe and not doubt, because the one who doubts is like a wave of the sea, blown and tossed by the wind. That person should not expect to receive anything from the Lord. Such a person is double-minded and unstable in all they do.

Today's devotion is a follow up to yesterday's devotion about "I wish I hads."

God's word contains the answers to most (if not all) of life's complexities. The problem of ending our lives with a "wish I had" on our lips is something most of us would like to avoid. The above Scriptures tell us how to do it.

Realize, appreciate and apply God's word to the immediate things in our lives (the lamp for our feet) as well as the direction (goals/plans) for our future (light for our path).

Desire and ask God to give you wisdom and understanding for the immediate (urgent) things in your life as well as what may be important but not urgent

Discipline ourselves to apply God's words to our immediate situations while keeping ourselves focused on who we are and want to be IN CHRIST.

Be earnest and consistent in applying God's word in your life. Resist wasting time and doing things that have little eternal significance. Refuse to be double minded (saying one thing and doing another)

Live in the expectation of being a New Creation in Christ - where the old has passed and all is new — and where the "wish I hads" are no more.

Lord, lead us to read, study, and apply Your word to our lives. Thank You.

41.NOTICE

Matthew 7:3 (NIV)

Why do you look at the speck of sawdust in your brother's eye and pay no attention to the plank in your own eye?

I have read that we generally do not notice (see) much of what is right in front of us. Some of you are more detailed oriented and see quite a bit. People like me tend to look past the details. I am convinced there is much going on around me that I do not see.

I once met a man (to this day I think he may have been an angel) who stopped me and got me to look "inside a flower." I am so grateful for that person/angel as he helped me to see what I otherwise would not have noticed.

Sometimes, as today's scripture reminds us, it is far easier to point out the faults in others than to recognize our own. We buy a new car, a dress, or even a simple purse or shirt—and suddenly we begin to notice how many others have the very same thing. What once went unseen now catches our eye again and again, as if a light has been turned on.

Or have you had the "misfortune" of visiting someone's home that is meticulously kept and then come home and for the first time notice that your home needed some straightening up?

Our ability to truly notice is so often clouded by hurry, worry, and the endless noise of life. It is part of our human condition to overlook what is right before us. But what if, instead, we chose to pause—just for a moment each day—and opened our eyes with intention? What if we noticed, really noticed, the beauty in our surroundings and the sacred worth of the people near us?

Go ahead, I challenge you. Stop right now and take 60 seconds to truly notice your surroundings and/or the people you are with.

Lord, please help us to slow down and notice your incredible creation right here in front of us. Thank You.

42.POWER

Ephesians 1:18-21 (NIV)

I pray that the eyes of your heart may be enlightened in order that you may know the hope to which he has called you, the riches of his glorious inheritance in his holy people, and his incomparably great power for us who believe. That power is the same as the mighty strength he exerted when he raised Christ from the dead and seated him at his right hand in the heavenly realms, far above all rule and authority, power and dominion, and every name that is invoked, not only in the present age but also in the one to come.

Ephesians 6:12 (NIV)

For our struggle is not against flesh and blood, but against the rulers, against the authorities, against the powers of this dark world and against the spiritual forces of evil in the heavenly realms.

Romans 7:18-20 (NIV)

For I know that good itself does not dwell in me, that is, in my sinful nature. For I have the desire to do what is good, but I cannot carry it out. For I do not do the good I want to do, but the evil I do not want to do—this I keep on doing. Now if I do what I do not want to do, it is no longer I who do it, but it is sin living in me that does it.

Almost every day I marvel at myself and others as we choose to do what we know is not good/best for us. Not even the simple things like eating properly, spending time in the scriptures, following the speed limit, not smoking, exercising, fellowship with someone lonely, giving to the needy, cleaning the garage (attic, closet), giving away what you're not using, clearing the clutter from the dining room table, making your bed (oh, I better stop before you think I am meddling).

As you read Romans 7, can you see yourself? Surely you can. When we consider Romans 7, we realize there is a spiritual battle going on. There are powers and authorities in this dark world that are warring against your good intentions ("I will try.")

I often wonder, *"Will I ever reach the place where I choose what is good all the time?"* In this life, probably not (see Philippians 1:6). Yet I rest in knowing that the final victory is already certain. Ephesians 1 reminds us that Jesus is seated *far above every rule and authority, every power and dominion.* The very forces we struggle against each day have already been defeated in Him. Our hope, our strength, and our victory flow not from ourselves but from being firmly rooted in Christ—where His triumph becomes our own.

Dear Lord, do I even understand what it really means to be 'In You?' Teach me, lead me to be victorious in You every day. Thank You.

43.FORGOTTEN

Luke 12:6-7 (NIV)

Are not five sparrows sold for two pennies? Yet not one of them is forgotten by God. Indeed, the very hairs of your head are all numbered. Don't be afraid; you are worth more than many sparrows.

You've probably heard the saying "out of sight out of mind." I know that this saying is not always 100% true but my experience has been that when something, or even someone, is out of sight for a while I tend to forget them.

I once heard the story of a young boy who asked his father, "What was the name of your grandfather, and what did he do?" The father gave a sad reply—he knew the name, but nothing more of the man's life. In my own case, I do not even know the names of my great-grandparents, let alone their stories. Now that May and I are blessed to be great-great-grandparents, I cannot help but wonder how quickly we too will fade from memory. My prayer is that, even if our names are forgotten, the love we have sown into our family will live on.

Perhaps that is why some people expend all kinds of energy and financial resources to build memorials to themselves? The reality, however, for the vast majority of us, is that we will be forgotten.

But that is not the end of the story. We will not be forgotten by the Lord and Creator of the Universe, the One who recorded all the days of our lives even before we were born: (Psalms 139:16-17 (NIV) Your eyes saw my unformed body; all the days ordained for me were written in your book before one of them came to be. How precious to me are your thoughts, God! How vast is the sum of them!

God knows us and He will not forget us. We are His children for all eternity. Therefore, let us live for the One who will remember us.

Lord, thank You for bringing us into Your Ohana (family), and for not forgetting us. Thank You

44.PAU
(FINISHED)

Genesis 2:2 (NIV)

By the seventh day God had finished the work he had been doing; so on the seventh day he rested from all his work.

John 19:30 (NIV)

When he had received the drink, Jesus said, "It is finished." With that, he bowed his head and gave up his spirit.

For some reason, the word *"pau"* has been resting heavily on my heart. In Hawaiian it speaks of something finished, brought to completion.

When Jesus surrendered His Spirit, He declared that the work of salvation for all humanity was complete. The work was *pau*, finished, final, nothing left to add and nothing left undone. No further sacrifice required, no lingering debt unpaid. The price was covered fully, once for all.

And when the work is truly finished, it is time to enter into rest. Not the kind of rest that waits for tomorrow to resume the burden, but the deep rest of gratitude, pausing to appreciate, to give thanks, and to rejoice in the fruit of what has already been accomplished.

As I reflect on this word, I keep thinking that we would do well to keep the finished work of Jesus constantly before us, reminding ourselves that the work is done. It is time to be thankful and to rest in the Messiah, Jesus.

Father, thank You that Jesus completed the work. Help us to find rest for our souls as we reflect on this most perfectly completed work of Jesus the Messiah.

45.DIRECT

2 Thessalonians 3:5 (NASB)

May the Lord direct your hearts into the love of God and into the steadfastness of Christ.

Recently I heard a pastor say, "when Jesus is Lord of you, you are not in charge of the clock." He was making the point that, as servants of the Most High God, we are not the ones who chose the timing of events in our lives.

As His servants, we do not even get to decide which events are to be part of our lives. At least we should not. After all, isn't a servant to do the bidding of the Master? Isn't it the Master's decision to decide what is to be done, when it is to be done and how it is to be done?

Perhaps that was understood in the days of Jesus when slaves and servants were common. Today, we seem to think that servants have certain "rights". That may be true in our secular culture, but do you think that is acceptable in your relationship with the Lord Jesus?

I suspect that many would answer "no." But then I ask why are you continually trying to direct your life? Consider the decisions we make such as where we want to go to school, our vocation, our choice of a mate (or not), where to live, what church to attend, when to move, who to be friendly to, where to shop etc. I could go on and on. Many of the things we choose to direct may seem inconsequential, but maybe they are not.

What if God has a master plan for our lives and we keep going on detours? What if there are people we are supposed to meet but we have directed ourselves somewhere else? What if Jesus was truly Lord of ALL of your life - what might be different?

Father, I know we call You Lord, but are You really Lord of all of me? Please let me see the incongruity between what I say and what I do and redirect my steps. Thank You.

46.EXCESS

Exodus 16:18 (NASB)

When they measured it with an omer, he who had gathered much had no excess, and he who had gathered little had no lack; every man gathered as much as he should eat.

Proverbs 25:16 (NASB)

Have you found honey? Eat only what you need, that you not have it in excess and vomit it.

Is excess something good or not so good? The word excess means to have more than is necessary. We probably agree that it is not good to have an excess of something negative (like anxiety), but what about something that is perceived as neutral or even good? Consider food. Is having excess food in our pantry good or not? How about having excess clothes in our closets? Or how about excess space in our homes? Or excess cosmetics etc. on our bathroom counters? Or excess pots and pans in our cupboards? Or how about excess money or time?

I think the above scriptures are giving us a word of caution about accumulating excess in our lives, even the good things. The accumulation of excess is never free. It costs us financially but, even more importantly, it takes time and effort to acquire and maintain all our excess. Time and effort that would otherwise be available to do what is important. The excesses in our lives limit our ability to be all that God intends for us to be.

They are like the "little foxes" that steal away the little (but important) things in our lives.

"Your life is a canvas for limitless potential. Every stroke matters. With every unnecessary item we buy, we trade a bit of our freedom. We trade our focus, our resources, and even our potential. Here is the challenge for all of us: Stop pursuing anything that distracts you from your greatest values and highest potential. If an item doesn't serve a purpose or bring joy, then consider freeing yourself from it. Start today. Start now. Unburden yourself of the excess and see how much more room you have to grow, to breathe, and to pursue what genuinely matters to you. Reclaim your time, your resources, and your potential. I can't think of anything more valuable than that." Joshua Becker

Dear Lord, in a culture that often sees excess as normal, help us ignore those voices that encourage us to think this way. Teach us to see things as You do, and to want a simple and content life that follows the example of Jesus. Thank You for guiding us back whenever we start to lose focus on what really matters.

47.MARGIN

Acts 4:34-35 (NASB)

For there was not a needy person among them, for all who were owners of land or houses would sell them and bring the proceeds of the sales and lay them at the apostles' feet, and they would be distributed to each as any had need

I felt prompted to select the word "margin" for today's devotional as a way of balancing yesterday's word of excess. To live a peaceful life one of the things we must learn to do is balance the opportunities this life offers. I am using the word "margin" to mean "having a little extra." Not excess, but more than you might need at the moment.

Our secular culture suggests this is a good thing. I am mostly inclined to agree. Examples include setting aside some cash for emergencies. Or little extra food or water in case of a storm or other emergency. The concept is to have a "little extra" set aside for the unexpected and the unplanned.

I have ascribed to this principle practically my whole life and it is a great stress reducer when faced with the unexpected emergency. Margin helps us get through the difficult period. Margin in our lives also makes it possible for us to help others when they experience "life's surprises."

The challenge is to know the difference between margin and excess. If we earnestly seek God's wisdom, His Spirit will give us the understanding we desire.

In today's scripture, we see believers modeling a way of life that speaks to us even now. They remind us how to handle both abundance and margin with wisdom and humility. Teach us, Lord, to "live beneath our means" with consistency and trust, creating space not only for our families but also to extend generosity to others. May our stewardship reflect Your heart, so that truly, "there may not be a needy person among us."

Father, quiet our restless minds and open our hearts to truly grasp this concept and its place in every part of our lives. Show us that it touches not only our finances, but also the way we spend our time, the talents we develop, and the gifts You have placed within us. Teach us to remember that all we have belongs to You, and shape our hearts to use every blessing for Your service and glory. Thank You for entrusting us with so much and for guiding us in how to use it well.

48.GIFT

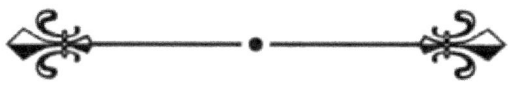

Ephesians 2:8-10 (NASB)

For by grace you have been saved through faith; and that not of yourselves, it is the gift of God; not as a result of works, so that no one may boast. For we are His workmanship, created in Christ Jesus for good works, which God prepared beforehand so that we would walk in them

Does a gift truly come without strings? In much of Western culture, we are taught that a gift is freely given, expecting nothing in return. And yet, have you noticed how often our hearts whisper otherwise? When a gift is placed in our hands, there can rise a quiet pressure, a sense that gratitude must be proven, that somehow we owe something back. Instead of resting in the generosity of the moment, we may find ourselves wrestling with the unspoken weight of repayment.

A simple example. Someone treats you to a meal or a cup of coffee. Do you not feel a little obligated to do the same? Or someone is especially kind and thoughtful. Don't you want to return the favor? Now I know there are exceptions, but in general rarely do we accept gifts without a sense of obligation.

I once read the story of a new missionary who was warned by a seasoned one, "Whatever happens, do not accept gifts from the natives." Curious, he asked why. The older missionary explained, "Because by tomorrow they will be at your door—expecting, perhaps even demanding, that you give something back. In their culture, a gift is never truly free; it always carries with it the expectation of return."

In **Ephesians 2:8-10** we are told that we have this gift given to us because of nothing we have done. However, in verse 10 we have a spoiler. The gift is not free but creates an obligation (to walk in good works prepared for us to do).

We might say that God's saving grace is an unconditional gift (no works can earn it). Yet receiving this gift of grace puts us under obligation.

I think this is the principle of reciprocity - as one gives it comes back to them (see Luke 37). As God has given grace to us it is only natural that we give to Him through our good works (which have already been prepared for us to do).

Dear God, thank You so much for the gift of Your grace - may we in turn show our appreciation for the gift as we live our lives for You.

49.HELPER

John 14:16 (NASB)

I will ask the Father, and He will give you another Helper, that He may be with you forever;

Some years ago, I was praying about something (I have no clue what it was) and I asked God to "help me" with something. I was stopped in my tracks as I clearly heard God tell me (rather harshly as I remember) - "I am not your helper."

I wrestled with confusion, for the Scriptures clearly reveal that God helps us in countless ways. Over time, I began to see more deeply what He was showing me—His position and His majesty. Yes, He graciously helps me, yet above all, He remains the Lord Almighty, the Sovereign King over all creation, the One who reigns forever.

My prayers have changed significantly since that event. I refrain from asking God to help me and instead I ask Him to lead me, to direct my paths, to strengthen me, to give me courage and boldness. Yes, I am still asking for help, but I try to place Him in the proper position as the Head and Lord of my life and not as my helper.

Something else became clearer from this experience. God is not as interested in helping me get what I want as He is vitally interested in my maturity and growth in the Body of Christ.

Lord, I rest well knowing that You are not my helper but, rather, Lord of the universe. Yet it is still Your pleasure to help me to be in Christ and to live out the fruits of the New Creation. Thank You.

50. THANKFUL

Ephesians 5:4 (NASB)

And there must be no filthiness and silly talk, or coarse jesting, which are not fitting, but rather giving of thanks.

Have you ever wondered why "giving thanks" can be a deterrent to living an immoral life? The above scripture does not seem to make sense - or does it?

My observation is that the one character trait shared by dedicated followers of Jesus is thankfulness. When times are good, they are thankful and when times are bad they are still thankful. Why? I suggest it is because their eyes are not on their circumstances but rather on whom they have become in Christ.

I wonder, is this the "secret" to a godly life? When we are genuinely thankful for all things we are much less likely to be drawn away by our own desires and/or the temptations placed before us by the world. We are much less likely to grumble and complain about the difficulties in life.

Being In Christ we are designed and enabled to devotedly love one another and to love God. When we yield our bodies to immorality we undermine the new creation we have become.

Lord, cultivate in us deeply grateful spirits. Let our gratitude overflow in ways that draw the attention of those who do not yet know You, stirring curiosity about Your goodness. Thank You for filling our lives with blessings seen and unseen, and for being the greatest gift of all.

51.SUBMISSION

Ephesians 5:21 (NIV)

Submit to one another out of reverence for Christ.

Now here is a word that causes much difficulty for many Christians. There are many views about what Paul "really" meant. For many, "submission" has a negative connotation. But I think that Paul wants us to "unlearn" what we think we know about relationships and to learn what it means to be new creatures living out a new Creation.

The Greek word translated here as *submit* is ὑποτάσσω **(hypotassō)**, a term that carries the sense of willingly placing oneself under another. Paul's instruction goes beyond mere hierarchy; he is inviting us to view others as more significant than ourselves and to let that perspective shape our daily actions. This isn't about diminishing our worth but about embodying humility—choosing respect, service, and love in the way we interact with those around us.

Let me explain. We may strongly disagree with someone holding a high office (like the president of the United States). However we can still recognize that they are of a higher social standing than we are. Thus, we owe them a certain amount of honor and respect - even though we might not like them.

That concept was revolutionary in Paul's day, and it is equally revolutionary today. What a difference it would make if we honored and respected one another in the body of Christ as if they were of a higher social rank than ourselves. It requires a little humility but I would like to see how our Christian Communities would be transformed.

Lord, begin with me. Let me be willing to actually submit myself to every believer I encounter as if they were of a higher - more important - social standing than myself. Lead me to honor them and to respect them - even if (when) I do not agree with them or even if I do not like them. Please Lord, make this especially so in our marriages and family relationships. Thank You

52.COMMUNION

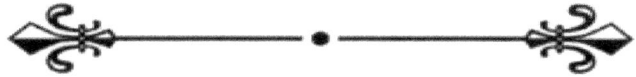

Matthew 26:26-28 (NASB)

While they were eating, Jesus took some bread, and after a blessing, He broke it and gave it to the disciples, and said, "Take, eat; this is My body." And when He had taken a cup and given thanks, He gave it to them, saying, "Drink from it, all of you; for this is My blood of the covenant, which is poured out for many for forgiveness of sins

Yesterday my small group gathered for communion and fellowship. After a summer break it was encouraging to be together again.

I firmly believe this is how the early church shared the Lord's supper (Holy Communion as part of gathering with a meal). When we spend time with friends around food it is generally a festive, pleasing and encouraging experience.

In many American churches, that practice is no longer common, often because of the size of congregations and the challenges of organization. Yet within the warmth of our homes and the closeness of small groups, it remains not only possible but deeply meaningful.

If you are not actively part of a small group, I encourage you to join one (or start one yourself). If you are part of a small group, I urge you set aside time for the group to celebrate communion and enjoy the fellowship of sharing life together.

As our culture drifts further from its moral compass, remind us that this is not optional. Impress upon our hearts the urgency to actively strengthen and encourage one another in faith, especially as we see the day drawing near.

1 Thessalonians 5:11 (NIV)

Therefore encourage one another and build each other up, just as in fact you are doing.

Hebrews 10:24-25 (NASB)

and let us consider how to stimulate one another to love and good deeds, not forsaking our own assembling together, as is the habit of some, but encouraging one another; and all the more as you see the day drawing near.

Father, lead us to make time - to adjust our schedules as necessary - to make it a priority - to be with and to encourage one another.

53.FOCUS

Philippians 3:14 (NASB)

I press on toward the goal for the prize of the upward call of God in Christ Jesus.

"Turn your eyes upon Jesus - look full into His wonderful face - and the things of this world will grow slowing dim in the light of His beauty and grace"

I remember the last 500 yards of the 1982 Honolulu Marathon. I was exhausted and my body was too tired to even take another step. But I could see the finish line. It seemed far away - but it beckoned me to finish the race. So, I took another step - and another and another. I saw nothing else as I kept my focus on the finish, determined to complete the race. And that is how we finish well - we focus on the prize of the upward calling to God in Christ Jesus.

You see my dear friends, in this life there are many, many distractions and they hinder us from getting the prize. Yes, we are assured of eternal salvation but there is another prize for the here and now and the yet to be. A prize for those who are not distracted in the race of life. It is the prize given to those who have learned to keep their eyes upon Jesus - of living now as if being "In Christ" was something obtainable in the "here and now" - not only in the "by and by".

Let us fix our eyes on the Lord Jesus, asking Him to quiet the countless distractions that compete for our attention. As we draw near, the pull of lesser things begins to fade, and what once seemed important loses its grip. Though the path may feel narrower—and others may even call it less exciting, the joy of walking with God in the "here and not yet" opens the way to deeper adventures, rich with purpose and free of regret.

Father, quiet the thoughts that distract and scatter us, and train our hearts to fix their gaze upon Your Son. Teach us to look steadily to Jesus, trusting Him as our guide and Savior. Thank You for never letting us lose sight of Him when we call on Your name.

54. TODAY

Joshua 24:15 (NASB)

If it is disagreeable in your sight to serve the LORD, choose for yourselves today whom you will serve; but as for me and my house, we will serve the LORD.

Last night, our son-in-law Jimmy took his final breath on this earth and entered into God's eternal rest. The loss of someone we love always leaves an ache, and my heart especially grieves for our daughter Bobbi. Yet for Jimmy, the struggles of this life, of which he had many, are now over, and he is embraced by the peace of God's perfect presence.

Life, however, still stretches before us. Though the weight of sorrow presses heavily, we continue on, strengthened by the hope that when the moment came to choose, Jimmy chose God, and that choice has carried him home.

The Time for Choosing - **C.S. LEWIS**

"God is going to invade, all right: but what is the good of saying you are on his side then, when you see the whole natural universe melting away like a dream and something else – something it never entered your head to conceive – comes crashing in; something so beautiful to some of us and so terrible to others that none of us will have any choice left? For this time, it will be God without disguise; something so overwhelming that it will strike either irresistible love or irresistible horror into every creature. It will be too late then to choose your side. There is no use saying you choose to lie down when it has become impossible to stand up. That will not be the time for choosing; it will be the time when we discover which side we really have chosen, whether we realized it before or not. Now, today, this moment, is our chance to choose the right side."

Source: Mere Christianity

Lord, please comfort the hearts of all who grieve for their loved ones. Thank You that we have chosen You as our Lord and Savior.

55.CONFIDENT

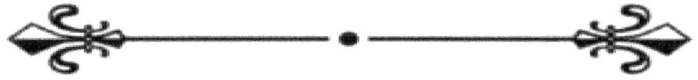

Ephesians 3:12 (NASB)

...in whom we have boldness and confident access through faith in Him.

When I was younger, I really enjoyed challenges - especially situations that seemed to puzzle others. I had an inner confidence that "I could figure it out". Fast forward a "few" years and I much prefer fewer challenges. I would be perfectly content to have updates to our phones every decade or two. It seems my phone gets "updated" again before I can even learn all the new features.

I was influenced by someone who told me "Paul, if you are facing a daunting challenge, and you do not seem to know what to do – act. Act as though you do know; because inside of you, you really do know." I considered his logic to be flawed; however, it settled into my spirit. Somehow, inside, I really did know. I just needed to find it and I was confident that I could.

Now many years later I have discovered that the advice was perfectly logical and wise - in the context of Christianity. You see we are filled with the Spirit. The Spirit lives inside of us and the Spirit knows all things. So, it is true - when I do not think I know, inside, I really do - for the Spirit guides me into all truth.

Please let me be clear, however, that this "confidence" can be little more than pride wrapped up in a more pleasing wrapper. I believe that we face our greatest challenges in the areas where we are most competent. God is exalted in our weaknesses not in our abilities, accomplishments or even our confidence. The great danger of confidence is that we start to think it is about us rather than God.

So next time you are stumbling around wondering what to do, how to act, or what to say - take this little bit of advice. Act. Act as though you do know because you really do know - through the Spirit of God living in You. But be very careful to understand and acknowledge this "knowing" does not come from you but the Spirit of the living God in you.

Oh Lord, life can be such an adventure in you. It matters not that I am weak in the knowing, because You know everything, and I am confident that the great work You have begun in me will be completed. Thank You.

56.OVERWHELMED

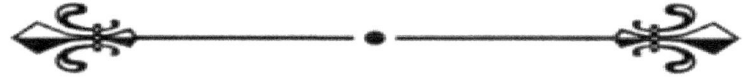

Matthew 11:29-30 (NASB)

Take My yoke upon you and learn from Me, for I am gentle and humble in heart, and YOU WILL FIND REST FOR YOUR SOULS. For My yoke is easy and My burden is light.

I have a tendency to feel overwhelmed. Mostly it stems from having more on my plate than is necessary or creating unnecessary personal deadlines, or from circumstances that I have no control over but seem to press in on me. And then there are times when my melancholy personality seems to do it all by itself.

Feeling overwhelmed is a negative emotion, but it has at least one positive attribute: it tells me I am not resting in the Lord. Somewhere along the way, I moved out from under His yoke of rest and placed myself under my own yoke, which can lead to unwanted pressure.

I have had much practice dealing with this and here is what works for me and might be helpful for others.

- Stop whatever you are doing, if possible, even if it is "important"
- Move to a place that you perceive as peaceful. For me it is usually outside in the garden
- Have a conversation with God. Express what is going on. Be honest. He already knows anyway
- Listen. Be still. Know that He is God
- Wait for His Spirit to tell you when it is time to rise and resume the day
- Repeat as necessary

When I feel overwhelmed, it is a reminder to put aside my own agenda and return once again to my knees in prayer — looking to the Savior of all humanity for His rest and for His peace.

Lord, thank You for Your reminders that in my weakness You can show Yourself strong. Thank You.

57.HOUR

Ecclesiastes 9:12 (NIV)

Moreover, no one knows when their hour will come: As fish are caught in a cruel net, or birds are taken in a snare, so people are trapped by evil times that fall unexpectedly upon them.

John 16:33 (ESV)

I have said these things to you, that in me you may have peace. In the world you will have tribulation. But take heart; I have overcome the world.

The writer of Ecclesiastes understood that life can suddenly take an unexpected turn, and Jesus warned us to expect difficulties in this world.

The answer lies in understanding whom we have become in Christ. You see, the "powers" that cause our difficulties have been disarmed - they were disarmed at the cross. Oh, yes, they may still buffet us and cause us pain and grief, but in the final analysis the "powers" have been defeated at the cross.

Colossians 2:15 (NIV)

And having disarmed the powers and authorities, he made a public spectacle of them, triumphing over them by the cross.

We live in the time of "now and not yet." A time when the work of the cross is complete, yet still requires us to cooperate with God to crush the "powers" of the air.

Ephesians 6:11-13 (NIV)

Put on the full armor of God, so that you can take your stand against the devil's schemes. For our struggle is not against flesh and blood, but against the rulers, against the authorities, against the powers of this dark world and against the spiritual forces of evil in the heavenly realms. Therefore put on the full armor of God, so that when the day of evil comes, you may be able to stand your ground, and after you have done everything, to stand.

Lord, let us not be so foolish as to think we can stand against the powers that war against us without the armor of God. Lead us to be prepared for battle and when we have done all - to stand. To stand in the expectation of Your deliverance. Thank You.

58. WONDERFUL

Isaiah 29:14 (NIV)

Therefore once more I will astound these people with wonder upon wonder; the wisdom of the wise will perish, the intelligence of the intelligent will vanish.

Isaiah 9:6 (NIV)

For to us a child is born, to us a son is given, and the government will be on his shoulders. And he will be called Wonderful Counselor, Mighty God, Everlasting Father, Prince of Peace.

1 Peter 2:9 (NIV)

But you are a chosen people, a royal priesthood, a holy nation, God's special possession, that you may declare the praises of him who called you out of darkness into his wonderful light.

I awoke yesterday morning with this word - wonderful - on my heart and mind. There it remained for the entire day. I thought to myself "wonderful means full of wonder." So I asked myself "am I full of wonder?"

Sadly, I have misplaced some of my wonder. The gospel and life as a follower of Christ has, in some ways, become predictable and common place. Please do not misunderstand me - the Christian life is an adventure. It is a joy to be a child of God. Yet I ask myself where is the wonder, the surprise, the excitement, the exhilaration of knowing another has paid all my debts and has given me freedom from sin and freedom to serve the One True God? Where is my amazing admiration for the One that loves me so much, He became the Suffering Servant and died for me?

Somehow the wonder and beauty of the Lord has faded. My thankfulness for the unexpected and undeserved gift of deliverance has diminished. I seem to take so much for granted as a Christian of nearly 50 years. Where, I wonder, has the wonder gone?

I long once again to experience the wonder of my first days as a believer. A time when I was "wonder filled." I want to be wonderfully delighted in His presence once again.

Psalms 51:11-12 (NASB)

Do not cast me away from Your presence and do not take Your Holy Spirit from me. Restore to me the joy of Your salvation and sustain me with a willing spirit.

Lord, there are many distractions. I ask You to please remove from my life anything that keeps me from fully experiencing the wonder of Your presence. Thank You.

59.WANT

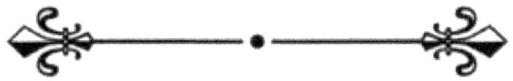

Mark 6:25 (NIV)

At once the girl hurried into the king with the request: "I want you to give me right now the head of John the Baptist on a platter."

Mark 10:51 (NIV)

"What do you want me to do for you?" Jesus asked him. The blind man said, "Rabbi, I want to see."

May and I enjoy watching the "house hunter" programs, especially the ones looking for homes all around the world. The more I watch, the more I feel content staying right here. Please do not get me wrong - many of the homes are very beautiful (and usually very expensive) but there is a pervasive theme of "I want."

It seems that no matter how nice the new home is, the prospective buyer feels the need to change something or have something updated or remodeled. It is seldom good enough. I think it must be the "American" way to want the latest and greatest in just about everything.

I often wonder why we feel discontented with what we have and what drives us to desire what we do not? Do you think we have been conformed to our culture? **(Romans 12:2)**

Jesus told us what is most important, the one thing we should want above all others —

Matthew 6:33 (NIV)

33 But seek first his kingdom and his righteousness, and all these things will be given to you as well.

Could it be that when we ignore this "advice" we risk being forever discontented with what we have?

Lord, lead me to never seek what I want in my life but rather to always seek first what You want. Thank You.

60.CONNECTED

1 John 5:4-5 (NIV)

For everyone born of God overcomes the world. This is the victory that has overcome the world, even our faith. Who is it that overcomes the world? Only the one who believes that Jesus is the Son of God.

When I place my Bluetooth earbuds in my ears and it hooks up with my computer I hear the word "connected." I hear nothing until the connection is made. There is zero communication going on until a digital link is established and I am "connected."

The word connected has the connotation of being associated with people of influence. I often hear people say "it is not so much what you know but whom you know." This is often true in many of life's situations and it could not be more true in the Christian's life.

Today's scripture promises that "everyone born of God overcomes the world." May I suggest a caveat? I have no issue with the end result of our promised deliverance — eventually we will die, and we will find that in Christ we have indeed overcome the world - not by anything we have done – but by the simple blessing of deliverance.

What I would like us to consider is the journey along the way. I know a lot of professing believers that are constantly struggling with all sorts of issues. They desperately need to hear from God and it seems like they do not. I wonder, could their problem be that they are not connected?

Let's face it, life is demanding, and it takes a lot of effort just to keep pace with everything that is going on. Being and staying connected to God can be challenging. I am convinced that a believer who lives life without purposefully staying connected to Savior is destined for more drama than I ever would like to experience.

Dear Father, staying connected to You is a two-way process. I know You want to connect with me. Lead me, Lord, to want to connect with You and to arrange my life to be still, to know You are God and to stay connected.

61.INSPIRATION

Jeremiah 32:40 (NIV)

I will make an everlasting covenant with them: I will never stop doing good to them, and I will inspire them to fear me, so that they will never turn away from me.

1 Thessalonians 1:3 (NIV)

We remember before our God and Father your work produced by faith, your labor prompted by love, and your endurance inspired by hope in our Lord Jesus Christ.

Have you given any thought lately to what inspires you? What is it that excites you about life and the work you do? What moves you to do more, to do better, or to keep going when life gets difficult?

What would get you out of bed early in the morning, excited for what is ahead? What makes your heart a little swishy and your mind think of all sorts of ideas? What is it that makes you feel young again, excited about life and what is ahead?

What is it that makes life worth living and living it to its fullest?

Inspiration comes from many sources. Yet there is one Source greater than all the rest. It is the inspiration birthed within us by the Holy Spirit, stirring our hearts to live lives that honor and please the Lord our God.

Lord, I set myself before You to seek Your inspiration to live a meaningful life. Thank You.

62.PRESENT

Titus 2:11-12 (NIV)

For the grace of God has appeared that offers salvation to all people. It teaches us to say "no" to ungodliness and worldly passions, and to live self-controlled, upright and godly lives in this present age.

The word "present" can be used several ways but for this devotion I am using it to mean what exists or is occurring now. In other words, I mean right now, at this very moment.

Consider the following: Hannah Tatum Whitall Smith (February 7, 1832 – May 1, 1911) was a lay speaker and author in the Holiness movement in the United States and the Higher Life movement in the United Kingdom. She also wrote the classic book The Secrets of a Happy Christian, which was very influential in my early Christian life. She often said that it is relatively easy for us to have a "future faith," but it is an entirely different matter to have faith for the present, a "present faith," as she called it.

What she meant was that it is much easier for us to have faith for something in the future than to have faith for the crisis of the moment.

For example, we may find it easy to have faith that when we die (someday) God will bring us into His presence. But, it is more difficult to have faith when one is unable to take a breath, is in excruciating pain, or perhaps being tortured to death, to have the "present faith" to believe all is well.

On a personal level, when I have trouble breathing, I can relate to the fear that can quickly eclipse faith. I "know" that s I will be OK but the panic is still very present as I struggle for the next breath.

Let us consider a common Christian experience. We know we should give generously, yet there is often no money left at the end of the month to cover the bills. The challenge is to have present faith— to do what God calls us to do even when we "know" it cannot be done.

Or our health fails and despite all the doctors and pills and protocols nothing seems to help. Can I have a present faith when everything is seemingly hopeless? Of course there are many other examples.

Dear Lord, I know I "talk a good faith" about the future but please strengthen me and give me courage to "live a present faith" in the here and now.

63.DISSIPATION

1 Peter 4:4 (NASB)

In all this, they are surprised that you do not run with them into the same excesses of dissipation, and they malign you.

This is an unusual word for me. I don't think I've ever used it in writing or conversation, but it came to mind the other day when I read an article, originally written over twenty years ago—that used it. It surprised me because I don't recall ever encountering the word outside of the Bible before.

Dissipation has to do with being drunk and disorderly. However, it also means to waste and squander our money, energy, or resources.

Have you ever been accused of dissipation living? Probably not, but since yesterday I have begun thinking that dissipation may be a fair characterization of the lives of many of us who profess to be Christians.

Think about it - have you and I not at times wasted what God has given us? I am immediately aware of when I have spent my money and time on self-satisfaction - things unnecessary and not needed. I have also wasted time. There are many ways to distract myself — is this not also dissipation?

I expect some of you will want to push back. Surely, I don't mean you, do I? Well, I'm not so sure. When does taking a needed break, a rest, or a little self-indulgence cross the line into dissipation? Perhaps that's a question only the Holy Spirit can answer. Of course, if we never ask, we'll probably never know.

Lord, once again I pray as David prayed - reveal to me anything in my life that is not useful to You and Your kingdom. Please continue Your most perfect work in and through me. Thank You.

64.LAMENT

Exodus 5:22-23 (NIV)

Moses returned to the LORD and said, "Why, Lord, why have you brought trouble on this people? Is this why you sent me? Ever since I went to Pharaoh to speak in your name, he has brought trouble on this people, and you have not rescued your people at all."

Joshua 7:7-9 (NIV)

And Joshua said, "Alas, Sovereign LORD, why did you ever bring this people across the Jordan to deliver us into the hands of the Amorites to destroy us? If only we had been content to stay on the other side of the Jordan! Pardon your servant, Lord. What can I say, now that Israel has been routed by its enemies? The Canaanites and the other people of the country will hear about this and they will surround us and wipe out our name from the earth. What then will you do for your own great name?"

Judges 6:13 (NIV)

"Pardon me, my lord," Gideon replied, "but if the LORD is with us, why has all this happened to us? Where are all his wonders that our ancestors told us about when they said, 'Did not the LORD bring us up out of Egypt?' But now the LORD has abandoned us and given us into the hand of Midian."

Jeremiah 14:8-9 (NIV)

You who are the hope of Israel, its Savior in times of distress, why are you like a stranger in the land, like a traveler who stays only a night? Why are you like a man taken by surprise, like a warrior powerless to save? You are among us, LORD, and we bear your name; do not forsake us!

Do you ever complain to God? Many Christians believe we shouldn't. Yet when we look at the Old Testament, we see that there was plenty of complaining, and not just a little (the examples above are only a few).

A lament is a heartfelt, honest, and passionate expression of grief, sorrow, complaint, regret or disappointment. The laments we find in scripture are heartfelt honesty being expressed to God. Was not Jesus' lament at the cross the greatest lament of all? **Mark 15:34 (NIV)** "My God, My God, why have You forsaken me?"

Should not our prayers at times contain a lament or two?

Lord, help us to be fully honest before You. When we need to lament, remind us that You can handle our pain and confusion, and that You alone can heal them. Thank You.

65.SUNRISE

Habakkuk 3:4 (NIV)

His splendor was like the sunrise; rays flashed from his hand, where his power was hidden.

Psalms 30:5 (NIV)

For his anger lasts only a moment, but his favor lasts a lifetime; weeping may stay for the night, but rejoicing comes in the morning.

Psalms 59:16-17 (NIV)

But I will sing of your strength, in the morning I will sing of your love; for you are my fortress, my refuge in times of trouble. You are my strength, I sing praise to you; you, God, are my fortress, my God on whom I can rely.

Do you recall your favorite sunrise? When I ask myself that question, I have this memory, which may be a composite of several memories.

Before I go on, I should admit that I'm not a morning person. I would much rather sleep in. The mattress and I do battle almost every morning. But one morning in 1959 remains etched in my mind. I was standing in an army reveille formation in Korea, watching the rays of the rising sun touch the golden fields of rice waiting to be harvested. Mist hovered above the paddies, caught between the earth and the soft, purple-hued mountains. I was just seventeen, and I had never seen anything so peaceful, so breathtakingly serene. The air was still. Korea is often called "the land of the morning calm," and for perhaps the first time in my life, I witnessed a beauty I hadn't known existed.

Many, many sunrises later I still appreciate early mornings. It is such a restful and rejuvenating time for me. I hope you too have experienced the special peace that comes from arising before dawn. It is a special time when the splendor of God's flashes anew.

It is a time to set aside the troubles of the night and to rejoice in the new day God has given to us. It is a time to renew our commitment of obedience and service to a God who has demonstrated His great love for us. It is a time to draw close to Him, to settle into the arms of God to be comforted and protected.

It is a time to sing praises to our Lord God - our fortress upon whom we depend . Yes, in the early morning, as I continue to do battle with the mattress, I arise from my slumbers and greet another day… Oh what a day this will be.

Lord God, thank You for every new day. Let the bed be for the weary. Awake me early each day, Lord, to spend time with You. Thank You.

66.MORE

Luke 6:38 (NIV)

Give, and it will be given to you. A good measure, pressed down, shaken together and running over, will be poured into your lap. For with the measure you use, it will be measured to you."

John 21:17 (NIV)

The third time he said to him, "Simon son of John, do you love me?" Peter was hurt because Jesus asked him the third time, "Do you love me?" He said, "Lord, you know all things; you know that I love you." Jesus said, "Feed my sheep."

How does one measure love? How does one know they have loved to the point that there is "no more love to give?"

Sometimes when May tells me she "loves me" I respond with "I love you more" and she answers, "there is no more." We have done this so many times that some of our friends are doing it too.

It is a very comforting exchange for both of us to know we love each other to the very best of our abilities. Please do not take this wrong, we have our "moments" (although they seem to be very rare these days), but we deeply care for one another, and we both know the other is the most important person in our lives.

As we read the scriptures and see God's great love for us, can we prayerfully say to Him "I love You more." If we did I suspect He might respond "but there is no more" and He would be absolutely correct. There is no greater love than the love of God for us His children.

Still, what can we say to express our love toward Him? Can we honestly tell the Lord that we love Him more than anything in this world, even more than our spouses, our children, our success, our friends, our church? Can we say we love Him above everything, with no exceptions?

Lord, look into the deep recesses of my heart - how much do I love You?

67.COME

Matthew 6:10 (NIV)

Your kingdom come, your will be done, on earth as it is in heaven.

Most of us have prayed today's verse as part of the Lord's prayer. When I hear these words, I often wonder "what would it be like if God's kingdom came NOW, and was manifested in my life NOW"?

Have you ever given that any thought? Just how is God's will done in heaven? How can we duplicate that here on earth?

I suppose in heaven God's will has no competition. Here on earth, we seem to have lots of distractions and we sometimes include God's will among a bunch of other choices we want to make.

And I suspect that in heaven God's timing is impeccable while here on earth there are a lot of other "priorities" that can sometimes be conflicting.

In heaven, God's will must be carried out perfectly without error, without weakness, without the flaws that come from human hands. There is no confusion there, no competing motives, no anxiety about how the work will get done. There is no shortage of time, talent, or resources. But here on earth, all of those limitations seem to stand in our way.

I think the reason Jesus taught us to pray this prayer is because it is truly a work of God and not a work of the flesh. Doing God's will here on earth as it is done in heaven is nothing short of a marvelous work of God.

God, give me a heart fully surrendered to You. Let Your will be done in my life so completely that it mirrors the perfection of heaven. Teach me to live each day in step with Your will—here on earth, as it is in heaven. Amen.

68.WOW

Mark 16:6-8 (NIV)

Don't be alarmed," he said. "You are looking for Jesus the Nazarene, who was crucified. He has risen! He is not here. See the place where they laid him. But go, tell his disciples and Peter, "He is going ahead of you into Galilee. There you will see him, just as he told you.'" Trembling and bewildered, the women went out and fled from the tomb. They said nothing to anyone, because they were afraid.

When was the last time you were truly astonished, so filled with admiration for someone or something that the word "wow" slipped effortlessly from your lips? I hope it wasn't too long ago, and I pray you find yourself saying that word often in the days to come.

After all the Lord has given us sight and hearing, and touch and taste and smell to experience His creation and there are wonders all around us. The trouble is that even the miracles become mundane as we continually encounter them, and we give them little thought.

I mean even simple things, like how does an acorn grow into a giant oak? Or how does a tiny egg become a human being after it is fertilized? In my mind both are incredible miracles, but they happen with such frequency that we rarely hear the word "wow" attached to these events.

Take a moment and read the above scriptures again. Do you notice something unusual? Normally, when we are "wowed" by something, our instinct is to share the experience with others. But what happened to the women?

Is it the same thing that happens to us as we encounter the incredible wonder of God's love and all His spiritual blessings? Do we go tell, or do we do as the women and say nothing?

Lord, I ask for two things: do not let me treat the profound as common and do not let my mouth be silent in telling others about You. Thank You.

69.PRETENDER

Psalms 139:1-4 (NASB)

O LORD, You have searched me and known me. You know when I sit down and when I rise up; You understand my thoughts from afar. You scrutinize my path and my lying down, and are intimately acquainted with all my ways. Even before there is a word on my tongue, Behold, O LORD, You know it all.

Early this morning, the word pretender came into my mind. It's been a long time since I've heard or used that word. Almost immediately, the lyrics of a song from my youth followed , "The Great Pretender" by The Platters. I could only recall a verse or two, so I looked it up:

"Oh-oh, yes, I'm the great pretender - Pretending that I'm doing well - My need is such, I pretend too much - I'm lonely, but no one can tell

Oh-oh, yes, I'm the great pretender - Adrift in a world of my own - I played the game but to my real shame You've left me to grieve all alone

Too real is this feeling of make-believe - Too real when I feel what my heart can't conceal

(Oh-oh-oh-oh-oh-oh-oh-oh-oh) - Yes, I'm the great pretender - Just laughing and gay like a clown - I seem to be what I'm not, you see - I'm wearing my heart like a crown — Pretending that you're still around"

On the one hand, sometimes we almost have to pretend that all is well even when it is not. Sort of "faking it 'till we make it". Or as May often shared, we just need to "suck it up."

On the other hand, who do we think we are fooling? Usually not others and certainly not ourselves (at least I hope not). What about God? Can we pretend with God that all is OK when it really is not?

All is not well with the world and yet somehow we go on and live our lives pretending that it is. All the while Christians around the world are being persecuted, innocent children and families are being destroyed by acts of terror and war. Families are starving in many parts of the world, floods and natural disasters abound here and all around the world.

So, I feel compelled to ask myself, am I a great pretender - pretending all is well when it is not? Am I adrift in my own world of surplus and entertainment and materialism while others are devastated and broken and lonely and at the mercy of those who would seek to kill and destroy?

Oh Father, please search my heart - is there any pretender in me? Lord, please break our hearts over what is breaking Your heart. Thank You.

70.TWO

Matthew 18:20 (NASB)

For where two or three have gathered together in My name, I am there in their midst.

Hebrews 10:23-25 (NASB)

Let us hold fast the confession of our hope without wavering, for He who promised is faithful; and let us consider how to stimulate one another to love and good deeds, not forsaking our own assembling together, as is the habit of some, but encouraging one another; and all the more as you see the day drawing near.

Yesterday my small group assembled at a member's home for our monthly gathering. I believe we were being faithful to the scriptures above as we had communion and shared a meal together just like the early church.

I am so thankful for those who took time out of their schedules to be there. Thankful to the hosts for opening their home to us. Thankful for the "visitors" who came and for the faithful that always seem to "be there."

These gatherings are open to anyone who want to attend; no need to be an active group member. It is open to anyone who wants to spend a couple of hours being encouraged and encouraging others in their walk with Christ. If you are not in a small group I strongly encourage you to find and join one (or start one yourself).

We live in a culture that encourages us to "stay busy" with all kinds of "opportunities." Many have told me, "oh, Paul, I would love to come to your gatherings but I am too busy right now." Why are we so busy? Perhaps it is because we have forgotten what is important in life or we are living lives without intention (or both)?

Father, I understand how difficult it is to make time in our schedules, but please lead us to put aside the seemingly urgent tasks in life to spend more time on what is really, really, important. Thank You.

71.DEPRAVED

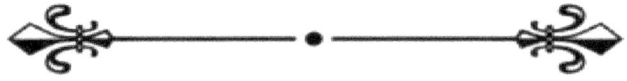

Romans 1:26-30 (NASB)

For this reason God gave them over to degrading passions; for their women exchanged the natural function for that which is unnatural, and in the same way also the men abandoned the natural function of the woman and burned in their desire toward one another, men with men committing indecent acts and receiving in their own persons the due penalty of their error. And just as they did not see fit to acknowledge God any longer, God gave them over to a depraved mind, to do those things which are not proper, being filled with all unrighteousness, wickedness, greed, evil; full of envy, murder, strife, deceit, malice; they are gossips, slanderers, haters of God, insolent, arrogant, boastful, inventors of evil, disobedient to parents.

Here is another one of those words that is not a normal part of my vocabulary. I read an article in the Oct 7 issue of World Magazine by Kim Henderson entitled, "Depraved Hearts." It is about the killing of a police officer in Jefferson County, MS. One of many police officers recently intentionally targeted and killed across the USA.

One statistic in that article has stayed with me: "In 2021, every birth in the county was to an unwed mother." A sign of the times? Yes, it is. We live in an age where Christian values and biblical principles are increasingly dismissed as narrow or divisive. What was once honored as good is now labeled evil, and what was condemned as evil a generation ago is now celebrated, even promoted by our own government.

One might ask, "What is going on?" Personally, I think that God is fulfilling today's scriptures as He gives many over to "depraved minds" (v28) resulting in murders, violence, and all kinds of evil.

What about you and I? How do we maintain a Christian witness with boldness, gentleness and convincing power? First off let us not be intimidated and silenced or overcome by evil. Instead let us counter evil by persistently doing good at every opportunity. (Romans 12:21 (NASB) Do not be overcome by evil but overcome evil with good).

Seek God with all our heart so that we might have something to say that comes from the Spirit of God and not from ourselves (but sanctify Christ as Lord in your hearts, always being ready to make a defense to everyone who asks you to give an account for the hope that is in you, yet with gentleness and reverence. **1 Peter 3:15 (NASB)**)

Pray earnestly for one another and for our government leaders, especially the ones you disagree with and the ones who seem opposed to godly principles. (First of all, then, I urge that entreaties and prayers, petitions and thanksgivings, be made on behalf of all men, for kings and all who are in authority, so that we may lead a tranquil and quiet life in all godliness and dignity. **1 Timothy 2:1-2 (NASB)**)

Let us understand that we are at war with the "powers of this present age." Do not become discouraged nor faint along the way. Put on the whole armor of God and when you have done all you can stand with the assurance of God and continue to pray. With all prayer and petition pray at all times in the Spirit, and with this in view, be on the alert with all perseverance and petition for all the saints. **(Ephesians 6)**

We cannot overcome the darkness of this age through our own strength or wisdom. This is a time to be still before the Lord and to know that He is God (Psalm 46:10). It is a time to draw close to Him, to know Him deeply and walk intimately in His ways (Philippians 3:10). It is a time to prepare for spiritual battle by asking God to fill us with His Spirit and lead us to represent Him faithfully in every encounter.

Lord, let us be still before You. You are God and we clearly are not. Draw us close to You so the world may see You are the transforming power in people's lives. Please empower us by Your Spirit to engage this world with undying devotion to You. Thank You.

72.APPLICATION

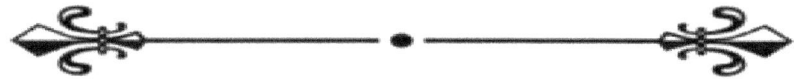

Proverbs 22:17 (NASB)

Incline your ear and hear the words of the wise, and apply your mind to my knowledge.

James 1:22 (NASB)

But prove yourselves doers of the word, and not merely hearers who delude themselves.

The other day I was talking to a neighbor about how some people pick up personally destructive habits and somehow fail to make changes even when they know it could destroy their lives. Smoking is a common example but excess in almost anything (like eating and sleeping) can be harmful.

As I mentioned in a previous devotion, I am often reminded of the Romans 7 dilemma, knowing what is good for me to do, yet still finding myself not doing it. Before you shake your head and say, "Oh, poor Paul," I truly believe this is a universal struggle.

I am very certain that if you stopped and gave it serious thought you would come up with at least one area in your life that you KNOW you should do differently and yet you do not. Please let me know if you are an exception to this.

So I ask the same question I asked in yesterday's devotion - "what is the Christian to do?." Is it OK if I (and you) as Christians continue living in this state of knowing what to do and not doing it? Consider what James said: therefore, to one who knows the right thing to do and does not do it, to him it is sin (James 4:17 NASB).

This is something I have not mastered so I am not about to tell you how to fi it. However, I can offer an approach that might be helpful.

First, realize that there are things you know are good for you to do and you are not doing them. Be honest ,name them, call them by their names, and know that they are sin. Humbly repent and admit your inadequacy.

Second, remember you really can overcome this sin through the power of God. (I can do all things through Him who strengthens me **Philippians 4:10 (NASB)**).

Third, earnestly seek the transforming power of God to always do what He has revealed to you is good for you to do. Keep Philippians 1:6 in mind: he is still working on us and never gives up.

Father, many are blind to this but to those that can see, please give them the power to be all they can be in You. Thank You.

73.ENJOY

Psalms 118:24 (NASB)

This is the day which the LORD has made; Let us rejoice and be glad in it.

Today's word came to my mind shortly after I awoke yesterday. The first thing I noticed was the early morning sun steaming onto a plant I have on my bed stand. "Oh," I thought, "this is going to be a really good day."

What I enjoyed the most about yesterday is that it was a quiet stress-free day. The sun was shining and there were just a few household chores to do.

I also noticed that when I turned on the water faucet, I had water heated to whatever temperature I wanted. The stove made cooking oatmeal quite easy, and the fruit I added tasted wonderful. And then, of course, there was the joy of sharing the day with someone who loves me, and let us not forget all the connections online.

We went out for dinner, enjoying the change of pace and the fact that we had the finances to do so. We also have a car to take us there, and let us not forget the people who are so kind to May and me — greeting us, holding the door open, or offering help in some other way. I would be remiss if I failed to mention the hugs we often receive from the wait staff and others.

Our evening was relaxed - a good cup of tea with a few treats. A time to reflect and read and enjoy a phone conversation with one or two of our children. Yes, a good day. A really good day.

As we said our evening prayers, I was most thankful for a day much like any other day except that I paused and took notice. I hope you have an enjoyable day also, taking time to notice the day that Lord has given to us, and to rejoice in it.

Father, we can easily overlook the mundane things of life, but I have a sense that in them often lie the hidden gems of a day enjoyed. Thank You.

74.EX-NIHILO

2 Kings 4:2 (NASB)

Elisha said to her, "What shall I do for you? Tell me, what do you have in the house?" And she said, "Your maidservant has nothing in the house except a jar of oil."

Jeremiah 32:17 (NASB)

Ah Lord GOD! Behold, You have made the heavens and the earth by Your great power and by Your outstretched arm! Nothing is too difficult for You.

Luke 1:37 (NASB)

For nothing will be impossible with God.

The word "ex-nihilo" means to create something from nothing. Perhaps its most popular use is how God fashioned life: exnihilo — out of nothing. Who can fashion anything "exnihilo?" Only God, of course. It is a mystery that perplexes all unbelievers - how did life begin? Nothing can be created from nothing unless there is a pre-existing (eternal) being that is all powerful and that is God.

So let me ask "where do our sleeping dreams come from?" Sometimes I have the strangest dreams that seem to come out of nowhere, but I know that is not true. I just do not have the right understanding.

What about "dreams" for the future? I notice that as people get older, they seem to have less "excitement" (dreams) about the future.

They often think their lives have been lived out and they are just waiting for the finish line to show up.

I wonder, is this normal for the Christian? Look around. Does it not seem like we are approaching the day of reckoning? Is this not the time to dream dreams? ("And it shall be in the last days," God says, "that I will pour forth of my spirit on all mankind; and your sons and your daughters shall prophesy, and your young men shall see visions, and your old men shall dream dreams" **Acts 2:17 (NASB))**

Come, Lord Jesus, come. In the meantime, let Your Spirit fall upon us, fill us to overflowing, so that we may be Your people, carrying Your prophecies, Your visions, and Your dreams. Thank You.

75.GENUINE

Jeremiah 29:4-7 (NIV)

This is what the LORD Almighty, the God of Israel, says to all those I carried into exile from Jerusalem to Babylon: "Build houses and settle down; plant gardens and eat what they produce. Marry and have sons and daughters; find wives for your sons and give your daughters in marriage, so that they too may have sons and daughters. Increase in number there; do not decrease. Also, seek the peace and prosperity of the city to which I have carried you into exile. Pray to the LORD for it, because if it prospers, you too will prosper."

It is hard to put ourselves in the same context, but let us imagine we have been forced to leave our homes and made to go to a place where we are truly aliens in every way. What if a prophet came to us and declared the words of Jeremiah? How would you respond?

I think I would be really upset. How dare he tell me to make the best of the situation when everything in me is screaming for revenge and to return quickly to my home. There is no way I would want to settle down for three generations in a place I do not want to be.

On the other hand, the distinction between genuine and imitation faith rises to the forefront. Will I do what I do not want to do for the sole purpose of being obedient to the Lord GOD? Even when I do not "feel" like it? Genuine faith chooses to be obedient regardless of feelings or possible negative consequences.

From a distance, the words of Jeremiah may sound like good advice but what about when God calls us today to be faithful to something we don't want to do? It might be something simple, like making a phone call to encourage someone, showing extra kindness to a person who irritates us, or helping a brother or sister in need, whether with money, time, or talent. Or it could be something harder, like forgiving someone who has hurt you and doing all you can to restore the relationship. And perhaps, for you, it's something even more difficult, you pick the example.

If we have genuine "present faithfulness" we will quickly surrender to the will of God. If on the other hand, we have an imitation faith there is no telling when we will be get around to doing God's will.

Father, please help us to be genuine Christians. Fill us with genuine "present faithfulness" to respond in obedience to every call you make on our lives. Thank You.

76.PEACE

Psalms 83:1-4 (NIV)

O God, do not remain silent; do not turn a deaf ear, do not stand aloof, O God. See how your enemies growl, how your foes rear their heads. With cunning they conspire against your people; they plot against those you cherish. "Come," they say, "let us destroy them as a nation.

Psalms 122:6-9 (NIV)

Pray for the peace of Jerusalem: "May those who love you be secure. May there be peace within your walls and security within your citadels." For the sake of my family and friends, I will say, "Peace be within you." For the sake of the house of the LORD our God, I will seek your prosperity.

Lord GOD, how does one undo thousands of years of animosity; where hatred has grown into bitterness resulting in terror and violence and all kinds of mayhem? How can there be peace in Jerusalem or anywhere else in the world?

Please Lord, Hasten Your return!

Father, as Hamas seeks the destruction of Israel - so satan seeks the destruction of Your people. Give us understanding that we struggle against powers and authorities that we know very little about but Lord You have come to make all things right. You came that there might be peace, a time when evil is sent to the abyss never to return.

Please, Lord, hasten Your return!

Father, I ask for Your compassion upon the suffering people on both sides of this conflict. They are being misled by dark, unseen forces that speak evil and hatred into their hearts.

Please, Lord Jesus, hasten Your return so that there may be peace in Jerusalem and throughout the world.

Thank You.

77.WELCOME

Mark 9:35-37 (NIV)

Sitting down, Jesus called the Twelve and said, "Anyone who wants to be first must be the very last, and the servant of all." He took a little child whom he placed among them. Taking the child in his arms, he said to them, "Whoever welcomes one of these little children in my name welcomes me; and whoever welcomes me does not welcome me but the one who sent me."

Have you ever gone to some place where you felt you should be welcomed (like a church) and were not? It has happened to May and I only a very few times in our lives. I am certainly glad about that because it is a very uncomfortable feeling.

On the other hand, have you ever been welcomed so warmly that the experience left a lasting, positive memory? May and I have felt that way a few times and often wish it happened more often. It's truly unforgettable to be greeted with such genuine warmth that even the memory of it brings a smile to my face.

Let me share one example. Our son Jon was stationed near Fayetteville NC. On our first visit we drove around looking for a church to attend. We ended up in the parking lot of Son Spot Baptist Church. As we were getting ready to get out of the car, we realized it was a black only church. I told May perhaps we should keep looking and she said "No, lets go in." (One of many, many times over the years when she has had better spiritual discernment than I.)

Long story short, we were welcomed so warmly that we both remember it clearly to this day (perhaps someday we'll share the longer version with you). Suffice it to say, over the next couple of years, whenever we visited our son, it was always Son Spot Baptist

Church for us. Each time we returned, we were greeted the same way like honored guests. What an amazing experience that was for us. We were the only white people in the church, yet we felt something that was just a little short of being in heaven.

I can only imagine how life would be different in the Christian community if this was the normal experience in our churches. Do you think it might be possible? It would have to start with you and me.

Father, we are so thankful for this experience - and the many others in our lives - where You have shown us what is possible when we are truly connected to you. Thank You.

78.FOOLISH

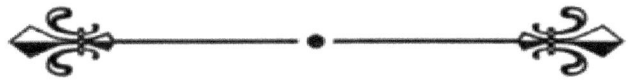

Matthew 7:26-27 (NIV)

But everyone who hears these words of mine and does not put them into practice is like a foolish man who built his house on sand. The rain came down, the streams rose, and the winds blew and beat against that house, and it fell with a great crash.

These verses in Matthew are at the end of the Sermon on the Mount **(Matthew Chapters 5-7).** When Jesus says, "hears these words," He is talking about what He just said as recorded in the previous chapters.

Have you ever seriously considered following everything that Jesus said? If you tried to live up to this "gold standard" how successful were you? Have you ever known anyone who consistently lived up to what Jesus clearly communicates is the straight and narrow way upon which true believers in God should be traveling? Perhaps there are a lot of professing believers that are acting foolishly? What do you think? How about you and me?

Let me ask again, how are your travels? Have you read John Bunyan's "The Pilgrim Progress"? If you have then you might remember how difficult it was to stay on the "straight and narrow" and how easy it is to wander off after "this or that."

All of us who proclaim to be followers of Jesus are on a journey of sorts. We inhabit a land that is hostile to us, a land where we are aliens, foreigners and strangers. Yet it is here that we press on to our eternal home. But beware, there are many distractions along the way.

The reality is that we are also foolish if we attempt this journey with our own strength. When we try to live up to the "gold standard" in the Sermon on the Mount in our own strength we are doomed to utter failure. It is not possible to live up to such a standard with consistency over a lifetime.

However, we do not travel alone. We have a traveling Companion that knows the way and knows all about us. As He leads, the glow of the "heavenly city" becomes brighter and brighter and, in time, we will enter into His eternal rest. The "secret" is staying connected to our Lord.

Father, sometimes this journey feels so difficult. Please don't let us grow weary or give up. Grant us the grace to keep pressing on, no matter how hard life becomes, knowing that in Your perfect time, we will be home in Your presence. Anything less would be foolishness. Thank You.

79.LIGHT

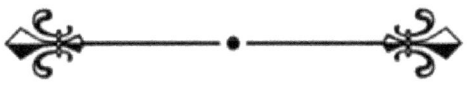

John 1:4-5 (NIV)

In him was life, and that life was the light of all mankind. The light shines in the darkness, and the darkness has not overcome it.

As a plant enthusiast I have learned the importance of light to plants. Most plants can manage when their lighting is not quite right. They are not at their best but most will survive (for a while anyway). However, very few things will grow without any light (fungus and mold are notable exceptions).

When May and I visited the sick and elderly we noticed that the light in their homes usually reflected their disposition. The dark homes seemed to have gloomy people. The brightly lit homes were mostly occupied by joyful people, even if they were dying or in a very difficult situation.

We often suggested to the folks living in dark, gloomy homes that open the shades and/or turn the lights on. Interestingly, they agreed it would be helpful but I cannot think of a single instance where they did it. They were still living in their dark and gloomy homes when we next visited.

I wonder if we Christians can be held captive by our feelings? Feelings can be so strong, powerful and overwhelming that we seem unable or unwilling to exert the strength and energy to overcome them.

Our physical surroundings have a powerful effect on our moods and dispositions. Take a moment to look around as you read this; do your surroundings reflect how you feel? If you don't like the way you feel, try changing your environment: add more light, breathe in fresh air, move your body. So many small things can influence our emotional state.

In our human nature, we often resist doing what we know would help us. Yet Jesus understands how we feel, and He remains the true source of joy in this life. When we stay connected to Him, even our most negative emotions can be transformed; I speak from much experience. The key is to be, and remain, connected to the Lord of the Universe.

Oh Lord, please break the bondage of negative feelings in our lives. Yes, life is hard and difficult but You have come to give us true life and to have it with an abundance of joy. Thank You.

80. CAN'T

Philippians 4:13 (NIV)

13 I can do all this through him who gives me strength.

Should the word "can't" be banned from the Christian's vocabulary? It seems to me "can't" is a contradiction to Philippians 4:13. Don't you agree? Perhaps you agree with me in principle but I doubt if you agree with me in practice.

I was talking to a younger Christian (younger than me) who's nurturing some tropical trees that are quite difficult to grow in this area. She called me for advice, and in the midst of our conversation, she said, "I don't have a green thumb, I can't grow anything." It struck me as a complete contradiction to what she was actually doing.

It might be the way we like to excuse ourselves when we are trying to do something difficult. Like, I can't lose weight. Or I can't find time to have devotions every day. Or I can't make new friends. Or I can't learn new things. Or I can't drive a stick shift. Or I can't keep track of things. Or I can't understand the scriptures. Or I can't learn a new language. Or I can't …

You get the idea. We all use this word. Sometimes a lot. The problem is that it immediately limits our potential. It cuts us off at the pass. No sense trying if "I can't, is there?

I think the words we should use in many of these cases is "I don't want to." In other words, we really are not interested in putting forth the energy/time/resources it would take to do something we do not naturally desire or are not naturally gifted in.

Over the years, I have often suggested to people that God might be calling them to do something outside of their comfort zone. The response often is, "Oh I can't do that." Press as I may, it seems once "can't" has been spoken, that is the end of the story. I sometimes wonder what "could have been" if they had said "How can I?"

What if Scripture is true? What if we really could do whatever God calls us to do? If God is calling us surely, He will supply whatever we need to do it. So perhaps "can't" is a word we should use with caution. Maybe it should be forbidden when responding to God's call on our lives.

Father, I so firmly believe Your call always comes with everything we need. Help us to trust You for what we cannot do ourselves. Thank You.

81.VENGEANCE

Romans 12:19-21 (NASB) Never take your own revenge, beloved, but leave room for the wrath of God, for it is written, "vengeance is mine, I will repay," says the lord. But if your enemy is hungry, feed him, and if he is thirsty, give him a drink; for in so doing you will heap burning coals on his head. Do not be overcome by evil, but overcome evil with good.

When the Russian Army invaded Ukraine, I felt angry and bitter toward the aggressors. At first, it seemed like a "righteous" anger, but I've come to realize it was not.

The atrocities of the Hamas terrorist attacks on innocent people brought the anger back with a desire for vengeance. Again, I felt justified at first, but I knew that my anger could never bring the righteousness of God. I also know that vengeance is reserved for God and never for the new creature that is in Christ.

The correct Christian response is to love even those who hate us and are our sworn enemies. How do we do this when our flesh so strongly wants to do differently? I offer the following for our devotion today. Please take it to heart. What choice do we have if we are truly disciples of the Messiah Jesus?

The following is taken from "The Gospel of Peace in a Time of Terror," Heinrich Arnold, dated 10/15/23 from the Brunderhauf.

"Last Friday was a day of festivity in Israel, as throngs of people attended synagogues to celebrate the end of Sukkoth and the beginning of Simchat Torah, 'rejoicing with the Torah.' As this joyful holiday dawned on Saturday, unimaginable evil was unleashed. Thousands of rockets struck nearby towns as well as cities as far away as Tel Aviv and Jerusalem. .... By now, everyone has heard of the shocking atrocities perpetrated by Hamas in Israel over the last week. In the face of this horror, how should Christians respond?

The New Testament calls on us to mourn with those who mourn (Rom. 12:14). At a time like this, we should grieve with the people of Israel, especially the survivors of the Hamas attack. And we should mourn too, with civilians in Gaza who are already suffering as collateral damage in the military response to it.

We must pray for peace. To say this may sound like a platitude. But if we believe in God's power to intervene in history, prayer remains vital all the same.

Beyond grieving and praying, what else should we do? From many corners, there are demands for stern action from world leaders. This is more than understandable because of the depth of fury, fear, and panic that Israelis feel at being violated in such terrible ways by an organization that has pledged to eradicate their country. The desire for a swift and severe reaction is at the core of our human response to evil.

I have traveled to Israel and the West Bank …. have made close friends on both sides of the long-standing conflict in the region. Many of them have spent years working for peace and dialogue in order to overcome the deep-seated hatred in their communities. When I've spoken with some of these over the last few days, they've described their incredible pain. They are living through a level of anger and dread of the future beyond anything I can imagine.

The only thing Christians can do with absolute certainty is to testify to Christ's gospel of peace. Our calling is to pray for peace and for all the victims of violence, to refuse to support violence ourselves, and to be peacemakers. As members of His church on earth, we are to be an embassy in the present world of the future peaceable kingdom. Jesus said, "Blessed are the peacemakers, for they shall be called sons of God" (Matt. 5:9). He taught: "You have heard that it was said, 'You shall love your neighbor and hate your enemy.' But I say to you, Love your enemies and pray for those who persecute you, so that you may be sons of your Father who is in heaven" (Matt. 5:43 - 45).

We should deplore all war; we can never cheerlead for violence, however justified it may seem to be. Christians should protest the barbarity of the attacks on Israel – the cold-blooded targeting of civilians, the rapes, the massacre of children, women, and elders. We should speak up, too, against depriving civilians of water and electricity and the bombing of residential targets. We should deplore all war. That is our duty; to be silent is sinful. Especially in moments when the public mood grows bloody-minded and vindictive, we can never cheerlead for violence, however justified it may seem to be.

What force can overcome such evil? Again, Jesus teaches us the answer: Only love can truly win over enemies."

My dear brothers and sisters in Christ, I implore you to harbor no hatred, bitterness, anger, or desire for vengeance. Instead, let us pray for the peace of Jerusalem and for the world. Let us overcome evil by doing good, and let us not grow weary as His day of return draws near.

82.NUDGE

Matt 13:11-13 (MSG) He replied, "You've been given insight into God's kingdom. You know how it works. Not everybody has this gift, this insight; it hasn't been given to them. Whenever someone has a ready heart for this, the insights and understandings flow freely. But if there is no readiness, any trace of receptivity soon disappears. That's why I tell stories: to create readiness, to nudge the people toward a welcome awakening. In their present state they can stare till doomsday and not see it, listen till they're blue in the face and not get it.

Have you ever been nudged? Given a gentle push or coaxing to get you moving in the right direction? I was thinking this could be a good commandment for all believers: "Thou shalt nudge your fellow believers to get on with it, to rightly live their lives as new creatures in Christ."

In Romans 7, Paul reminds us that our flesh seldom cooperates with the Spirit of God. Sometimes we even get stuck and need help to get dislodged from whatever hinders us. I believe you and I can be God's tools as we encourage one another, nudging each other along to stay on (or get back on) that narrow path that leads to the righteousness of God.

If you are reading this, you most likely have the insight to understand and appreciate God's kingdom and how it works. On the other hand, many in this world are confused and traveling down a path of personal and/or relational destruction. Do you have someone in your life like that? How might you nudge that person along?

Lord, sometimes we wander. Please bring people into our lives who will gently guide us back to You. And Lord, through the way we live, the words we speak, and the things we do, help

us to encourage one another along the narrow path that leads to eternal life. Thank You.

83.PRODIGAL

Luke 15:13 (NKJV) And not many days after, the younger son gathered all together, journeyed to a far country, and there wasted his possessions with prodigal living.

I am reasonably certain that when you read the word "prodigal," you immediately thought of the parable in Luke of the Prodigal Son. We generally would not encourage our children or one another to live like the Prodigal Son, but I want to stretch our imaginations just a little.

The essence of the word prodigal means to be unconcerned about keeping what we have and to spend with extravagance. It is a reminder of the scripture's admonition to be more concerned about Jesus than the things of this life. (But seek first his kingdom and his righteousness, and all these things will be given to you as well (Matthew 6:33 NIV)) And to give generously to others? Good will come to those who are generous and lend freely who conduct their affairs with justice (Psalm 112:5 (NIV))

What would life be like if we lived a life of extravagance for the benefit of others? If we freely gave what we have, whether it be money, time, talents, patience, love, kindness etc. with little to no concern for ourselves? If we trusted that Jesus spoke the truth when He told us, "if we seek Him FIRST, all we have need of in life will be provided by Him."

I just had a thought, can we ever "out-give" God? Could we possibly give away more than what He gives back to us? Would you dare to put that to the test?

Malachi 3:10 (NIV) "Bring the whole tithe into the storehouse, that there may be food in my house. Test me in this," says the LORD

Almighty, "and see if I will not throw open the floodgates of heaven and pour out so much blessing that there will not be room enough to store it."

Lord GOD of heaven and earth, help us live with generosity toward others, giving freely from all You have given us. You have blessed us, Lord, so that we may be a blessing to others. Make it so, Lord. Thank You.

84.CO-REGENTS

2 Timothy 2:11-13 (NIV) Here is a trustworthy saying: If we died with him, we will also live with him; if we endure, we will also reign with him. If we disown him, he will also disown us; if we are faithless, he remains faithful, for he cannot disown himself.

Revelation 5:9-10 (NIV) And they sang a new song, saying: "You are worthy to take the scroll and to open its seals, because you were slain, and with your blood you purchased for God persons from every tribe and language and people and nation. You have made them to be a kingdom and priests to serve our God, and they will reign on the earth."

Have you ever given real thought to what you will do in heaven? I suspect few of us have. After all, "we can only imagine".

On the other hand, some of us will be co-regents, ruling and reigning under the Lordship of Jesus Christ. When I think about that possibility the word that comes to mind is "WOW!"

I do not think I gave that serious thought before. Some years ago, on a particularly pleasant day attending to my plants, I asked God to let me be a gardener in heaven. I have this peace that it just might be so. However, whatever I get to do on the "other side" it will be the best "assignment" ever.

This life can bring its share of anxious thoughts, worries, and sorrows. But a day is coming—a day when you and I will stand in the presence of the Creator of the Universe. It will be the moment when all things are made right, and we receive our eternal assignments, those prepared for us since the foundation of the earth.

Lord, as that day draws near, and we see it approaching, let us not worry or fret but simply "trust and obey because there is no better way." Thank You.

Lord - we pray for peace in Jerusalem and Your soon return.

85.ENEMY

1 Peter 5:8-9 (NIV) Be alert and of sober mind. Your enemy the devil prowls around like a roaring lion looking for someone to devour. Resist him, standing firm in the faith, because you know that the family of believers throughout the world is undergoing the same kind of sufferings.

It is easy to focus on our "flesh and blood" enemies but they are not the real problem. They are pawns in a "spiritual chess game." They have lost their way, being manipulated by dark spiritual forces and they are MOSTLY clueless.

As people around the world seem bent on destroying one another, may God help us come to grips with the reality that our vengeful "righteousness" is just as deadly as what they are doing.

Ultimately, we have only one weapon: the Word of God, which commands us to love one another, even our enemies and those who persecute or spitefully use us. It may seem impossible to fight hate with love, and yet that is the only way we can truly win the battle against evil.

Let us be cautious about the evil "out there" while not forgetting that it is the vengeful evil in our own hearts that can be our undoing. We too can become pawns of the devil if we seek to "make things right" in our own strength. As disciples of Jesus, we are to love even those who would kill us. We cannot do this without an inner burning desire to be like Christ.

"Lord, make me an instrument of your peace: where there is hatred, let me sow love; where there is injury, pardon; where there is doubt, faith; where there is despair, hope; where there is darkness, light; where there is sadness, joy." (Francis of Assisi)

Father, please search our hearts, reveal our hypocrisy, and teach us the way of love. Lead us to sow peace, love, pardon, faith, hope, light, and joy. Thank You.

Jesus, we pray for Your soon return and the peace of Jerusalem.

86.CLUTTER

Matthew 5:6 (NIV) Blessed are those who hunger and thirst for righteousness, for they will be filled.

Have you noticed how clutter seems to come from nowhere? My desk, garage, work table, and shed all seem to get cluttered "by themselves." I like to think that I am not a clutterer, but the reality of my life tells me otherwise.

Most of the time, I don't even notice the clutter until it takes over the space, when I can't find anything on my desk or the shed is overflowing and I need to add something else.

When I finally give my energy to clearing the clutter it almost seems overwhelming, "where do I start?" On the other hand, when I walk into my office and see my clean desk, or go to the shed and find what I am looking for, it sure feels good.

You see my friend, physical clutter steals our energy. Try it. Clean a space (table, desk, closet, junk drawer), any space that is cluttered. Notice the energy you get back when the job is done. Much more than the energy you had to use to "de-clutter".

As troubling as physical clutter can be, spiritual clutter is an even greater issue. When we fill our physical spaces, we simply stack one thing on top of another. But when we crowd our minds and hearts with the distractions of this world, we leave no room to "hunger and thirst for the righteousness of God." Our inner lives become packed with the unimportant, leaving no space for what truly matters.

Father, help us to declutter our lives, both physically and spiritually, so that we earnestly hunger after You. Thank You.

Lord, we pray for the peace of Jerusalem and for Your soon return.

87.CHERISH

Proverbs 4:7-8 (NIV) The beginning of wisdom is this: Get wisdom. Though it cost all you have, get understanding. Cherish her, and she will exalt you; embrace her, and she will honor you.

What or whom do you cherish?

When we cherish someone or something, we protect and care for them beyond measure. We hold them close to our hearts, and they are often in our thoughts. To have someone to cherish is like possessing a treasure of immeasurable worth. It matters little whether we are rich, poor, or somewhere in between; when we are in the presence of a cherished one, the world feels right, even when it isn't.

However, even when we cherish another, life's demands have a way of interfering and can take the wonder away. Being too busy to spend time with a cherished one is too busy, way too busy.

Letting negative feelings interfere with being with a cherished one is pure foolishness. Why would we as believers allow satan to rob us of one of the most precious gifts of life?

As important and wonderful as it is to have a cherished one in our lives it is even more important, much more important, to cherish the presence of the Lord of the universe in our lives. If we do not cherish God's presence the world will invade the space, and we shall enter eternity wondering why we neglected such a treasured gift.

Father, thank You for the cherished ones in my life. Help me to be ever more present with them. And please, Father, place it in my heart to cherish You above all else, beyond anyone and anything. Thank You.

88.KIND

Ephesians 4:32 (NIV) Be kind and compassionate to one another, forgiving each other, just as in Christ God forgave you.

Kindness is such a wonderful virtue, don't you think? It may be hard to describe in the abstract but when someone is kind to us, we know it. Kindness takes many forms , a friendly smile, a generous nature, consideration for others, politeness, or simply being affectionate and loving.

I especially appreciate those acts of kindness that are unexpected, the ones that come "out of the blue." Like when someone pays your bill at a restaurant, lets you cut in line at the grocery store or the bank, or surprises you with a call or a card just to say hello.

Since May and I have gotten a little older and aren't quite as spry as we used to be, people often hold doors open for us. (Using a cane seems to work wonders in bringing out people's kindness.) What is even more precious is when someone notices we might need a little help and goes out of their way to help us. Maybe I am getting a little sentimental, but I notice kindness more and more around us. Maybe there are more Christians out and about just being obedient to the scriptures?

Regardless of the source, being kind is good for the giver and the receiver. I wonder how many acts of kindness we could do in a day? I bet a lot, especially with the Holy Spirit directing our thoughts and actions.

Dear Lord, as we go about our days, let us be aware of the opportunities all around us to be kind. Nudge us, or give us a little push, if necessary, but let us be kind to one another. Thank You

89. DEVOTED

2 Peter 1:3 (NIV) His divine power has given us everything we need for a godly life through our knowledge of him who called us by his own glory and goodness.

Have you ever spent time with someone who is devoted to something or someone? It does not take long to notice their devotion. They are committed to whatever they are devoted to. It is something or someone they are ready and willing to talk about (sometimes there is no end). They are enthusiastic, loving, caring, attentive, ardent, etc. all toward the object of their devotion.

I have often wondered how some people are able to accomplish so much in their lives. Yes, talent and gifting are important, but I believe the real factor is their devotion. Being devoted helps us to focus and accomplish great things. But we cannot be devoted to everything and everyone.

A most important aspect of a life "well lived" is knowing what is important. Our devotion to something precludes devotion to something else (every "yes" is a "no" to something else).

If we are not devoted to what is important, we will frequently find ourselves devoted to pleasing ourselves. It is just what we do. Look at our obsession with sports, social media and entertainment.

What is important? Who decides? If you are a disciple of Jesus, then what is important should be clear. You are to live a godly life.

The Scriptures promise that we have everything we need, even divine power, to live a godly life. So let me ask a probing question: Are you truly devoted to living a godly life, or are you simply devoted to doing what you want to do?

Lord, give us hearts that are devoted to living a godly life. Lead us with the details, the "little acts of obedience" that result in a godly life - a life well lived. Thank You

90.STRUGGLE

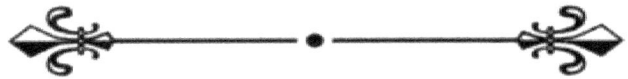

Hebrews 12:4 (NIV) In your struggle against sin, you have not yet resisted to the point of shedding your blood.

Ephesians 6:12 (NIV) For our struggle is not against flesh and blood, but against the rulers, against the authorities, against the powers of this dark world and against the spiritual forces of evil in the heavenly realms.

There is a story of a frog that was placed in a pot of boiling water. It hurt so much he struggled mightily and jumped right out. He was hurt but he survived. And then there is the frog that was placed in temperate water, "just right," he thought. Slowly, the heat was increased but the frog kept adjusting to the gradual change. He did not struggle as he boiled to death.

All of us are familiar with the outward and physical struggles of life. Broken relationships, financial problems, health issues, pain, disappointment. We understand that we are in a struggle to stay centered when so much seems to be in disarray. We are often like the first frog. We see the problem and we struggle; hopefully trusting in the One who has overcome the world as we deal with the trials of this life.

There is, however, the other frog. He did not know he was in a struggle and slowly but surely, he died. I think that happens to many professing Christians in America today.

Our culture has lost its way. Things that were considered evil and even abominations are now considered normal and acceptable. Think about the shows we watch on TV. Violence, sex, drugs, cohabitation, homosexuality, adultery, etc. are common themes.

Why are we still watching? Is it because we've failed to notice the moral decay around us, like the frog that doesn't realize the water is getting hotter?

As much as I would prefer to not struggle, it is clear to me that struggles make us stronger. They help us to rely on the Lord of the Universe. They enable us to comfort and help others.

The problem is that too often we Christians do not even know we are in a spiritual struggle. We "go with the flow" and soon find ourselves adapting to the culture until there is little difference between the professing Christian and our secular culture.

Father, we know what struggles are like in the physical realm. Please, Lord GOD, reveal to us the spiritual struggles that we seem not to notice. Thank You.

91.NICE

Isaiah 30:10-11 (NLT) They tell the seers, "Stop seeing visions!" They tell the prophets, "Don't tell us what is right. Tell us nice things. Tell us lies. Forget all this gloom. Get off your narrow path. Stop telling us about your 'Holy One of Israel.' "

Yesterday, someone paid me a sincere compliment. After the exchange was over, I thought to myself, "That was nice." And it was. I know I must receive compliments with a "grain of salt" (any good that comes from me is because of the Spirit of God), and yet it felt nice to receive such a sincere compliment.

But there's a kind of "nice" that isn't really nice at all. To be truly kind, our niceness must be rooted in truth, not in lies, deception, or empty flattery. Most of the time, we recognize the difference, but sometimes we'd rather not. We'd much rather settle for "nice."

The scriptures warn us that a day would come when people do not want to hear the truth but rather "nice" things that tickle their ears. (The time will come when people will not put up with sound doctrine. Instead, to suit their own desires, they will gather around them a great number of teachers to say what their itching ears want to hear. They will turn their ears away from the truth and turn aside to myths. 2 Timothy 4:3-4 (NIV).

Surely those days have arrived. Do you agree?

Two things come to mind. As followers of Jesus Christ, we must earnestly seek after truth, unlike our culture. Also, we should seek out opportunities to be genuinely nice to one another.

Father, I thank You for the "niceness" of a sincere compliment. Lead us to welcome the truth into our lives and to be nice whenever possible. Thank You

92.CARRIED

2 Peter 1:21 (NIV) For prophecy never had its origin in the human will, but prophets, though human, spoke from God as they were carried along by the Holy Spirit.

Remember the story of "Footprints in the Sand"? An individual arrives in heaven, and Jesus shows them the "footprints" of their life. They notice that, for most of the journey, there are two sets of footprints. "Whose are those?" the individual asks. Jesus replies, "They are mine, as I walked beside you."

Then they come across a particularly difficult time in the individual's life, and there is only one set of footprints. "Why did You leave me, Jesus, when I needed You most?" the person weeps. Jesus gently replies, "My child, that was when I carried you," as He wipes away the person's tears.

We see and know so little of the spiritual life on this side of eternity. Much must be understood through faith and trust. Let us indeed take hold of God's promises.

He can never forsake us or abandon us. His love for us runs deeper than we can comprehend. When life's heartaches become more than we can bear, He is there carrying us, holding us close to His breast. He encourages us as we make this journey. He whispers into our hearts "I am here - although you are weak right now, I am strong. I have overcome this world, and you will too as I carry you like the good Shepherd that carries the lamb."

Father, help us to be still and KNOW that you are God as You carry us through life. Thank You

93.ARTIST

Psalms 90:17 (NIV) May the favor of the Lord our God rest on us; establish the work of our hands for us— yes, establish the work of our hands.

We know we are God's chosen. Chosen to do the work that He has prepared for us to do. In a way we are all ARTISTS as we pursue God's purpose for our lives. I share the following prayer as our devotion for today:

"Oh Christ, through Whom all things have been made, meet me in this lesser making. Channel my creativity, guide my hands and heart. Give me discipline to steward well my craft.

Let me find a fertile place to sink my roots within the long tradition and continuing conversation of Your children who, across thousands of years have sought to display beauty, to articulate truth, to celebrate holy mystery, and to somehow echo eternal yearnings in the things we create.

Let me, in the short span of my life, contribute something more to that good conversation. And let me release my expectations of the times, and places and ways in which it might be received.

Let me, instead, simply craft the finest offering I can, within the limits of my time, skill, and circumstance, and then place it before You, to use as You will.

Let that be enough for me O Lord." (Every Morning Holy, Volume III)

Dear Lord, I join with my brothers and sisters in Christ, all over the world to ask that we be about the work You have given to each of us to do. May we do it to the very best of our abilities

and leave the results to You. Please Lord let it be enough that we are about the work You have given us to do. Thank You

94.DEBRIDE

Luke 6:41-42 (NIV) Why do you look at the speck of sawdust in your brother's eye and pay no attention to the plank in your own eye? How can you say to your brother, "Brother, let me take the speck out of your eye," when you yourself fail to see the plank in your own eye? You hypocrite, first take the plank out of your eye, and then you will see clearly to remove the speck from your brother's eye.

I am pretty sure that "debride" is a word you have not used lately. My friend Pete used it in a text recently and I had to look it up. It means to remove damaged tissue or foreign objects from a wound. In other words give it a good scrubbing and cleaning until all the rot is gone.

I told Pete it reminded me of a training session I once attended with the FAA. The instructor explained that unless the root issues in a relationship are truly resolved, they'll eventually resurface. He used a vivid illustration: when a pet does its "business" on the carpet, and instead of cleaning it properly, we simply pour honey over it. It might smell pleasant for a while, but the mess is still there, and it will show up again sooner or later, until we deal with it at the source.

It seems easier to notice the problem the "other person" is having, all the while not realizing that our noticing the problem is part of the problem.

You see, the "planks" in our own eyes obstruct our ability to see. But, and this is a big but, we generally do not believe it. I am not sure if this is pride or arrogance, but it is very common to the old nature and it seems to raise its head now and then among followers of Jesus.

So let us be most careful. There are times when we need to confront a believer. However, it is probably best to confront ourselves first.

Dear Lord, it is so easy to judge another. Please let me see my own hypocrisy. Reveal to me whenever I am about to act the fool; before Lord, please, not after. Thank You

95.INTENTIONAL

Ecclesiastes 9:10 (NIV) Whatever your hand finds to do, do it with all your might, for in the realm of the dead, where you are going, there is neither working nor planning nor knowledge nor wisdom.

Are you a day dreamer? Do you sometimes find yourself thinking about one thing while doing another? I do that a lot. I might be "busy" making lunch, but my mind is thinking about something else. Suddenly, I'll come back to the present and I'm not sure what I was doing or what I am supposed to do next.

Or I'm reading a book while thinking of something else. My eyes are going back and forth following the words, but I have no idea what I just read. Or how about when we were in school and the teacher was giving all sorts of life enriching information but our minds were somewhere else?

I am pretty sure you can relate to singing a song in church, mouthing all the right words, maybe even in the perfect pitch, while your mind was thinking about lunch, or the disagreement you had with someone, or who knows what.

I am often amazed at how we can be doing one thing physically while our minds are clearly elsewhere. It is a mystery to me. It is reading but not reading. It is learning but not learning. It is singing but not singing. And often it is praying but not praying. You see, my friend, we are not intentional about what we are doing. We live in an easily distracted culture.

Mentally, we often drift elsewhere, losing focus on the task before us. No matter how strong the case for multitasking may seem, you can never perform at your best unless you are fully engaged, heart, mind, soul, and body.

Maybe that is why God wants us to love with all of ourselves so we can do a "really good job" of loving Him and others? (Matthew 22:37-40 (NIV) Jesus replied: "'Love the Lord your God with all your heart and with all your soul and with all your mind.' This is the first and greatest commandment. And the second is like it: 'Love your neighbor as yourself.' All the Law and the Prophets hang on these two commandments."

Lord, help us to focus, to truly pay attention. Teach us to live with intention and purpose. Above all, show us the ways of genuine, devotion-filled love, for You and for others. Thank You, Lord.

96.ENTANGLED

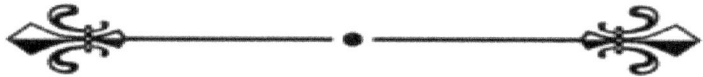

2 Peter 2:20 (NIV) If they have escaped the corruption of the world by knowing our Lord and Savior Jesus Christ and are again entangled in it and are overcome, they are worse off at the end than they were at the beginning.

Have you ever thought of what it might be like for a dolphin or other large fish to become entangled in a net? There is usually no way out, and every attempt to escape entangles them a little more.

When we were living in Palm Coast, May and I had a very productive patch of blueberries. They were so good and produced a LOT of berries. The only trouble was that the birds liked them even more than we did. So, a friend and I built a frame (that is another story unto itself) and we draped it with a net.

It worked! We had lots of berries, but every now and again, a bird would get in and get entangled. We were always able to get the birds out, though it took some effort. However, we created another problem. Snakes.

Apparently, they liked the berries too (or was it the trapped birds). Guess what? They too got entangled. As much as I tried, I was never able to untangle a snake. They all died of self-inflicted wounds as they struggled to get loose and continually caused more injury to their bodies.

What is the moral of the story? Be careful of becoming entangled in the affairs of this life. Some things in this life may seem tempting but extraction can be difficult, painful and even deadly.

Have you become entangled by trying to please God while also trying to please yourself? Getting entangled in our own fleshly desires might be the deadliest of all possible entanglements.

Lord, help us to see this life clearly through Your eyes and not our own. Keep us from all entanglements that would distract us from You. Thank You.

97.FALSE

2 Timothy 3:1-5 (NIV) But mark this: There will be terrible times in the last days. People will be lovers of themselves, lovers of money, boastful, proud, abusive, disobedient to their parents, ungrateful, unholy, without love, unforgiving, slanderous, without self-control, brutal, not lovers of the good, treacherous, rash, conceited, lovers of pleasure rather than lovers of God— having a form of godliness but denying its power. Have nothing to do with such people.

2 Peter 2:1-2 (NIV) But there were also false prophets among the people, just as there will be false teachers among you. They will secretly introduce destructive heresies, even denying the sovereign Lord who bought them —bringing swift destruction on themselves. Many will follow their depraved conduct and will bring the way of truth into disrepute.

When I read these verses, and I see today's headlines, it seems that they are practically the same. If these are not the "last days," then surely, they are a prelude to what is to come. Twenty years ago, I doubt if any of us would have anticipated such a radical moral decline in almost every aspect of society, including, sadly, some Christian denominations.

It is not uncommon to hear of preachers (teachers) perverting the gospel and bending to the dictates of the culture. They proclaim that what the Scriptures clearly state as sin is just another "normal" lifestyle. Beware, my brothers and sisters in Christ. Do not be deceived by false teachings.

Our flesh is very weak, and our human hearts are generally bent toward evil. Unless we are faithfully committed to prayer, God's word, and the leading of the Spirit, it is almost certain that we will be led astray by teaching that tickles our ears.

Lord, I know few of us think we could fall victim to false teachers. Please give us an understanding of Your word. Let us come to know You intimately, to be familiar with all Your ways lest we too be led astray. Lord, You are holy. Make us Your holy people. Thank You

98.EPIPHANY

2 Timothy 4:1-2 (NIV) In the presence of God and of Christ Jesus, who will judge the living and the dead, and in view of his appearing and his kingdom, I give you this charge: Preach the word; be prepared in season and out of season; correct, rebuke and encourage —with great patience and careful instruction.

The word "appearing" in the above verse is from the Greek Epiphanies, or in other words, Epiphany. The word means the manifestation (or revelation) of the divine (as to the Magi after Jesus' birth). The church celebrates this as the feast of the Epiphany on Jan 6th of each year. The word is also often used for a moment of sudden revelation, sometimes called a "rhema" word, such as when you notice something you never noticed before while reading the scriptures.

In today's verse, Paul uses this word to describe the second coming of Jesus Christ, the appearing, the Epiphany, the glorious revelation of Christ in all His splendor. Oh, what a day that will be!

It is good to know He is returning. How else might this world be "fixed"? Paul's charge to Timothy (and to us) is to be prepared (do not get caught sleeping and taking it easy). Preach the word (use words if you must). Always be ready to share with others the reason you have so much hope even though the world seems to be falling apart.

Engage in the lives of fellow believers so that they might listen as you correct, encourage, and even admonish if necessary. We are called to be patient (a lesson I continue to learn), and to be mindful in teaching and living the truth of the gospel, not our own version of it.

Let's ask ourselves a couple of questions. Are we truly excited about the return of Jesus? Are we prepared to share the gospel, and are we sharing it? Have we invited others into our lives so that we might mutually encourage, correct, rebuke, and teach one another?

Dear Lord, it is so easy to live our lives for ourselves. However, there is work to be done. Lead us, Lord, to be Your disciples not in name only but also in how we live. Thank You.

99.AROMA

2 Corinthians 2:14-16 (NIV) But thanks be to God, who always leads us as captives in Christ's triumphal procession and uses us to spread the aroma of the knowledge of him everywhere. For we are to God the pleasing aroma of Christ among those who are being saved and those who are perishing. To the one we are an aroma that brings death; to the other, an aroma that brings life. And who is equal to such a task?

Aromas can transport us back in time and to another place. The smell of honeysuckle immediately takes me back to Jackson, Mississippi, when we visited a family nearly 50 years ago. The smell of pikake (Hawaiian Jasmine) reminds me of Hawaii. The smell of the sea takes me back to the many times May and I walked the beaches in Hawaii and Florida. Many memories are quickly brought to mind simply by an aroma.

We – ourselves - are a pleasing aroma of Christ. Just our presence brings the blessings of Christ to our brothers and sisters. We bring an aroma of life, peace, love, kindness, gentleness, hope, and joy. We bring light to dark places. We bring joy where there is sadness. We bring comfort where there is pain and loneliness. We bring hope to the hopeless. We bring peace to the anxious and fearful. We are God's chosen to represent Him. What a wonder this is.

Read and note the last words in verse 16: "who is equal to such a task?" Be assured my friends, it is not you nor I. Rather, it is the living Christ in us as we are led by the Spirit of God.

Dear God, You are the aroma we bring to the world. Let us indeed be crucified as You live through us. Thank You

100.SCOFFERS

2 Peter 3:3 (NIV) Above all, you must understand that in the last days scoffers will come, scoffing and following their own evil desires.

This verse talks about the "last days." Perhaps the Lord is trying to tell us something? In reality, we have been in the "last days" ever since the resurrection of Jesus Christ. The longer we wait for the return of Jesus, the more loudly the scoffers will shout, "Where is the reality of His coming?"

Let us understand that these things are normal for the inhabitants of this world. Scoffing is easy to do when the focus is on ourselves and the blessings of the flesh. To others, our devotion to Jesus and living for Him seems like just so much wasted energy, perhaps bordering on being a fanatic.

Let us not shy away from our "fanaticism." Is it not a compliment in disguise? I am sure Jesus values fanaticism for Him far more than being "lukewarm". (Revelation 3:15-16 (NIV) I know your deeds, that you are neither cold nor hot. I wish you were either one or the other! So, because you are lukewarm—neither hot nor cold—I am about to spit you out of my mouth.)

My dear brothers and sisters, let us be careful to not be scoffers. It is easy to scoff at the lifestyles of those who are perishing, but that is not our calling. Our calling is to share the reality of Jesus Christ as we live out our days among them. When Jesus Christ is the Lord of us, others, in time, will notice and wonder, "What is it that makes you different?"

1 Peter 3:15 (NIV) But in your hearts revere Christ as Lord. Always be prepared to give an answer to everyone who asks you to

give the reason for the hope that you have. But do this with gentleness and respect.

Lord, let us not be intimidated by the scoffers. Give us boldness, strength, courage, and patience to live Godly lives in their presence. Please open the hearts of the scoffers to see You. Thank You

101.REALITY

Colossians 2:17 (NIV) These are a shadow of the things that were to come; the reality, however, is found in Christ.

In this day and age, some say there is no ultimate reality. Your truth is as valid as my truth. For those of us who call Jesus Christ Lord, He - and He alone - is the definer of truth and reality.

So, what is reality? It's the state of things as they truly are, not as we, as a society, might wish them to be. For example, the reality is that we are male and female. When our culture tries to redefine that, it inevitably collides with what is real.

I want to talk about two types of reality: primary and secondary. I once read an article where a 96-year-old gentleman was asked, "Where will you be in ten years?" He smiled and replied, "Oh, you mean where I'll be buried?" The interviewer clarified, "No, that's not what I mean. What I'm asking is, what will be the state of your afterlife in ten years?"

You see, the gentleman was answering a primary reality question with a secondary reality answer.

We often invest enormous resources in secondary realities, such as a wedding, while neglecting the primary one: the marriage itself.

Similarly, we immerse ourselves in our favorite shows, sports teams, or other forms of entertainment (secondary realities) while overlooking our physical and spiritual well-being (primary realities).

Can you distinguish between the secondary and primary realities in your life? Are you focusing on what is really important or are you squandering your life on secondary matters?

Lord, there are a lot of conflicting interests in this life. Give us the wisdom to discern the important and to focus on what should be primary in our lives. Thank You

102.TRUCULENT

Matthew 5:9 (NIV) Blessed are the peacemakers, for they will be called children of God.

James 3:18 (NIV) Peacemakers who sow in peace reap a harvest of righteousness

Today's word is new to me and, once again, comes from our friend Pete. It describes someone who's always ready for a fight or an argument, defiant, even hostile. Sounds a bit like certain parts of our culture these days, doesn't it?

May and I went out for lunch and found ourselves sitting next to a young mother and her pre-toddler child (who was as precious as can be). The woman's mom and dad (I assume) had joined her for lunch. The young mother did most of the talking as the mom and dad listened. He was describing her online "conversation" with an "activist" who seemed more eager to argue than to engage. His tone was aggressive, antagonistic, and combative, confrontational to the point of being downright truculent.

The young mother was obviously well educated, articulate and apparently a Christian (at least she was supportive of Christian principles) . As I listened, I could imagine the contentious, discourteous discussion getting nowhere. I wanted to say something, but I was pretty sure they were not interested in my input.

The real reason I didn't say anything is that I simply didn't know what to say. I'm fairly certain that online arguments rarely change anyone's mind; if anything, they often make people dig even deeper into their own positions. Still, I'm left with a dilemma: how should we, as Christians, handle confrontations of this kind?

I don't have a clear answer, only a few thoughts. The online world is not the best place for discussing contentious issues. Our calling is to be peacemakers, not to prove that we're right and someone else is wrong.

Jesus teaches us that the path to reconciliation is love. Preparation for a difficult discussion can be helpful, but it will always fall short unless it is accompanied by love, unless we truly "speak the truth in love."

Lord, lead us to really be the light. To seek to love rather than to be right. Thank You.

103.CONFORMED

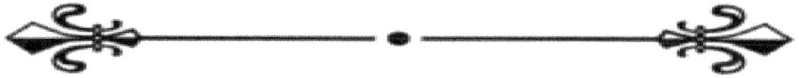

Romans 12:2 (NIV) Do not conform to the pattern of this world, but be transformed by the renewing of your mind. Then you will be able to test and approve what God's will is —his good, pleasing and perfect will.

Titus 2:11-12 (NIV) For the grace of God has appeared that offers salvation to all people. It teaches us to say "No" to ungodliness and worldly passions, and to live self-controlled, upright and godly lives in this present age.

Some verses stand out more than others. Romans 12:2 is one of those verses for me. I wondered how so many of us consider this verse to be true and yet many of us have already been conformed to this world. Even worse, many churches have and are being conformed to this world.

How can know what is right, even agree with it, and yet many of us are getting failing grades? I think part of the answer is that we do not want to do what is required to resist the world.

We know that the antidote to conformity is the Word of God. But knowing the Word and living by it are two very different things. A simple example many of us can relate to is falling into the trap of debt. Scripture is clear that debt is not a good thing and should be avoided whenever possible. Yet, who among us hasn't gone into debt for something we wanted?

Another familiar example is the challenge of contentment. We are encouraged to be content, yet few of us manage to remain so for long. The new phone, outfit, car, furniture, or streaming service seems to call our names, and who can resist?

I am confident that I could come up with a very long list of scripture principles that we ignore because we have already been conformed to this world.

Please allow me to share one more. Jesus told us to seek Him first above everything and everyone else. Why do we acknowledge the goodness of doing that, and yet we do not?

Perhaps we see God's word as suggestions? What do you think?

Oh Lord, please open my eyes and the eyes of all who might read this. Let there be an end to our hypocrisy. Thank You.

104.FOIBLE

Romans 15:1 (NIV) We who are strong ought to bear with the failings of the weak and not to please ourselves.

Colossians 3:13 (NIV) Bear with each other and forgive one another if any of you has a grievance against someone. Forgive as the Lord forgave you.

1 Peter 5:8 (NIV) Be alert and of sober mind. Your enemy the devil prowls around like a roaring lion looking for someone to devour.

Today, we have another word brought to us by our friend Pete: foible. It refers to those small, quirky habits or eccentricities we all have that sometimes irritate others.

I'm learning that what often bothers me about others isn't necessarily their behavior, it's my own disposition toward that behavior in the moment.

At times, someone can do something mildly annoying, and it doesn't affect me at all. Yet, when they do the exact same thing later, I find myself irritated. I have to smile and wonder at my own inconsistency.

Perhaps God truly understands the foibles we carry as human beings and calls us to bear with one another, to overlook small annoyances, to let go of grievances, and to live with grace toward each other.

Foible also has another meaning: the weaker point on a sword (from the middle to the point). It is the "breaking" point. Many of us have these foibles (breaking points) in our lives as we deal with grief, failing health, financial reverses, failed relationships etc. Guess who is out looking to attack us at these weak points? Yes, Satan knows our weak points and often strikes when we are at our most vulnerable.

Dear Lord, help us to genuinely overlook the foibles in others, for I know I am often the one with the problem. Please strengthen those who are facing life's trials. Guide us to encourage, comfort, and uplift one another whenever we can. Thank You.

105.CHEERFUL

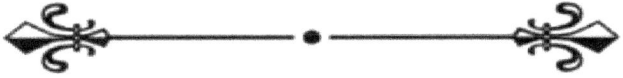

Proverbs 17:22 (NIV) A cheerful heart is good medicine, but a crushed spirit dries up the bones.

I have mentioned how May and I would visit the sick and dying and often leave feeling we got more out of the visit than they did. It is an amazing thing to visit someone to "cheer them up" and get "cheered up" yourself.

Being in good spirits and maintaining a sunny disposition has less to do with our circumstances than with our relationship with Christ. Imagine being gravely ill and facing the prospect of death, yet knowing with certainty that your suffering will soon end and that you will enter the presence of God for eternity, would you not, in such a case, still be cheerful?

I understand that the physical, relational and emotional pain we endure at times can seem overwhelming. But I am convinced it seems overwhelming because that is what we are focusing on. It is a measure of self-pity. Believe me, I know. I have been there a lot and it is a constant battle.

If our eyes were upon the Lord, why would we ever be downcast in our spirit?

Psalms 42:5 (NIV) Why, my soul, are you downcast? Why so disturbed within me? Put your hope in God, for I will yet praise him, my Savior and my God.

So let us put on our "happy faces," not because we are pretending but because our destiny is in the presence of God.

Dear God, The many distractions of life can easily lead us to discouragement and steal our joy. Guide us to keep our eyes fixed

185

on You and help us to be joyful, cheerful people who reflect Your love. Thank You.

106.READY

Luke 12:40 (NIV) You also must be ready, because the Son of Man will come at an hour when you do not expect him.

As we know, our days are numbered, and we can never know how many we have. The passing of our niece, Nani, a young woman of 49, brings this truth home once again.

Barely a week ago we were talking on the phone and the subject of dying came up. She expressed her expectation (partly because of her good genes like her Aunty May) to live to be 107. I told her I was not sure that would necessarily be a good thing. She chided me a bit, suggesting I might need more faith. And now she is gone. So quickly. A life cut off in her prime.

Nani was one of those people who never sat still. She was deeply involved in her community, her church, her family and her work. She was a sought-after professional, an author, and always, always in good spirits. She was perhaps the most energetic, engaging, and happy person I have ever known. She will be missed by many.

Yet this is the reality of life. Soon it will be our turn. Will we be ready?

Dear Father, we grieve the loss of our dear Nani. Please comfort her parents and her two brothers. Keep us mindful Lord, that Your call to come home can come at any moment. Thank You.

107.SMILE

Psalms 43:5 (NIV) Why, my soul, are you downcast? Why so disturbed within me? Put your hope in God, for I will yet praise him, my Savior and my God.

When I am out and about, I make it a point to smile and greet people, especially strangers or people who seem downcast. I am sometimes amazed at how easy it is to turn a frown upside down with a simple smile and a friendly word.

Yesterday I must have been a bit more reflective than usual. While in Publix, a stranger got my attention, put on a big smile, and pointed from her face to mine. I was startled at first, not realizing how inwardly focused I must have been. I had to smile. I have been witnessing the hand of God at work among His children, reminding me that all is well, even when circumstances suggest otherwise.

Father, I thank You for this stranger who reminded me of Your presence, that You hold this, that You hold all of life. May my countenance always reflect the depth of my relationship with You. Thank You.

108.LOOKING

2 Peter 3:14 (NIV) So then, dear friends, since you are looking forward to this, make every effort to be found spotless, blameless and at peace with him.

You know that looking and seeing are not the same thing, don't you? Our family sometimes has problems seeing. Once in a while we refer to each other as "potato eyes." It must be something to do with the water...

For instance, often when I am looking for something in the grocery store I can look right at it and not see it. Maybe they changed the label or the location? It's a bit embarrassing to ask a store clerk for help, only for him to reply, "It's right in front of you."

In today's verse, Peter encourages the believers (that would be you and I) to be "spotless, blameless and at peace" as they "are looking forward to this." What is "this"?

2 Peter 3:13 (NIV) But in keeping with his promise we are looking forward to a new heaven and a new earth, where righteousness dwells.

As we see the turmoil the world is in let us not fail to see the hand of God still at work among us. Especially as He does a more perfect work in you and me. Yes, this world is full of misery but in Christ the victory is assured.

My dear sojourner in Christ, as we travel the pilgrim's path to the eternal kingdom, let us keep our eyes upon Jesus, the Author and Finisher of life. The One who will bring us safely into the presence of the Father.

Lord, keep us from being dismayed or discouraged but rather give us a radiant joy that belies the circumstances of life. Thank You.

109.BEFORE

Colossians 1:17 (NIV) He is before all things, and in him all things hold together.

John 1:1 (NASB) In the beginning was the Word, and the Word was with God, and the Word was God.

John 8:58 (NASB) Jesus said to them, "Truly, truly, I say to you, before Abraham was born, I am.

Who can comprehend today's scriptures? We cannot understand eternity with the capacity that God has given us. What was there before there was anything? Jesus is fully Divine, and He is the exact representation of the Sovereign Lord Almighty. We, on the other hand, in our present physical bodies, are passing through the confines of time; bound for eternity, but not there yet.

The scientific community mainly agrees that nothing cannot be made from nothing. This creates a dilemma for those who refuse to believe there is a God. If there is no God, then how was something created from nothing? Look around. There is plenty of "somethings" everywhere. Where did it all start?

Even if we accept the "big bang" explanation for the universe's existence, where did the matter contained in this "big bang" come from?

And that is just about "stuff." Where did life come from? I wonder how otherwise seemingly intelligent people can believe that over millions of years it just happened. Surely that takes more faith than faith in God.

How is it that before there was anything there was God? God has always existed throughout the eons of eternity. He never was created because He always has been. And He is the Creator and the sustainer of all that is, including you and me.

Lord God, I rarely reflect about the expanse of eternity. I think you put this word "before" in my consciousness to help me come to grips with how big you are and how small I am. Thank You.

110.PROCLAIM

1 John 1:1 (NIV) That which was from the beginning, which we have heard, which we have seen with our eyes, which we have looked at and our hands have touched —this we proclaim concerning the Word of life.

As I read these words during my devotion time, I could only imagine what it must have been like to be one of the Apostles. Here is John, exclaiming, "I am an eyewitness, I heard Him speak, I have seen Him with my own eyes, I have touched Him, and I declare to you, without hesitation, He is the Word of life."

Stop a moment. Can you imagine the wonder and privilege of actually touching God? To audibly hear Him speak directly to you? To literally reach out and touch the Creator of the universe? We may never experience these things this side of heaven. However, we have the assurance that what is written is worthy of proclaiming.

John penned today's verse roughly fifty years after the death, burial, and resurrection of Jesus. By then, he was an elderly man who had endured much for his faith and for living as a faithful example of Christ. Would John have remained such a steadfast witness if he knew his testimony were false? Highly unlikely. His faith in Jesus was unwavering, after all, he had walked alongside the Lord Himself.

Although we have not walked with God physically, as His disciples, we are walking with Him in faith. Trusting Him in all situations and obeying Him as we understand His will. May He lead us to proclaim the Lord Jesus wherever we find ourselves.

Lord, thank You for men of old, eyewitnesses to the incredible incarnation. Give us strength to stand fast as we

resolve to trust and obey. After all, "there is no other way." Thank You.

111.DISREPUTE

2 Peter 2:2 (NIV) Many will follow their depraved conduct and will bring the way of truth into disrepute.

If we are awake, we can see that in many ways the Christian faith is in disrepute in America. Christian principles that were deemed to be good and wholesome just a generation or ago are now often seen as bigoted, repressive or even evil.

The scriptures warned us that this day would come. A day when leaders of prominent denominations will align with the culture and condone and promote deviant sexual behavior and even hide malicious abuse within their own spheres of authority.

As I reflected on these matters, I couldn't help but realize that there might be an even subtler and perhaps far more significant problem lurking within the ranks of Christianity.

I think that a big reason Christianity has and continues to fall into disrepute is because of one simple thing. Our hypocrisy. We fail to represent Christ in our everyday lives. We follow the principles of the world instead of following Jesus with practices that have become commonly accepted among Christians (like cohabitation, divorce, indebtedness, materialism, mindless entertainment, etc.). The list can get very long, but maybe even that is not the real problem.

The real problem may be that we fail to make Jesus lord of our lives. Yes, we proclaim with our lips that He is Lord but what do our checkbooks and calendars tell us? Are we blessing those who oppose us? How do we treat people not like us in our own churches and communities? Are we truly His, or are we professing Christians and practicing atheists?

Father, this is a harsh word. I pray it comes from You, not from myself. Begin with me, Lord, that I may bow in humility before Your Lordship. Thank You.

112.CLAIM

1 John 1:6 (NIV) If we claim to have fellowship with him and yet walk in the darkness, we lie and do not live out the truth.

To claim that something is true does not make it so. A claim is merely an assertion that something is the case, often made without evidence to support it.

John is saying that we who profess (claim) that we are in fellowship with God must also have proof that our assertion is, in fact, the truth. What is the proof that we are in fellowship with God? Simply that we no longer live in the darkness of our own understanding and fleshly desires. Instead, we "live out" the truth of a life that has been transformed by the Lord Jesus.

John is saying that "our walk" much match "our talk". Anything else is hypocrisy or, as John states, "we lie".

Some years ago, I heard the question, "Is there enough evidence in your life to convict you if you were on trial for being a Christian?" This might seem like an abstract question, but as I write, fellow Christians around the world are on trial for being a follower of Jesus.

Let us ask ourselves, does our walk match our talk? Is there enough evidence in our lives to prove (not just claim) that we are in the right relationship with the Lord of the universe? What is the evidence? Will it hold up in a court of law? Will it hold up at the Judgment Seat of Christ?

Father, I know that we can easily be fooled, and even worse, we can fool ourselves. If our claim of fellowship with You is false in any way, please reveal it to us and lead us to fully submit to Your Lordship. Thank You.

113.TRUSTED

James 5:12 (NIV) Above all, my brothers and sisters, do not swear—not by heaven or by earth or by anything else. All you need to say is a simple "Yes" or "No." Otherwise you will be condemned.

I read that there was a time in America culture when written contracts were the exception and that many (if not most) contracts were oral. People would "seal a deal" with a handshake and everyone knew they were bound to what they had agreed to.

It is my understanding that oral contracts, except in the case of real estate agreements can still be legally binding, provided the parties can demonstrate what was agreed upon.

I believe this principle should be a natural norm within the Christian community. When we say, "we will" or "we will not," our word should carry the same weight as a written contract that has been signed, sealed, notarized, and delivered. In other words, the words of a Christian should be trustworthy and reliable, our commitments should be ones others can depend upon. We should be known for following through on what we say. Wouldn't you agree?

I would like to apply this principle to us, especially in our homes and/or other close relationships. For example, when we tell a child we will do something favorable to or for them we should be sure to do it. Otherwise, we are teaching them that our words are unreliable and cannot be trusted.

When we tell a child he/she will be disciplined if they do/don't do something and we do not do what we say, again we are teaching them that our word is not dependable.

When we tell a friend, fellow employee, boss, spiritual leader, counselor or anyone else we will do something and then do not, we are teaching them that our words are not to be trusted. We are not dependable and what we say does not really matter that much.

When we tell a person that we love them and then treat them in any other manner we are hypocrites, showing by our actions that we are not dependable and that our words are meaningless.

Lord, it is easy to speak words that sound good but the "proof is in the pudding." Lead us, Lord, to always keep our word as much as it depends upon us. Let us become known as people who can be trusted to keep our commitments. Thank You.

114.BLUSTER

Job 6:24-27 (MSG) Confront me with the truth and I'll shut up, show me where I've gone off the track. Honest words never hurt anyone, but what's the point of all this pious bluster? You pretend to tell me what's wrong with my life, but treat my words of anguish as so much hot air. Are people mere things to you? Are friends just items of profit and loss?

Please re-read that first phrase of verse Job 6:24

This is so unlike our culture today. When was the last time you saw someone confronted with the truth and they simply "shut up"? More often, the opposite occurs. Rather than reflecting on the truth, there is a growing tendency toward bluster, including aggressive, indignant, overbearing, ranting, and even bullying speech, especially in today's public forums.

Most of us, if not all, have developed behavioral patterns over time that have generally proven effective in helping us achieve what we want.

For instance, children learn early on that if they cry, have a tantrum or throw their food on the floor they will often get their way. Young adults learn they can manipulate one parent against another so they can do what they want.

Spouses learn that shutting down or distancing oneself will usually wear the other person down. Employees learn how to butter up their boss. Bosses learn how to exploit their workers. There must be a million other ways that we have found successful in manipulating people.

Most of these "rackets" are simply learned behaviors. Ways in which we have been conformed to our culture.

Now back to blustering. How do we as Christians respond? Perhaps with a soft word? (Proverbs 15:1 (NIV) 1 A gentle answer turns away wrath, but a harsh word stirs up anger.) Sometimes, however, we need to remain quiet, and at other times we are called to give a reasoned response (see 1 Pet 3:15).

Yet my point goes far beyond how we respond to bluster. All of our "rackets" deserve careful examination, and many may need to be set aside, for we are called to a far higher standard, the standard of love.

Father, we have learned many behaviors that conflict with how we are to love one another. Please lead us in the way of love so that the world will know we belong to You. Thank You.

115.DECAY

Romans 8:20-21 (NIV) For the creation was subjected to frustration, not by its own choice, but by the will of the one who subjected it, in hope that the creation itself will be liberated from its bondage to decay and brought into the freedom and glory of the children of God.

Have you ever wondered why a bad apple placed in a basket with good apples turns the whole basket of apples bad? Why don't the good apples overcome the bad apples and turn them good?

Or why does the human body run down over time and give up and die? Why does it not become stronger and stronger over time and live forever?

Why does everything ever created eventually deteriorate and fade from existence? Why do cars age and need to be replaced? Why do relationships require constant care, or else they falter? Why does standing water grow stale and putrid over time?

By now, you must be wondering about me. What am I thinking? Perhaps these things just happen. Yes, but why? What would life on this earth be like if it was the opposite? What if one bad apple could be "cured" by the good apples? What if water stayed fresh forever? What if the sun and the stars show forever? What if love never stopped, but only grew stronger and more beautiful with each passing moment?

Perhaps I am dreaming of a time when this world, and all of God's creation, will be fully redeemed, and everything returns to the way it was meant to be. A day when sadness has vanished, tears are no more, and death holds no sway. Oh, what a day that will be.

((Life Application Bible Commentary New Testament) "The created order functions in spite of its flaws, but diseases, deformities, and suffering constantly remind us that all is not right with us or with the world.) I dream of the day when all will be made right in this world."

Oh God, I eagerly look forward to the new earth as You have promised. When this old world passes away and we are united with You in the new creation, there will be no decay there. Thank You, Lord.

116.RESPECT

1 Peter 2:17 (NIV) Show proper respect to everyone, love the family of believers, fear God, honor the emperor.

1 Peter 3:15 (NIV) But in your hearts revere Christ as Lord. Always be prepared to give an answer to everyone who asks you to give the reason for the hope that you have. But do this with gentleness and respect.

I was praying for someone who is in a difficult relationship when the word "respect" came to mind. I do not know if this is the issue between them, but I do know that mutual respect is very hard to achieve when two or more people are struggling in their relationships.

When I am offended (disrespected) my impulse is to be disrespectful in return. It is one of those "automated" responses according to the flesh that I have observed over the years. I know to be disrespectful in return is not a useful option if my goal is reconciliation. Even knowing what I know, the impulse is there and sometimes I do not squash the feeling in time and I say or do something that is not useful. I am often reminded of Paul's struggles ("Oh what a wretched man that I am (Romans 7)).

If I want to be respected, I must give respect. Oh, how difficult that is! When I am offended, the last thing my flesh wants to do is be respectful. Yet that is the way of love. It is God's way. With the empowerment of God's Spirit (the same Spirit that raised Jesus from the dead — the same Spirit that lives in me) I can do this.

All I need to do is take up my cross in the moment and die. Die to my impulses and fleshly desires for "revenge" or to "get even" or to "make things right".

The next time you are engaged in a conversation that is turning disrespectful remember the principle of reciprocity. Give what you want to receive (Luke 6:38 (NIV) 38 Give, and it will be given to you. A good measure, pressed down, shaken together and running over, will be poured into your lap. For with the measure you use, it will be measured to you.")

Lord, this is another one of those principles that is so easy to agree with yet so difficult to put into practice in real life. Please help us to remain respectful, even when we disagree or face attacks. We cannot do this on our own, Lord, but You can. Thank You.

117.HATE

1 John 2:9-10 (NASB) The one who says he is in the Light and yet hates his brother is in the darkness until now. The one who loves his brother abides in the Light and there is no cause for stumbling in him

I know that in many ways this devotion is for me. However, I am sure that others share the same dilemma. When faced with the awareness of pain being caused by others my immediate inclination is to hate not only what has been done but also the perpetrator. One might say that is a natural human response. However, it is not the way of love nor is it the way of Christ.

Some might argue that it is acceptable if the hate is not directed toward brothers and sisters in Christ. Yet Jesus clearly commanded us to "love our enemies." I believe, therefore, that any desire for revenge or any expression of hatred toward another is sin. It reflects arrogance and foolishness. How can anyone truly call themselves a child of God if hatred lingers in their heart?

I understand that loving our enemies can feel beyond reach, but that does not make it impossible. To live without love for my enemies is to live in the flesh. If I am truly a child of God, and if I am to walk in the light rather than in darkness, then I cannot, and must not, harbor hatred toward anyone.

Lord God, how greatly I need a heart transplant. Thank you for making me aware of a part of me that is still not aligned with You. Change my heart, please Lord. Thank You.

118.OFFERINGS

2 Chronicles 13:11 (NIV) Every morning and evening they present burnt offerings and fragrant incense to the LORD. They set out the bread on the ceremonially clean table and light the lamps on the gold lamp stand every evening. We are observing the requirements of the LORD our God. But you have forsaken him.

Matthew 7:22-23 (NASB) Many will say to Me on that day, 'Lord, Lord, did we not prophesy in Your name, and in Your name cast out demons, and in Your name perform many miracles?' And then I will declare to them, 'I never knew you; DEPART FROM ME, YOU WHO PRACTICE LAWLESSNESS.'

Difficult words to grasp: "Observing the rules, but forsaking God." It is possible to perform "good deeds" (offerings) and yet remain outside the will of God. It presents a kind of paradox.

If we have genuinely been saved, then it is "normal" to do "good things" as part of our daily lives. One naturally follows another. God has been extravagant toward us and, since He is our Lord, we should follow His example and be extravagant toward others. Surely you agree, don't you?

On the other hand, doing "good things," whether individually or collectively, does not mean Jesus is Lord of our lives. Many organizations and individuals do good but deny that God exists. Or they claim that God is not involved in our daily lives. Many say that religion is a "worthless crutch." Yet few deny that their humanitarian efforts relieve the suffering of many.

What are we to make of this? We cannot judge others by outward appearances. It is a matter of the heart, and only God truly knows the heart. However, we need to look closely at our own motives. If our "good things", our offerings, are done for any reason other than the glory of God, then our motives may be suspect. We can fool others, we can even fool ourselves, but we cannot fool God.

Dear Father, please search our hearts and reveal any motives that are less than pure. Thank You.

119.TEARS

Psalms 126:5-6 (NIV) Those who sow with tears will reap with songs of joy. Those who go out weeping, carrying seed to sow, will return with songs of joy, carrying sheaves with them.

I must be getting a little sentimental in my old age. Yesterday, I found myself thinking about our life, May's and mine, and suddenly tears welled up in my eyes. And now, here they are again. It is a deep sadness, one without a cause that I can discern.

I wipe the tears away and they return. "Oh my soul, why are you so downcast?"

God has given us a most wonderful life and a love that has matured and deepened with the years. Are these tears of happiness? Are they tears of pending loss? I do not know. It is not like me to shed tears so easily.

I cannot write more. My soul feels overwhelmed.

Lord, thank you for all things, including the tears and friends who care.

The above was written yesterday. Soon after I stopped writing, I was distracted by life's demands, and the tears and the sadness returned to their hiding places. The sadness that seemed to engulf me was just a very short season. My hope is that no one has to live in such a place. On the other hand, my brief visit seems to have lightened my soul.

Father, thank You for the tears and for the comfort of wiping them away.

120.GONE

2 Corinthians 5:17 (NIV) Therefore, if anyone is in Christ, the new creation has come: The old has gone, the new is here!

Today our son, Lee, returns home to his wife, cat, dog, and chickens in Tennessee. He has been with us for two full weeks, but in just a few hours, he will be gone. Gone. That word does not feel right at this moment. To be gone feels like to be no longer here. Whatever opportunities existed before are no longer available once they are gone.

May and I are deeply thankful that Lee was willing to spend this time with us. Being away from home for such a long period is never easy.We so appreciate his willingness to sacrifice to be with us. May and I know we will be gone soon (so will you by the way). We are confident that Lee will have no regrets as far as reaching out to us. He has done well in showing honor to his parents and I am confident God has taken notice.

But what about the rest of us? Are we doing well with the relationships we have? Will God say to us "good job, you were faithful in this or that relationship?" Or will we have regrets for things not said or perhaps things we have said that we should have made right?

My hope is that we will live our lives deliberately attending to each relationship as God leads us. May there be no regrets when either they or we are gone. Let us lift one another up and encourage each other, especially as we witness the day of the Lord drawing near.

Father, You dwell outside of time, yet we are bound by its limits. When the right moment passes, it is gone forever. Help us

to be about Your work, sowing seeds of love, compassion, mercy, and care wherever and whenever we can. Thank You.

121.KNOW

1 John 2:14 (NIV) I write to you, dear children, because you know the Father. I write to you, fathers, because you know him who is from the beginning. I write to you, young men, because you are strong, and the word of God lives in you, and you have overcome the evil one.

Proverbs 24:3-4 (NIV) By wisdom a house is built, and through understanding it is established; through knowledge its rooms are filled with rare and beautiful treasures.

Colossians 1:10 (NIV) so that you may live a life worthy of the Lord and please him in every way: bearing fruit in every good work, growing in the knowledge of God,

John points out two really important things if we are to live lives worthy of who we are (saints). He reminds us that the way to overcome evil is to KNOW God and have God's word LIVING in us (actively applying it).

Proverbs reminds us that as we grow in wisdom and knowledge, our lives will reflect greater spiritual fruit and abundant blessings.

Colossians reminds us that pleasing God and living a life worthy of our calling requires us to grow in the knowledge of God.

We must answer two questions. First, how do we grow in the knowledge of God? Is there a set of books we can study, or perhaps a course or two we could take?

The second question is, how does the Word of God come alive in us? Do I need to go to church more often, pray more/better, etc.?

The reality is that we come to know someone more intimately when we spend quality time with them and they choose to reveal themselves to us. When we are in a relationship, and do not share who we really are and what is going on in our thought and emotional lives, we cannot have an intimate relationship with that person. To have an intimate relationship requires that we truly come to know that person.

It is the same with God. We must first spend time with Him and wait for Him to reveal Himself. I do not mean simply praying more or studying the Word more, though both can be valuable. What I mean is that we must sit quietly before Him, earnestly seeking to know Him and listening attentively to His voice. We are called to be still and wait with expectation, allowing God to reveal Himself to us more deeply over time.

To answer the second question, we must consider what happens as we get to know someone with great intimacy. The more that happens, the more we want to please them. Why? Because we come to love them.

I am reminded of the song lyrics, "to know, know, know, Him is to love, love, love him, and I do." The same is true in our relationship with God. As we come to know God, we fall increasingly in love with Him, and our desire, more and more, is to please Him. The Word of God naturally comes alive in us as we respond to the reciprocal love between God and ourselves.

Oh, Father, please work into our hearts a desire to know You intimately. To become familiar with all of Your ways. To want to please You more than anything else in this life. Please do not allow the many distractions in our lives to keep us from having the intimate relationship with You that You desire for us. Thank You.

122.COACH

Hebrews 5:12 (NASB) For though by this time you ought to be teachers, you have need again for someone to teach you the elementary principles of the oracles of God, and you have come to need milk and not solid food.

Have you ever had a good coach or mentor? They can be very helpful in getting us to accomplish things that seem out of reach. They can teach us how to discipline ourselves or to stretch and do what seems impossible.

I read an article about a study to determine if a life coach could make a difference in the quality of life for the elderly and reduce the incidence of heart attack, stroke, and dementia. The results were very promising.

According to the article, individuals who volunteered to work with a life coach did relatively better in all areas than the control group. While some only did marginally better, many considerably improved their quality of life. The difference seemed to be the level of enthusiasm in working with the coach and the willingness to tackle difficult areas (such as smoking, obesity, and inactivity).

When May and I did marriage counseling, we saw very similar results. If the couple engaged in the process, followed our instructions, and in general did their best, progress was substantial and, in some cases, amazing. On the other hand, sometimes May and I found ourselves working harder than the couple. In general, the results reflected the effort applied.

I contend that "life coaches" should be "mandatory" for Christians. I am frequently reminded of the Paul, Barnabas Timothy interactions described in the Bible.

Paul was clearly a gifted teacher, mentor, and coach. Timothy was his student. Yet Paul still needed a spiritual friend and encourager, and that role was filled by Barnabas, among others. It is valuable for all of us to have someone who speaks truth into our lives, just as it is important for us to mentor others along the journey of Christian maturity.

No matter what our role (teacher, encourager or student), we all need people to help us on our journey.

Father, please bring into our lives a Paul, a Barnabas, and a Timothy. Thank You.

123.SELF-CONTROL

1 John 2:16 (NIV) For everything in the world—the lust of the flesh, the lust of the eyes, and the pride of life—comes not from the Father but from the world.

Technically, today's word could be two words, but the hyphen brings them together.

The world we live in often presents us with such a pleasing array of choices that we want to join it. We think we can place a hyphen between the world and the Christian life and live in both. However, there is grave danger in wanting to do this. Jesus warned us that it is not possible to love this world and to love God.

We cannot have it both ways. Even knowing this, we still sometimes lose control over our desires.

We live in a time and culture that insists that Christian virtues are outdated and no longer relevant. Do not believe that for even an instant. We are foreigners and aliens living in a corrupt culture that wants us to assimilate its values of materialism, open sex, and worldly success. As enticing as these things may be, they are from this world and not from the Lord Jesus, whom we are to serve.

This problem affects us because we have been subtly shaped by the world's influences. The other day, May and I were watching a Hallmark movie, which was heartwarming, but there was a moment in the dialogue where one woman flirted with another. It was very subtle, barely noticeable. I do not think May even picked up on it.

The world uses this quiet, almost invisible process to guide us toward its agenda. It is very sneaky. "Just a little sin, how can it hurt?" or "Just a little innocent play here and there" seems harmless. These things go largely unnoticed, yet they slowly infiltrate our mindset and shape our worldview.

I have two suggestions. First, pay attention to what you are taking in, whether it is TV, movies, books, friends, news commentaries etc. The source doesn't matter. Ask yourself whether what you are taking in aligns with the word of God?

Second, exercise your free will while you are still able. Reject everything coming into your life that does not reflect the word of God.

Father, please open our eyes. Help us recognize where the world is trying to deceive us. By Your Spirit, empower us to exercise self-control and live according to Your ways. Thank You.

124.ALIENATED

Galatians 4:17 (NIV) Those people are zealous to win you over, but for no good. What they want is to alienate you from us, so that you may have zeal for them.

Ecclesiastes 7:29 (NASB) Behold, I have found only this, that God made men upright, but they have sought out many devices.

To be alienated is to be alone and separated. It is not a good feeling, and I suspect it has a lot to do with the mental crisis and increasing suicide rates in America. People feel their alienation from God. From days of old, men have sought ways to relieve this pain.

(My Daily Pursuit Devotions for Every Day) "Behind every invention of instruments, and every sort of entertainment, is a simple reason. Mankind, who was created to have fellowship with God, and is now alienated from God, is trying to deal with that alienation. Maybe, so they think, the noise and activity will drown out that inner longing for something they cannot explain. They know something is wrong, even though they may not be able to explain it."

We who profess Jesus as Lord are also alienated, not from God, but from this world. Or, at least, we should be.

1 Peter 2:11-12 (NASB) Beloved, I urge you as aliens and strangers to abstain from fleshly lusts which wage war against the soul. Keep your behavior excellent among the Gentiles, so that in the thing in which they slander you as evildoers, they may because of your good deeds, as they observe them, glorify God in the day of visitation.

So, yes, we may feel "out of sorts" because of our alienation from this world, but we must remember that although we are in the world we are not of the world. Sometimes this is difficult but do not be discouraged. Keep your eyes on Jesus as He completes the perfect work He is doing in you and me.

Father, I do so thank You for Your strength to stay the course and not to give up. Thank You.

125.IMPENDING

1 John 2:18 (NIV) Dear children, this is the last hour; and as you have heard that the antichrist is coming, even now many antichrists have come. This is how we know it is the last hour.

Have you ever suddenly awakened from a dream with an overwhelming sense of calamity or profound joy? The dream felt so real that you were unsure if you had truly been dreaming. The event that seems imminent, at least in your mind, can evoke fear and anxiety or the anticipation of great happiness, depending on your perspective.

Imagine that you knew, I mean really knew, that Jesus' return was imminent, very close at hand, really soon. Approaching from the East and about to be seen on the horizon all around the world. Imagine you had absolute certainty that His return was for You to experience soon, no longer looming in the distance. The last hour has arrived, and all is about to submit to the complete Lordship of Jesus of Nazareth, the Anointed One, our Savior and Messiah.

If you truly had this over whelming sense of Jesus' impending return, would you feel anxious or joyful?

The Apostle John is urging us to live with that level of awareness of Jesus' impending return. I wonder, "what would I do differently if I knew this for sure"? I hope the answer for both you and me is nothing. If I am truly living with the expectation of Jesus' imminent return, then there would be nothing I would need to do differently when that hour comes.

Given our human tendencies and the ways we often neglect what is truly important, I suggest we help ourselves by intentionally remembering His impending return. This could become a meaningful part of our morning and evening quiet times. Perhaps a short prayer, such as, "Lord, given today might be the day of Your return, what are my priorities? What do I need to do today for Your honor and Your glory and the advance of Your kingdom"?

Lord, it has already been a long wait, and we may still wait a long time before Your return. I know our days are numbered, and we do not know what that number is. Help me to live each day with the awareness that it could be my very last on this earth, or it could be the day of Your return. Maranatha, Lord Jesus. COME SOON (1 Corinthians 16:22b). Thank You.

126.PURPOSE

Romans 8:28 (NASB) And we know that God causes all things to work together for good to those who love God, to those who are called according to His purpose.

Not too many years ago, the book "The Purpose Driven Church" was very popular in the Christian community. It certainly seemed to make sense. If we do not know our purpose, we will squander our life and will have little sense of direction for our lives. After all, if we do not know where we are going how will we ever know when we get there?

But this can be a little misleading if we begin to think of our purpose as a destination rather than a process. I believe that what we accomplish on this earth is not nearly as important as who we become as followers of Christ. The transformation itself is our true purpose, a purpose that shapes us and places us right in the center of God's will for our lives.

"Purpose is for me to depend on Him and on His power now. If I can stay calm, faithful, and unconfused while in the middle of the turmoil of life, the goal of the purpose of God is being accomplished in me. God is not working toward a particular finish; His purpose is the process itself."

(Excerpt from My Utmost for His Highest, Oswald Chambers)

We can consider purpose from two perspectives. The first being where we are heading in life. If we know God's purpose for our life, we can be assured we are aligned with His will as we allow that purpose to lead and guide us in life.

On the other hand, our true purpose is to bring glory to God. It is the process of being transformed into the nature of the Spirit of God that lives inside of us.

Father, please give us clarity and understanding of our individual purposes for this life. Also, Lord please let it be most clear that our main purpose is to submit, to surrender to You; transforming our lives into the Divine nature. Thank You.

127.GOLDEN

Luke 6:31 (NASB) Treat others the same way you want them to treat you.

Luke 6:38 (NASB) Give, and it will be given to you. They will pour into your lap a good measure.

The golden rule is not unique to Christianity or Jewish culture. It appears in one form or another in many cultures and religions. It is often considered to be a form of "ethics reciprocity" (Wikipedia). In other words, we can generally expect to get back what we give out. If we want to be treated well, then we need to treat people well and mostly it will be returned.

Life Application Bible Commentary (LABC) "The well-known Rabbi Hillel, when challenged to teach the entire Law while standing on one foot, said, "Whatever angers you when you suffer it at the hands of others, do not do it to others, this is the whole law." But Jesus stated this in a positive manner, making it even more powerful. While it may be possible to not do evil to others, it is much more difficult to take the initiative to actually do good."

My dear friend, are you a follower of Jesus? Good. Then go forth and do good. Show your love for Jesus by doing good for someone else, perhaps even for someone you do not care for very much.

Thank you, Lord, for so many guiding principles that bring peace and harmony when we follow them. Thank you.

128.DIFFERENCE

Luke 6:32 (NASB) If you love those who love you, what credit is that to you? For even sinners love those who love them.

Luke 6:35 (NASB) But love your enemies, and do good, and lend, expecting nothing in return; and your reward will be great, and you will be sons of the Most High; for He Himself is kind to ungrateful and evil men.

I have often told believers that if people do not notice that you are "different" then something is wrong. Jesus tells us clearly in John 13:34-35 that our love distinguishes us from the world and causes people to take notice. Loving those who do not like us or even actively oppose us is surely the most radical evidence that we are sincere followers of the Master.

I suggest that we begin where we are. Learn to love the emotionally distant husband, the nagging wife, or the neglectful parent or child. Yes, let us begin in our homes, becoming examples to one another as we express God's love.

But do not stop there. Let us show love to the cashier who works slowly, or the waiter who is careless or forgets what we need. Let us also show love to the traffic officer who pulls us over. Perhaps we can practice with the telemarketer who irritates us so much. Maybe if we keep practicing love, we will reveal God's presence within us.

(LABC) the difference is that God's people are willing to love, do good, and lend even when there is no promise of return, even when it results in abuse. Such actions will mark Jesus' followers as different from the world, different even from the religious leadership.

Dear Father, please move upon us so to that the world can see that we belong to You. Please let the difference in us become obvious to the most casual observer. Thank You.

129.ANOINTED

1 John 2:20 (NIV) But you have an anointing from the Holy One, and all of you know the truth.

Some Christians mature, and some do not. There are many causes for this but I believe we all have the capability to become all God intends us to be. On the other hand, I also believe many Christians are living way below the capacity God intended. Why is this? Consider the following:

(Believer's Bible Commentary, ref. 1 John 2:20)

"When John tells his young readers, 'you know all things,' he does not mean this in an absolute sense. It is not that they possess perfect knowledge, but that they have the capacity to recognize what is true and what is not. Even the youngest and simplest believer has a level of discernment in spiritual matters that an unsaved philosopher does not have…

In the physical realm, when a baby is born, he is immediately endowed with all the faculties common to the human race. He has eyes, hands, feet, and a brain. He does not receive these later. Although these faculties grow and develop, the whole person is present from the very beginning. In the same way, when a person is born again, he receives at that moment all the spiritual capacities he will ever possess, even though there will be endless opportunities for their growth and development."

Read the last two sentences again. When we are born again, we receive all the faculties to do the "work that God has prepared for us to do" (See Ephesians 2:8-10). They may need refinement but the problem is not capacity. It is development (or lack of) of our capacities that makes it possible (or not) for us to carry out God's assignment(s) for our lives.

What do you think? Have you developed and reached maturity in the spiritual gifting God has given to you?

130.MISTAKE

Jeremiah 42:19-21 (NIV) "Remnant of Judah, the LORD has told you, 'Do not go to Egypt.' Be sure of this: I warn you today that you made a fatal mistake when you sent me to the LORD your God and said, 'Pray to the LORD our God for us; tell us everything he says and we will do it.' I have told you today, but you still have not obeyed the LORD your God in all he sent me to tell you.

Have you ever looked back on something you did and thought it was a mistake? I am pretty sure most of us have had that experience one time or another. But what if I told you that ultimately "a born again believer" cannot make a mistake" Consider:

Romans 8:28 (NIV) And we know that in all things God works for the good of those who love him, who have been called according to his purpose.

"All things" includes my foibles, misdirections, indecisions, and procrastinations. Everything. But, did you notice that there is a condition? This promise applies only to those who love God. If I am genuinely in love with God and genuinely want Him to be Lord of my life, then I do not need to fear making a mistake because, even if I don't "get it right," He will "make it right." Please understand that does not mean I do not have to deal with the consequences of my mistakes but I can be assured that in the end God will make it right.

A word of caution here. Notice the warning in the scriptures from Jeremiah. This promise to make things right falls away when we know what God wants us to do but choose not to do it. That, my dear brothers and sisters, may be a "fatal mistake."

Father, as Your children, let us approach life and the decisions we make with great confidence. You promise to guide

us and grant us wisdom when we seek Your direction. If we earnestly desire You and submit to Your Lordship over our lives, then You will be a lamp for our footsteps and a light for our path. And if we fail, we trust that You will use even that for our good and for Your glory. It is a truly wonderful thing to be Your child. Thank You for making everything right in the end.

131.REMAIN

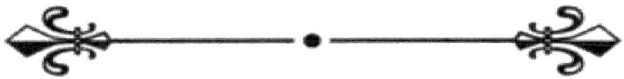

1 John 2:24 (NIV) As for you, see that what you have heard from the beginning remains in you. If it does, you also will remain in the Son and in the Father.

John 15:4 (NIV) Remain in me, as I also remain in you. No branch can bear fruit by itself, it must remain in the vine. Neither can you bear fruit unless you remain in me.

To remain means to stay put. To not wander off somewhere, perhaps exploring and going on adventures. We are frequently tempted to check out what seems to be greener pastures "over there"?

In some ways, to remain seems kind of boring. The same old same old day after day. I look around and see others seeming to have fun and enjoying life. Maybe I too could wander off and "follow my heart" like our culture encouraging me to do.

It sounds good and might even be exciting. But the reality remains. Only those who abide in Him will bear good fruit. You see, God understands and warns us about the evil in our own hearts. We have hearts that are prone to evil. So much so that we often fool even ourselves.

Jeremiah 17:9 (NASB) "The heart is more deceitful than all else And is desperately sick; Who can understand it?.

If we fail to remain in Christ, we allow rot to grow in our hearts. That is all one should expect from a heart that is evil and has become detached from Christ.

I could write a list of disciplines that would help us to remain in Jesus, but I am pretty sure you already know these things. They might be useful but none of them will be very helpful unless we really want to remain in Him. This is the place we must begin and stay. Are we motived to remain in Christ? Do we really want to remain in Him more than we want anything else in this life?

Father, the distractions are many and to remain in You may mean saying "no" when I want to say "yes" or saying "yes" when I want to say "no." Please, God, may every decision I make from the time I get up in the morning until I go to bed enable me to draw closer to You and to remain in You, forever thankful for Your Lordship in my life.

132.ALONE

Psalms 23 (NIV) The LORD is my shepherd, I lack nothing. He makes me lie down in green pastures, he leads me beside quiet waters, he refreshes my soul. He guides me along the right paths for his name's sake. Even though I walk through the darkest valley, I will fear no evil, for you are with me; your rod and your staff, they comfort me. You prepare a table before me in the presence of my enemies. You anoint my head with oil; my cup overflows. Surely your goodness and love will follow me all the days of my life, and I will dwell in the house of the LORD forever.

In the early morning, as I wait for May to rise from her slumber, I like to log onto "praycast.com" and watch or pray along with a prayer video for different nations around the world. I use my earbuds so I do not disturb her. Sometimes my music app opens on its own, even when I do not want it to.

Yesterday it opened unexpectedly, and a song began to play that I had not heard in a long time. Its melody made me pause and listen. Here are the words:

I AM NOT ALONE (Joni Erickson Tada)

"I'm alone, yet not alone. God's the light that will guide me home. With His love and tenderness, Leading through the wilderness, And wherever I may roam, I'm alone, yet not alone.

I will not be bent in fear. He's the refuge I know is near. In His strength I find my own. By His faithful mercies shown. That so mighty is His shield, All His love is now revealed.

When my steps are lost. And desperate for a guide, I can feel His touch, A soothing presence by my side. Alone, yet not alone. Not forsaken when on my own. I can lean upon His arm And be lifted up from harm. If I stumble, or if I'm thrown, I'm alone, yet not alone.

He has bound me with His love, Watchful angels look from above. Every evil can be braved, For I know I will be saved. Never frightened on my own, I'm alone, yet not alone. I'm alone, yet not alone"

If you have a chance, listen to this song reflectively. I also suggest you check out "prayercast.com."

Lord, when we feel alone and lonely, by Your Spirit remind us that we are NEVER, EVER alone. You are by our side all the time. Thank You.

133.RIGHTEOUS

Jeremiah 23:5 (NIV) "The days are coming," declares the LORD, "when I will raise up for David a righteous Branch, a King who will reign wisely and do what is just and right in the land.

1 John 2:29 (NIV) If you know that he is righteous, you know that everyone who does what is right has been born of him.

Did you know that there is a difference between being right and being righteous? For many years, May would tell me "You always have to be right." I would counter with my defense of "I am right." To me it was not a matter of "having" to be right, it was just the way it is.

Pretty arrogant, don't you think? Well, I still think "I am right." And, you know what? So do you. Here is my thinking: If we knew we were not right we would change our position or argument or whatever we are dealing with. Few would intentionally do or say what we do not think is "right." Agree?

But being "right" is a far cry from being righteous. May's objection points to the root cause of my failures. I delivered my "right thinking" without the essential ingredient of love.

Have you ever made pumpkin pie without sugar? It happened once in our family, and I do not recommend it. That is what it feels like when we do what is "right" but forget to stir in love, kindness, gentleness, patience, and all the other virtues of the Holy Spirit.

Lord, the Scriptures remind us that we are only resounding symbols when we do anything without love. Please perfect Your love in us. Thank You.

134.NOW

1 John 3:2 (NIV) Dear friends, now we are children of God, and what we will be has not yet been made known. But we know that when Christ appears, we shall be like him, for we shall see him as he is.

NOW BUT NOT YET! Yesterday this came up in our small group meeting. It was unplanned but seemed to have fit with God's leading. It began with a heartfelt prayer that literally brought tears to my eyes.

It was not until recently that I noticed this reality in the scriptures. Today's verse is a good example. We know we are children of God right now but there is more to the story. As John puts it, "what we shall be has not yet been made known." Clearly there is more to being a child of God than we are now able to realize or appreciate.

We are God's children right now but the "now" of being a Christian includes troubles and difficulties, and some weigh us down to the point of breaking.

What is this "not yet" that we will one day experience? In John's words, "we shall be like Him." Amazing. Beyond incredible. Absolutely mind boggling, especially given our current condition. It will be a time when all is fulfilled in Christ. When we take on our new glorified bodies there will be no more pain, no more anxiety, and no more pressure. Oh Lord, please hasten that day.

This reminds me of one of our favorite scriptures (Philippians 1:6 (NIV) Being confident of this, that he who began a good work in you will carry it on to completion until the day of Christ Jesus.

Some days I wish God would hurry, but everything will happen according to His plan and His timing. He knows what is best. Let us trust Him in the midst of our daily struggles.

It seems to me that God has plans to do a complete makeover for His "kids." Oh! What a day that will be.

Oh Lord, we look forward to the "not yet" even as we live in the "now.". Please Lord, let us live a life worthy of who we are and whom we will become. Thank You.

135.SURPRISE

1 Thessalonians 5:4-6 (NIV) But you, brothers and sisters, are not in darkness so that this day should surprise you like a thief. You are all children of the light and children of the day. We do not belong to the night or to the darkness. So then, let us not be like others, who are asleep, but let us be awake and sober.

Have you ever been surprised to the point where it took your breath away? Like a bolt of lightning from the sky, so close and unexpected that it leaves you astonished and amazed? A jolt you will never forget.

I think for any of us still alive when Jesus returns for His people, it will be the "surprise of a lifetime." Can you imagine? One moment you are doing the mundane chores of life and in the next instant you are caught up in the air in the presence of Jesus?

1 Thessalonians 4:16-17 (NIV) For the Lord himself will come down from heaven, with a loud command, with the voice of the archangel and with the trumpet call of God, and the dead in Christ will rise first. After that, we who are still alive and are left will be caught up together with them in the clouds to meet the Lord in the air. And so we will be with the Lord forever.

Or perhaps I am mistaken? Maybe we will not be surprised at all. If we are awake and looking with expectation for God to fulfill His promised return, then why would we be surprised? On the other hand, if we have busied ourselves with the affairs of the world it might be the shock of a lifetime.

Do you like surprises? Then sleep away

1 Thessalonians 5:6 (NIV) So then, let us not be like others, who are asleep, but let us be awake and sober.

If we are awake, let us look to the horizon for our redemption is drawing near.

Oh Lord, please wake us from our slumber and keep us from being distracted by the busyness of our lives. The day of standing in Your presence is drawing near. Come, Lord Jesus, come. Thank You.

136.GUILE

John 1:47 (KJV) Jesus saw Nathanael coming to him, and saith of him, Behold an Israelite indeed, in whom is no guile!

1 John 3:5-6 (NIV) But you know that he appeared so that he might take away our sins. And in him is no sin. No one who lives in him keeps on sinning. No one who continues to sin has either seen him or known him.

I am reminded of the saying, "you get what you see." In other words, there is no hidden agenda or deception in any shape or form. It is interesting that only one of the twelve disciples got this commendation from Jesus.

The word guile is not very common these days. It means deceit or not being completely honest. I think we can also apply it to being double-minded, or perhaps the word "pretense" is appropriate.

Why do you think only Nathanael got this commendation? I do not know the answer for sure, but I suspect the other eleven disciples were like most of us - a little double-minded, pretending we are what we are not, or having motives that are hidden deep in our hearts, etc..

As I read 1 John 3:5-6 this morning, I was reminded of how often I still stray from the righteousness of God. Impatience is a big struggle for me, and at times I judge others or even do something good with a hidden motive. You name it, the "old man" in me has not fully died yet. Sometimes I wonder if he ever will in this life. Do you know what I mean? Get up on the cross and stay there.

I am reminded once again that it is grace that saves me, not anything I am or anything I can do. Even when I do good, it is touched by my old nature. But (oh, how I love that word!) the day is coming when I will finally be set free from this old nature and live for all eternity in the presence of Almighty God.

Lord, I want to do "more better," and I know You are working on me. Thank You.

137.CONTRIBUTE

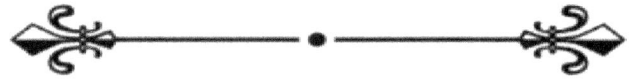

2 Kings 15:20 (NIV) Menahem exacted this money from Israel. Every wealthy person had to contribute fifty shekels of silver to be given to the king of Assyria. So the king of Assyria withdrew and stayed in the land no longer.

Romans 12:12-13 (ESV) Rejoice in hope, be patient in tribulation, be constant in prayer. Contribute to the needs of the saints and seek to show hospitality.

Tribute and contribute have similar actions but entirely different beginnings. In today's verse, the word used in the NIV version is "contribute," but if you consider the context, the Israelites are really paying a tribute. Do you agree?

What is the difference? When we pay a tribute, we are being "forced" to make a "contribution." I doubt if the wealthy people in Israel had a choice. If they wanted to live in peace they had better "pay up."

On the other hand, we followers of the Living God are instructed to give (contribute) generously. (1 Timothy 6:18 (NIV) Command them to do good, to be rich in good deeds, and to be generous and willing to share.)

Do we have a choice? Well, yes and no. We can choose to not contribute to the work of God. But it is kind of tricky to say "no" to God and then claim Him as Lord. Can you see the conflict? I think we owe the "tribute" to God but everything works better in our lives when we "volunteer" and contribute with a joy-filled and generous heart.

Often when I hear the word "contribute," the first thing that comes to my mind is money. However, that is a very limited understanding. As followers of Jesus, we should give more than money. We should give ourselves – our time, talents, skills, empathy, prayer, forgiveness, gentleness, patience, love, etc.. All that we have should be shared with others. How else will we be a fragrant aroma to one another?

Lord, thank You for Your generosity to us. Lead us to do likewise and freely give of whatever we have received. Thank You.

138.PERNICIOUS

Luke 12:1 (NIV)1 Meanwhile, when a crowd of many thousands had gathered, so that they were trampling on one another, Jesus began to speak first to his disciples, saying: "Be on your guard against the yeast of the Pharisees, which is hypocrisy."

I suspect that most of you are unfamiliar with today's word. Pernicious means that something has a harmful or destructive effect, often in a gradual or subtle way. Something pernicious is dangerous and can spread like malignant cancer, eventually being lethal. It is like yeast that eventually takes over and transforms the loaf of bread

As one reads Luke 1:1-12, there is a sense that hypocrisy is pernicious to an honest relationship with God. We can pretend to the point that we fool everyone around us, and even fool ourselves, but we cannot fool God. Hypocrisy is deadly but it takes its victims slowly and sometimes unsuspectingly.

I included the following in a devotion I wrote in June 2019, I think it is useful to share once again:

"I have wondered for some time why it is that, although we know what is good we do not do it. Simple things like knowing something is not good to eat and eating it anyway. Or knowing exercise is good for us but not doing it. Knowing that saving for the future is important but failing to save. I am sure you can go on with your own personal examples.

When we fail to do what we know is good, we are hypocrites. Being a hypocrite about the kind of things I mentioned often results in negative consequences but they are minor compared to when we act the hypocrite with God's word.

For example, pretending to obey God in the most important things (loving people and justice, being compassionate, helping others, spending time in God's presence). This pretending can have eternal consequences."

Lord, I join with David and many other saints of old and ask you to give us pure hearts that are fully devoted to You. Please reveal to us anything in our lives that is pernicious to our relationship with You. Thank You.

139.COMPELLED

1 Corinthians 9:16 (NIV) For when I preach the gospel, I cannot boast, since I am compelled to preach. Woe to me if I do not preach the gospel!

Have you ever felt compelled to do something? It is like an irresistible force that cannot be resisted. The word is often used for adverse circumstances (e.g. my lack of finances compelled me to skip lunch). In today's verse, the Apostle Paul seems to be compelled by his own conscience or ultimately by God.

When I think about this word, I am reminded of a time more than 30 years ago when I decided to learn how to juggle. I do not remember what sparked it, but once I began, it no longer felt like something I simply wanted to do. Instead, I felt compelled to master it. I did not think much of it back then; however, looking back now, that compulsion nearly took over my life. I practiced everywhere I went: at the airport while waiting for a flight, standing in line at the store, walking, and even while rollerblading. I practiced every chance I got.

I found a book that promised to teach me. (Have you ever tried to learn how to juggle from a book? There must be a better way, don't you think?)

To this day, I remember the first lesson. "Toss a ball into the air and let it drop to the ground. Repeat 100 times." I am serious. The rationale was that there would be a LOT of failures and I needed to practice failure so it wouldn't phase me.

My initial goal was to juggle three items ten times without a mishap. That took a while, believe me. My next goal was 100 catches. That took a really long time, but I remember exactly where I was when I accomplished it. I really felt like I had accomplished something. Although it was difficult, and took a very long time, the sense of accomplishment stays with me to this day.

Why am I telling you this story? Because when we are compelled to do something we do it regardless of the odds, effort, time or resources needed. When we are compelled, we will do it, and no one must remind us.

Similarly, Paul was compelled to preach the Gospel. What a difference it made in His life - and ours. There was no suffering, expense, difficulty or persecution that could stop him. How about you and me? How compelled are we to live lives that are pleasing to God?

Father, we have many, many distractions. Please, God, compel us to seek You first, always. Thank You.

140.QUINTESSENTIAL

Colossians 1:22 (NIV) But now he has reconciled you by Christ's physical body through death to present you holy in his sight, without blemish and free from accusation.

Did you know that you are the quintessential representation of God? I know that seems like a stretch at times, but that is what the scriptures say. That is our position in Christ even if not our practice. Look at today's scripture. We are described as "holy in His sight - no blemish or accusation."

If we are holy and without blemish, then we must be close to perfect. That means we are pure and the essential essence of God. We are the perfect embodiment of the Creator of the universe. How can this be? Simple. Through the death of our Lord Jesus Christ.

The Hebrews used the word "perfect" to describe something that fulfilled its purpose. Those who are wholehearted, sincere, and in right relationship to God are described as perfect in Scripture. (NIV Commentary)

Simple right?

Are you wholehearted in your relationship with God? Not half in and half out, but fully committed to God.

Are you sincere in your walk with God. Do you purpose to do His will even when it is difficult? No hidden motives?

Is Jesus your Lord? Have you surrendered your life, acknowledging His sacrifice as full payment for everything that has and will go wrong in your life?

As I reflect on this, I recognize my own—and perhaps your—foibles. It is all too easy to be swayed by our emotions. Yet, in our relationship with God, we have become far more than what meets the eye. We are created to be the living reflection of a Holy God.

Oh Lord, when I look at my life, I see countless shortcomings, failures, and wrong turns. But this is not how You see me. I am in Christ, and You see me as Your child. Oh, thank You so much.

141.SPEECH

1 John 3:18 (NIV) Dear children, let us not love with words or speech but with actions and in truth.

Have you ever thought about how wondrous is the gift of speech? I know I have taken it for granted. We often take things for granted until the day they are gone. God has blessed us with many wonderful things, including our ability to communicate with one another to tell someone you love them.

But the apostle tells us that loving with only words is not enough. When we love someone, we must have more than "hot air." When that is all we have to give to our loved ones then much more is still desired.

We must put on attitudes of forgiveness, mercy, patience, kindness, joy, peace, self-control, mercy and goodness. The fruits of the Spirit must accompany our speech when we say we love someone.

And our speech should be thoughtful. The next time someone says, "I love you, " STOP. Do not respond with just, "I love you." Instead, be thoughtful about what you can say that truly expresses how you feel about them. Do not just parrot the words "I love you." And, when you can, close the physical distance between you and your loved one.

Do you and your spouse still hold hands? If not, why not? Is there someone you have been meaning to visit and have not? When was the last time you spent time with a loved one doing what they want to do? Physical presence, even without words, communicates a lot. Make it a point to be physically close to those you love whenever you can.

Do not be only physically present. Also be emotionally and mentally present. Do you listen intently when your loved ones have something to say? Do you care about what they are saying? Hopefully you do, so listen closely. Not only to the words but the emotions behind the words.

Does your loved one need some encouragement? Be there for them if you really love them and do not let any unwholesome words come out of your mouth.

Father, let the words of our mouths truly reflect your heart and lead us to love you with more, much more, than with just our speech. Thank You.

142.LEISURE

Acts 17:21 (NIV) All the Athenians and the foreigners who lived there spent their time doing nothing but talking about and listening to the latest ideas.

Mark 6:31 (NASB) And He *said to them, "Come away by yourselves to a secluded place and rest a while." (For there were many people coming and going, and they did not even have time to eat.)

Do you see the contrast between today's two verses? In the first, there was too much leisure and not enough attention to the day-to-day issues of life. In the second, it is just the opposite. The people were so busy attending to the details of life they did not even have time to eat. Two extremes of lives that are out of balance (which could be the topic for another devotion). But today my thoughts turn to "what is leisure anyway?"

I recently read an article to May about this topic. A number of examples were given of people who spent their careers in mostly mundane, lowly-valued occupations (servants, housewives, garbage collectors, factory workers, etc.). Their occupations and their lives kept them well occupied and they had precious little time for leisure. What was so interesting is what they did when they were able to find a little leisure time.

One studied classic literature, another solved mathematical problems, and another wrote poetry. In their leisure, they sought to do things that many of us might not think were leisure at all. The point being that they did not let the mundane reality of their "real world" keep them from pursuing what they found to be truly important and meaningful.

I wonder what did Jesus do in His leisure time? He often went off by Himself and prayed. What about the Apostle Paul? He wrote - a lot. What about Mary? She contemplated the events in her life. What about the psalmists? They journaled a lot. How about David? He got alone with God a lot.

What is leisure for one person may seem like work to another. Those who know me consider my attention to plants to be way too much work. To me it is one of the most relaxing and refreshing things I can do. Some people like to binge on TV series or sports. I feel anxious when I do either one.

What about you? Where do you go and what do you do for your leisure time?

Here is the crux of the matter. If you are a disciple of Jesus and if He is truly the Lord of your life, then your leisure time does not belong to you. If He is truly your Lord, then He is also Lord of whatever you do when you are not doing "real life."

Father, we want to do what we want to do. Please, even in our leisure, give us hearts to do what You want us to do. Let us not squander the precious time You are giving us. Thank You.

143.PUTTER

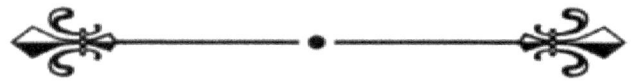

Isaiah 40:29-31 (NIV) He gives strength to the weary and increases the power of the weak. Even youths grow tired and weary, and young men stumble and fall; but those who hope in the LORD will renew their strength. They will soar on wings like eagles; they will run and not grow weary, they will walk and not be faint.

For years, May and I have used the term "putter" to mean going to see what needs to be done, without any specific objective in mind. It is simply doing the little things we notice need attention, with no agenda, no rush, and no time frame—just following what God brings to our minds and eyes.

I deeply enjoy "puttering," and almost always, when my puttering is complete, I feel refreshed and encouraged by what has been accomplished with seemingly little effort. Although we have been "puttering" for many years, I never considered it a form of leisure (see yesterday's devotion) until just the other day.

I read an article that encouraged people to learn how to putter in order to build balance in their lives while, at the same time, doing what needs to be done. It suggested that "puttering" is an antidote to being weary. As I read the article, it dawned on me that puttering is a very satisfying kind of leisure. It requires little effort but produces a great sense of satisfaction and accomplishment. I am surprised I never saw this before. The "right" kind of leisure not only gives rest for the weary it also replenishes the soul.

A couple of years ago, I wrote the following for a devotion. I had done some "puttering" that day and it helped to create a day of peace and contentment.

"Today was one of those days that just seemed to flow along nicely. May and I had time together, we puttered in the yard a bit, went out for breakfast, got our taxes completed, ate delicious leftovers for lunch, took a nap and watched a movie while enjoying dinner together.

Nothing special, but a really good day. The good Life? Yes, I would say so, because with Jesus as our Lord we can be content and delight in the simple things of life since the really important things have already been handled."

Father, I know how easy it is to become weary. Thank You Lord for the gift of "puttering." Help us to incorporate the principle into our daily lives so we live lives that are rest-filled while also accomplishing what needs to be done. Thank You.

144.RECIPROCITY

2 Thessalonians 3:13 (NIV) And as for you, brothers and sisters, never tire of doing what is good.

Titus 3:8 (NIV) This is a trustworthy saying. And I want you to stress these things, so that those who have trusted in God may be careful to devote themselves to doing what is good. These things are excellent and profitable for everyone.

1 Peter 2:15 (NIV) For it is God's will that by doing good you should silence the ignorant talk of foolish people.

There seems to be a lot of anger and even hatred in the world today. The principle of reciprocity indicates that we often get back what we give. Luke 6:38 (give and it will be even to you …) is perhaps the clearest passage in the New Testament that speaks to this principle.

In the gospel of Luke, the message is clear: when you do something good, it will be returned to you, often many times over. This principle also holds true when harm or negativity is given. For example, the conflict between Hamas and Israel illustrates what happens when hate is spread. Hatred, once given, often begets more hatred in return.

Followers of Jesus are called to sow good seeds and never grow weary of sharing goodness, compassion, and kindness at every opportunity. This is our purpose while alive on this earth. It is the way we are meant to live under the Lordship of Jesus Christ.

I understand it can be most difficult to sow good seeds in a hostile environment, but do not let that stop you. The principle of reciprocity and the law of the harvest both assure us that our good seeds will bear fruit in God's timing and in His way.

Keep in mind the law of the harvest we reap after we sow (not before) and we have a harvest much larger than what we sow. If you do not sow, there will be no harvest.

Lord, You have given us simple instructions to "overcome evil by doing good." Let us be about the business of Your kingdom. Thank You.

145.MINDFUL

Psalms 8:4 (NIV) what is mankind that you are mindful of them, human beings that you care for them?

Psalms 26:3 (NIV) for I have always been mindful of your unfailing love and have lived in reliance on your faithfulness.

This devotion was written for Christmas Day 2023. My hope is that you will find your next Christmas Day to be one of the most blessed you have ever experienced. Why? Because I am praying you will be mindful of the Savior whose birth you are celebrating.

Amidst the gift giving, fellowship, and good food, my prayer is that you will be conscious of something that is more incredible and amazing than all of the gifts or food or fellowship could ever bring into your life.

I am praying that you will live this day with great intention to honor the One whose birth we celebrate at Christmas. The One whose love for us exceeds all bounds. The One whose love for us is without limit.

I pray you will live this day and every day with intention. That you will be constantly mindful of whom you have become in Christ Jesus and whom you will soon be when you meet Him face to face.

I pray that we may be ever mindful of the One who is able to keep both you and me from stumbling. Mindful of the One who can present us before the glorious presence of God, blameless, faultless, and filled with joy beyond our understanding. Yes, let us remain mindful of our Father God and our Savior Jesus the Messiah, and of their majesty, power, and authority. For all eternity, Lord, make us mindful of You through Jesus Christ our Lord—yesterday, today, and forever. Amen. (Jude 1:24-25)

146.CONTEMPLATE

2 Corinthians 3:18 (NIV) And we all, who with unveiled faces contemplate the Lord's glory, are being transformed into his image with ever-increasing glory, which comes from the Lord, who is the Spirit.

Luke 2:19 (NIV) But Mary treasured up all these things and pondered them in her heart.

I want us to consider two words today: contemplate and treasure. Both are related to yesterday's word, mindful.

To be mindful is to be conscious of your world. I have often noticed that people seem drift from one event to the next with little purpose or direction. They are led by the events of the moment with no goal in mind, no purpose except perhaps to make it to another day.

Then there are those who slow the pace down and consider their lives and what is going on. They give thought (contemplate) where they are and where they are going. They are mindful of what is good and what is not and, hopefully, act accordingly and live with intention.

Then there are those who treasure and ponder things. They think deeply about their meaning and value to their lives and to the kingdom of God. They treasure those things that are useful, good, helpful, uplifting and encouraging. Despite the troubles around them and in their own lives, their hearts are filled to overflowing.

Which one are you? Are you unconscious, asleep at the wheel, or are you awake and fully aware of who you are in Christ and the purpose He has given you? Are you someone who reflects deeply on life in general and on your own life in particular?

Are you someone who has learned to treasure life, embracing both the good and the not-so-good? Do you value your position as God's child above all else?

Oh Lord, help us discover purpose and meaning in our lives. May we slow down, reflect, and learn to cherish our relationship with You. Thank You.

147.CONNECTED

John 15:5 (NIV) I am the vine; you are the branches. If you remain in me and I in you, you will bear much fruit; apart from me you can do nothing.

Have you ever sat down to write something but did not know for sure what it would be? Well, that is me right now. I have been mindful of the many ways today's word is used, and I have contemplated the wonder of being connected with the God of the universe. Now I am looking for a treasure to share today.

I read that "people do not come to church looking for a friendly church. They are looking for friends." It reminded me of the pang of loneliness a person feels when they want to be connected but are not. Instead of feeling connected, they feel like they don't fit in.

Have you ever felt that way? It's not a good feeling. It is better to be alone than to be in a crowd and feel like you do not belong. Don't you agree?

For some time, I have read/heard that our modern culture has largely forgotten its elderly. I have never given this much thought (and I do not fully agree).

I suppose you can count May and I among the elderly (93 & 82) so maybe that is why I am thinking about this? May recently told me that "she feels left out when she is a part of a gathering of people." It is like she no longer fits in. Interestingly, when she said that I immediately identified with her.

Please do not take me wrong. People that know us are kind, friendly, supportive and encouraging. The problem is mostly us.

We have entered the winter of life and, unless you are too, it is hard to explain. I guess it is harder for others to relate to us. The word "connect" helps me to see the core of the issue. Although we have many people in our lives, we are not really connected to most of them. Very few really know us, and perhaps that is OK, because we know the One who really knows us.

Lord, getting on in age keeps bringing surprises for me. I know being connected to You is the only connection I need to be concerned about. I ask You, Lord, to deepen that connection until we are in Your presence, "soon and very soon Lord"? Thank You.

148.CONNECT (2)

1 John 3:18 (NIV) Dear children, let us not love with words or speech but with actions and in truth.

We connect with others in many ways (work, sports, play, eating, drinking, church, neighbors, etc.). Most of these interactions are superficial. Although "connected," we are not really "connected" in the sense of knowing one another.

This morning, I am thinking about being connected in the sense of intimacy. Not sexual or romantic intimacy but in the sense of knowing someone deeply. Similar to how God knows us.

Intimacy is rare these days, at least in my little world. I think it is because intimacy demands openness, vulnerability, and acceptance between people. It also requires a significant investment of time, patience, forgiveness, and sometimes mercy. Our culture does not encourage openness and vulnerability, and I cannot recall a single sermon that addressed either of these qualities in my life.

Being truly connected in the sense of intimacy takes courage. As it has been said, "It is better to hide who I really am than to risk being rejected."

Intimacy requires people who are willing to accept one another exactly as they are, including their foibles. Some 40+ years ago someone told me I was afraid of intimacy. I immediately rejected that comment with some energy. Afterwards, I wondered why it had upset me so much. Over time I came to realize it was because it was true.

How about you? Do you think you might be afraid of great intimacy? What is the evidence for your answer?

May and I have over 50 years of sharing and doing life together. Some people think we have "gone overboard" and want nothing to do with our life-style. I wonder if that is because they fear intimacy?

On the other hand, many admire what we have. It is something special and we thank God for it every day. It is the wonderful type of intimacy that comes to those who are willing to pay the cost of pursuing it.

Lord, thank You so much for the gift of intimacy. You have enriched our lives "over the top." It is a most wonderful adventure for those who experience it. Thank You.

149.RESCUE

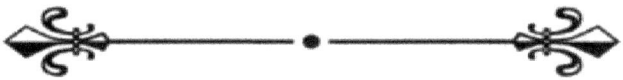

Colossians 1:13-14 (NIV) For he has rescued us from the dominion of darkness and brought us into the kingdom of the Son he loves, in whom we have redemption, the forgiveness of sins.

Have you ever been rescued? Today's word reminds me of a time 50 years ago when May and I, newly married, were camping, along with her brother Tom and his new bride at Haleiwa beach park on the north shore of Oahu. Hawaii.

May and I got caught in a current and we were in trouble. I told May, "I can get us back to shore," but she was not too sure (tell you the truth I am not sure I was sure either - but I could not let my new brother-in-law think I was a wimp). May called out for help. Sure enough, here comes brother Tom, a very big, husky man in his late 30's. I was both embarrassed and very happy to be rescued.

I think the relationship between a rescuer and the rescued is unique. There is a sense of appreciation and thankfulness that literally lasts a lifetime. Although I was reluctant to be rescued in the moment, I am so thankful to May for doing the right thing (this was the first of many, many such times).

It is real wisdom to know when we need rescuing. So many today are lost and in need of spiritual rescue. But, like me, they are either too proud to admit their need or too busy being lost to understand their lostness.

Our spiritual rescue is not just something that happened in the past but something that continues to happen day by day as we live out our lives in a culture that does not know it is lost. Consider the following:

"He (Paul) is thankful that God has "rescued" us from having to live as the world does. We are no longer bound to find entertainment in places that mocks God. We are no longer bound to pursue pleasure and comfort in worldly pursuits. We are no longer bound to partake in lifestyles that the present evil age promotes. We have been rescued from all of that by a God who gave himself for our sins. May we live as such." (Joshua Becker)

Yes, Lord, thank You so very much for our rescue. Keep us from the attractions of our carnal nature so that we live as examples of rescued folks. Thank You.

150.CONFIDENCE

1 John 4:16-17 (NIV) And so we know and rely on the love God has for us. God is love. Whoever lives in love lives in God, and God in them. This is how love is made complete among us so that we will have confidence on the day of judgment: In this world we are like Jesus.

Confidence is the feeling or belief that one can rely on someone or something. A firm trust with little or no doubt. Confidence in someone, something, or self (i.e. self-confidence) enables people to accomplish things that cannot otherwise be accomplished. It enables people to take risks because they feel success is assured.

If you have ever experienced love, you know it is like magic and can change our personalities overnight. One of the changes that just about always occurs is great confidence in the relationship. It can seem like nothing is impossible together and the world can be conquered.

Mutual love between God and us should produce something very similar in our lives. The apostle John is telling us that the love we have for Jesus and the love Jesus has for us produces a confidence that makes us secure. It enables us to trust what is not seen. Confidence is one of the characteristics that separates those who want to accomplish something from those that do accomplish something.

There is a little "hidden" principle attached to this scripture. Love cannot be static if it is to produce confidence. In the words of the Apostle, "this is how love is made complete." How is it made complete? By the continuing mutual expressions of love from us to God and God to us as we live lives of obedience. Our confidence grows as God continually reveals more and more of His nature as we honor Him in how we live.

Our confidence in our relationship with God should always be maturing as we pursue loving God with all that we are able.

Father, life changes as we earnestly seek You. Thank You for Your love for us. Please lead us to reciprocate and grow with confidence in our relationship with You. Thank You.

151.PRESENCE

Psalms 16:11 (NIV) You make known to me the path of life; you will fill me with joy in your presence, with eternal pleasures at your right hand.

Well, the New Year has arrived. The season of gift giving has passed until the next marketing extravaganza (Valentine's day?). Over the years I have often been lost for words when someone asks, "did you enjoy the gift I sent you last ….?" I am lost for words because I do not remember the gift, much less if I enjoyed it or not. Gifts are only memorable if they are considered valuable by the recipient.

I have been thinking about which gift I value the most. I concluded it is the gift of presence, whether in person, on the phone, text, letters, sharing a meal, having a cup of coffee, etc.. Sometimes talking about nothing in particular, other times sharing a need or celebrating something joyful. Sometimes even with strangers. Many of you know that I am an introvert and highly value my alone time. Yet, I find a place of deepening joy when someone gives me the gift of presence.

I have two examples I want to share. The first is from the book/movie "Tuesdays with Morrie." An ex-student visits his retired professor who is dying from ALS. He gives the gift of presence to someone whose "numbered days" are but a few.

The other example is from my friend, Pete. We have a mutual friend that suffered a stroke and is virtually unable to communicate. Pete, over an extended period, visited and read him the scriptures. I see it as an example of a living sacrificial offering (See Romans 12:1). As Pete often encourages, "be the church."

We do not have to wait until someone is close to death or suffering a serious physical issue. Why not "be the church" wherever and whenever we can? Consider giving the gift of presence to the people in your life.

Oh, Father, we are often caught up in the mundane of life, or nursing our own wounds, or feeling sorry for ourselves. Please, Lord, do not let us get stuck in the things that steal our joy and keep us from giving joy to others. Put it in our hearts to give the gift of presence. Thank You.

152.OVERCOME

Psalm 42:5a (NIV) Why, my soul, are you downcast? Why so disturbed within me?

1 John 5:3-5 (NIV) In fact, this is love for God: to keep his commands. And his commands are not burdensome, for everyone born of God overcomes the world. This is the victory that has overcome the world, even our faith. Who is it that overcomes the world? Only the one who believes that Jesus is the Son of God.

My dear friend in Jesus, which of these two spirits do you identify with today? Are you feeling downcast, or are you an overcomer?

The Psalmist offers guidance for those moments when we are downcast. Psalm 42:5b (NIV) says, "Put your hope in God, for I will yet praise him, my Savior and my God." Often, when we feel downcast, it is because our focus is on our difficulties—troubles, struggles, failures, broken relationships, loss, financial challenges—you name it.

There are many reasons to feel downcast, but my dear friend, let us remember that we are not of this world. We are merely passing through, and our times of sorrow and struggle are temporary. When we turn our hearts and focus back to God, we encounter a peace that overcomes anxiety, fear, sadness, and feelings of failure. His peace surpasses human understanding and stands firm against every trouble, offering comfort and assurance that, in the end, everything will be okay.

On the other hand, if today you are an overcomer, share the joy and victory with another. Encourage one another, even more so as you see "the day" approaching. There are only a few that have learned that in Christ we can overcome the world and all its drama and trials. Since you are one of the blessed ones, be about the work of ministry wherever you might find it.

Dear God, I am so thankful for the outlook of eternity. It puts today and all it might bring into perspective. Let us not succumb to our feelings that cause us to have a downcast soul. Instead, Lord, we look forward to the victory In Jesus. Until that day is fully realized, let us live by faith in You. We are over comers IN CHRIST. Thank You.

153.RADICAL

Acts 19:4 (MSG) "That explains it," said Paul. "John preached a baptism of radical life-change so that people would be ready to receive the One coming after him, who turned out to be Jesus. If you've been baptized in John's baptism, you're ready now for the real thing, for Jesus."

I know many who are reading this would like their lives to be modeled after Jesus. Do you realize that you must take on a radical lifestyle to do that? Many believers consider themselves to be conservative and some think they are progressive. Maybe some consider themselves liberal. Jesus, however, was clearly a radical. To be progressive, liberal, or conservative does not quite cut, it in my opinion.

Consider Jesus' teachings in the Sermon on the Mount (Math. 5-7). In these three short chapters Jesus' teaching is nothing but radical. For instance, when was the last time you gave somebody something after they stole from you? Or have you ever offered the other cheek? How are you doing with loving those that you do not like (much less your enemies)?

I know some of His teachings seem like high ideals to us today but in Jesus' day they were truly far out. I mean really far out, very radical concepts. Some have reduced these chapters to unattainable ideals that are unattainable. To think that we could actually live by the principles of the Sermon on the Mount is indeed radical.

If you doubt what I say, try slowly reading through these chapters and asking God to reveal any way(s) you are falling below the standards set by Jesus. If by some chance you are 100% compliant then I would classify you as a radical in today's culture.

But there is another point here. As much as we want to model and be like Jesus, even being obedient in all venues of our lives, it is not enough. Jesus must be the object of our worship. Not just someone we admire or want to imitate. Yes, He is a great radical teacher, but He is so, so much more than that.

Lord God, what would it take for us to become true radicals for You? Will you do it? Thank You.

154.ASTONISHED/AMAZED

Acts 4:13 (NIV) When they saw the courage of Peter and John and realized that they were unschooled, ordinary men, they were astonished (thaumazō;) and they took note that these men had been with Jesus.

Matthew 7:28 (NIV) When Jesus had finished saying these things, the crowds were amazed (ekplēssō;) at his teaching,

These verses were brought to my attention from two different sources. I found it interesting (and a little confusing at first) that the NASB translates two different Greek Words (thaumazo & ekplesso) as amazed. The NIV translates the former as astonished and the latter as amazed. Both words seem to be very similar in meaning. (No charge for that little freebie.)

Jesus astonished/amazed His hearers and so did His followers. I wonder how we are doing with astonishing/amazing others? And then, a couple of hours later May and I had the following experience.

We were leaving Publix with a cart half full of groceries. We reach our car and I heard a voice behind me saying, "can I help you?" I turned around and there was an older woman (turns out she is 71) wanting to know if she could help us put the groceries in the car. Now, those of you who know me surely know my response, don't you?

"Oh, thank you, but I'm OK. I don't need any help." The lady insisted "are you sure?" In that instant I heard the small voice in my head saying "wrong answer." So I relented. It was a little strange letting a 71-year old lady load my car with groceries while I just stood there, perfectly able to do it myself. I thought, "we must really be getting old to need an older lady to help us." To me it was a funny thought, an interesting revelation of how much and how quickly we are slowing down.

Well, after the car was all loaded, we shared a pleasant little chat. Her name is Barbara, and I am certain she is one of His. So sweet, unassuming, and genuinely kind. She even invited May and me to a free (I like that) church dinner. As she walked away, we exchanged mutual blessings. It was all so simple and yet so remarkable. A simple act of kindness received, and a joy-filled conversation with a stranger.

And now I hear the small voice again saying, "do likewise and be amazing."

Father, a simple act of kindness became such a blessing. Lead us to do the same. Thank You.

155.NEW

2 Corinthians 5:17 (NIV) 17 Therefore, if anyone is in Christ, the new creation has come: The old has gone, the new is here!

Since I am prone to melancholy from time to time, I have to confront my emotions and remind myself whom I have become in Christ Jesus. Melancholy seems to come from nowhere and can be very difficult to overcome. Sometimes I seem to get that way for no particular reason. Other times are driven by circumstances or just being lonely. Regardless of the source I have found that the "funk" is not nearly so deep, nor so long, when I remind myself of whom I am in Christ Jesus.

The one thing I know for sure is that we are not to live under the circumstances of our lives. Not even under any negative personality foibles we may have. In Christ we are new creatures. As such, we have the power of the Holy Spirit in us to live by the Spirit and not by circumstances. We have been set free from the domination of sin and even our own negative emotions. Do you believe this? Do you act on it?

I came across the following yesterday in the Life Application Bible Commentary. I think it applies.

"Look around you. People are searching for something to give their lives a boost. Few people seem content within themselves. A strange and often hard-to-identify inner vacuum gives most people an uneasy sense of incompleteness. But Christ fills the vacuum. As Jesus' person is fully divine, so we, united by faith to Jesus, find personal fulfillment in him. We are complete in Christ. Some days may not feel like it, but, in fact, in Jesus the vacuum is gone; the full power and presence of God has taken up residence in your mind and heart. You are a new person, equipped for life and satisfied in God. So . . .

Take more risks—God will guide you

Give more generously—God will supply you.

Love more freely—God will energize you.

Say "can do" more often—God will amaze you."

Oh, Father, in Christ we are a New Creation. What a most wonderful thing you have done for us. If our humanity gets in the way of our living for You remind us once again whom we have become in Christ. Thank You.

156.TURN

Psalms 119:37 (NIV) Turn my eyes away from worthless things; preserve my life according to your word.

I was reading an article about the loneliness epidemic in America. According to the article, being lonely is more than just a sad emotional state. It can impact our physical and mental health. The article mentioned how important it is for us to "turn" our attention to one another. Simple gestures like phone calls, notes, even texts can help people feel connected to one another.

I agree. I find the exchange of texts, phone calls, notes, cards and visits by my small group to be encouraging and supportive. Letting people know we are thinking about them, praying for them and wishing them well can go a long way to encouraging people. These are not just simple acts of kindness. They carry a lot of value in God's kingdom. Let us look for and take advantage of every opportunity to "turn to another" and be an encourager.

However, as important as it is to turn to another it is much, much, more important that we turn toward the risen Savior every day. It is from our Lord Jesus that we receive the grace to do anything. When we spend time with Him, even simple acts of kindness have a way of being multiplied for the giver and receiver. We live in a society that is really lost. That makes our little acts of love even more special. In dark times it is easy for us to be the light.

Keep in mind, however, that we cannot give what we do not have. Our time spent in the presence of the Creator of the Universe enables us to give to others even when we are not trying. Loving others becomes the most natural thing of all as the love of Jesus overflows from our lives to others.

Lord, thank You so very much for the way of love. Let us draw close to You so we can love others as You love us. Thank You.

157.EVERYTHING

Philippians 4:6 (NASB) Be anxious for nothing, but in everything by prayer and supplication with thanksgiving let your requests be made known to God.

I was thinking about this verse when I was reminded of an incident that I experienced many years ago. May and I had been married a few years, and I was a relatively new Christian. We were on our way to the post office to mail a package when May said, "we should pray that the package arrives OK."

My first thought was, "that is really foolish and unnecessary." I think I asked her, "why would we do that?" Obviously May was light years ahead of me spiritually and I still had a lot to learn. I remember praying but feeling very awkward about it.

That was nearly 50 years ago. I have since learned that it is very foolish not to pray about everything. Even the smallest detail of our lives can become an act of worship when we take it to God in prayer.

Recently, I came across a formal prayer book, Every Moment Holy – Volume III – The Work of the People. It contains prayers for nearly everything you can imagine in our daily lives: praying before a meal, tending the garden, enjoying leisure time, engaging in a hobby, or even going shopping. Honestly, I usually don't think about praying for some of these things—I just do them. But how much richer would it be to invite the Sustainer of life into these moments first?

What are you doing right now? Have you prayed about it?

Lord, keep us mindful that even our very breath is a gift from You. Thank You for transforming the mundane affairs of our lives into acts of worship when we turn our hearts and minds toward You. Thank You so much.

158.EVERYTHING (PART II)

1 Corinthians 10:31 (NIV) So whether you eat or drink or whatever you do, do it all for the glory of God.

Today's verse came to mind as I considered yesterday's devotion on the word "everything." Paul used the words "whatever" and "do it all." We could substitute the word "everything" in their place, yes?

Yesterday we discussed our success and failures when we try to pray about everything, especially things we think we have a "handle on." We are pretty good about praying for things we need (like lost glasses and keys). However, we seem to need some work when it comes to praying about the mundane everyday things.

I expect we could come to the same conclusion with the admonition in today's verse about doing everything for the glory of God. Think about it. How much do you do intentionally for the glory of God "from the rising of the sun until the setting of the same"? How much did you do simply because it was in front of you or because you "felt like it"?

A friend mentioned that what we are striving to have an ongoing conversation with God, about everything, even the smallest of things in our lives. In other words, inviting God into our lives, seeking His partnership in our days, for the big and little things, and letting Him guide and direct us in all (i.e. everything) we do.

Dear Father God, do not let us wander through our days just doing what is in front of us to do. Today, remind us to pray about whatever we are about to do. Give us hearts that are determined to bring glory to You. Please do not let us waste the gift of time. Every moment can be precious when offered up to You. Thank You.

159.BEGIN

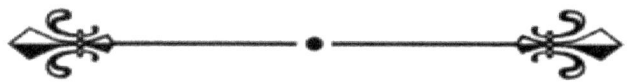

Psalms 81:1-2 (NIV) Sing for joy to God our strength; shout aloud to the God of Jacob! Begin the music, strike the timbrel, play the melodious harp and lyre.

Luke 21:28 (NIV) When these things begin to take place, stand up and lift up your heads, because your redemption is drawing near.

In a way, today's devotion is a continuation of the prior two devotions about "everything." You see, "everything" in the sense of eternity has no beginning but for us humans "everything" must have a beginning.

If we are to pray about everything and if we are to do everything for the glory of God, then we must start the process at the very beginning of each day. Even before we open our eyes in the morning. As we slumber in that twilight zone between awake and asleep, it is time to begin.

Many of you know that I love the mornings but getting out of bed is always a struggle with the mattress. It just does not want to let me go. One part of me wants to get up and get going and another part of me just wants to be left alone and go back to sleep. So, who wins?

It depends. If my heart and mind are focused on me, you can be sure that I will roll over for another wink or two (or three or four). But if my focus is on God and His plans for my day, than I'm likely to rise from my slumbers and start the day.

At the first moment of being conscious that God is giving me another day, I turn my focus to Him. I ask Him about His plans for me this day. I go over my plans for the day and ask Him to walk beside me. I go over my prayer list as God brings to my consciousness what He wants me to pray for. I admit that this is not always a straight-forward process. It is not unusual for me to nod off for a few minutes (or longer) but that is of little concern because I have begun the day with God.

Perhaps your early morning routine would look much different to mine. I do not think it matters much. What matters is that your first conscious thoughts are directed toward the Creator and Sustainer of the universe.

Oh Father, please put it in our hearts to begin the day with You. Thank You.

160.END

Psalms 113:3 (NIV) From the rising of the sun to the place where it sets, the name of the LORD is to be praised.

Isaiah 45:5-6 (NIV) I am the LORD, and there is no other; apart from me there is no God. I will strengthen you, though you have not acknowledged me, so that from the rising of the sun to the place of its setting people may know there is none besides me. I am the LORD, and there is no other.

Let us continue on this theme of "everything." Let us pray about everything. In everything let us purposefully bring glory to God. When our day is over and the sun has set, it is time to consider our day.

I have found it most useful to have a little reflective quiet time each evening. It is a time to review the day. Was it a "good" day? Did I do what was in front of me? Did I mess up in something I said or did not say? How was my attitude?

When I have this conversation with God while already in bed, I often fall asleep somewhere in the middle of it. Not to worry, though, because it usually resumes when God awakens me to finish the conversation.

It is a wonderful way to end the day. It does not matter whether the day was "good" or "not so good." Talking it over with God seems to be a comforting way to let my anxious thoughts drift into His care.

Lord, please help each of us to intentionally begin and end each day with our focus on You. Guide us, Lord, to pray about everything and in everything to bring glory to You. Thank You.

161.HALFHEARTED

Haggai 2:15-17 "'Think back. Before you set out to lay the first foundation stones for the rebuilding of my Temple, how did it go with you? Isn't it true that your foot-dragging, halfhearted efforts at rebuilding the Temple of GOD were reflected in a sluggish, halfway return on your crops—half the grain you were used to getting, half the wine? I hit you with drought and blight and hail. Everything you were doing got hit. But it didn't seem to faze you. You continued to ignore me.' GOD's Decree.

Revelation 3:15 (NIV) I know your deeds, that you are neither cold nor hot. I wish you were either one or the other!

God is not impressed with halfhearted efforts, especially when it comes to our relationship with Him. Jesus' relationship with His Father was completely wholehearted. What are we to make of our halfhearted attempts to live a life for God?

Are we "all in" in our relationship with Jesus? Are we pursuing the best relationship possible with our spouse, children, and other loved ones? Are we fully dedicated to knowing God as He is revealed in the scriptures? Are we fully committed to loving people who offend us?

Anything done halfheartedly leads to results that are less than amazing. As children of the Creator of the Universe, should not your life and my life have some amazing things going on?

I think it goes back to the first two of the 3 "D's" of the Christian walk: DESIRE and DISCIPLINE. If we do not deeply desire something we will not discipline ourselves to be wholehearted about getting it. Whether it is a relationship, hobby, sport, or anything else.

What "lights your fire"? Are you passionate about knowing God intimately? Do you desire and seek Him more than anything?

Lord God, please give us hearts that earnestly seek after You. Nothing less will do. Thank You.

162.BEAUTIFUL

Ecclesiastes 3:11-13 (ESV) He has made everything beautiful in its time. Also, he has put eternity into man's heart, yet so that he cannot find out what God has done from the beginning to the end. I perceived that there is nothing better for them than to be joyful and to do good as long as they live; also that everyone should eat and drink and take pleasure in all his toil—this is God's gift to man.

As I tried to decide what would be today's word, I happened to look up from my chair and see a beautiful orchid in full bloom. It has been in bloom for a few weeks, and it gives off a fragrance that I can only describe as heavenly. It is so beautiful I cannot help but wonder how beautiful heaven will be.

I have nurtured this plant for years to get it to bloom so beautifully. This is a fallen world where God's creation has been marred by evil. What would this world be like if there was no evil? How beautiful it could be. How amazing it will be when finally evil is done away with and all is made new.

This world is full of things that are not beautiful, yet there are glimpses of God's glory that will one day settle upon the earth when the Lord Jesus returns. Oh, what a day that will be! Until then, let us nurture one another in love, allowing God's beauty to shine through our lives.

It is always good to take time to "smell the roses." Today, pause to notice God's creative beauty all around you.

Lord, thank You that You have made all things beautiful. What a wonder it will be when You restore things as they should be. Help us to see and to respond to the beauty of Your creation. Thank You.

163.CONDONE

Revelation 2:2-4 (NIV) I know your deeds, your hard work and your perseverance. I know that you cannot tolerate wicked people, that you have tested those who claim to be apostles but are not, and have found them false. You have persevered and have endured hardships for my name, and have not grown weary. Yet I hold this against you: You have forsaken the love you had at first.

A pastor shared that he had received a phone call from someone who attended a recent service. She was upset and told the pastor that, "she would no longer be coming to his church if he would not condone her lifestyle."

Condone means to accept or allow behavior that is considered morally wrong or offensive. I looked up the word condone and could not find it in the scriptures. Perhaps "tolerate" is close. God placed two thoughts in my mind:

First, as followers of Jesus we are in great danger of condoning lifestyles promoted by our culture that are morally wrong according to the scriptures. Ready examples include co-habitation, materialism, and watching sexually explicit and/or violent media.

The second point is that even when we refuse to condone or tolerate any morally compromising behavior we are still in great danger. Danger of what you ask? Of forsaking our first love, which is Jesus. We do this when He is not first in our lives.

You might ask if it is possible to do good and refuse to tolerate evil and still get in trouble? I say yes.

Remember Jesus' words:

Matthew 7:21-23 (NIV) "Not everyone who says to me, 'Lord, Lord,' will enter the kingdom of heaven, but only the one who does the will of my Father who is in heaven. Many will say to me on that day, 'Lord, Lord, did we not prophesy in your name and in your name drive out demons and in your name perform many miracles?' Then I will tell them plainly, 'I never knew you. Away from me, you evildoers!'

What is the point of this devotion? Simply this, God must be first in our lives. When we make Him first everything else will fall into place.

Oh Father, I know many people who are Christians and seriously distracted by our culture and/or their busyness. Please, Father, draw them to You so that you are first in their lives. Thank You.

164.COMPELLED

Jude 1:3 (NIV) Dear friends, although I was very eager to write to you about the salvation we share, I felt compelled to write and urge you to contend for the faith that was once for all entrusted to God's holy people.

My dear friends, I feel compelled to write to you. My heart is full and I am obliged to share with you.

First of all, thank you for your faithfulness to God and for striving to serve Him and walk in the light He gives us. I am filled to overflowing by your willingness to spend time seeking after God.

I so appreciate your patience with me. I know I can "wax eloquent" (talk too long) on some things. Yet you listen and never give me any flack.

Your generosity in helping others has gone beyond anything I could have ever hoped for. I wonder what the future holds in this area as we all continue to give as God directs our steps? Your gifts of kindness to one another and to neighbors and friends is a joy to behold. In so many ways you are being the church. I know God has a lot of work yet to do in us, but I see so much progress. Thank you for your commitment to becoming more and more Christlike.

Oh, and your prayers! What a joy to know that you pray for all sorts of things. Whenever a need is expressed, you are quick to pray. And thank you for your vulnerability in sharing your own prayer requests. God is surely doing a work in our midst.

Thank you for your care and concern for May and me as we engage this "winter" season of our lives. How wonderful it is to know that we have a family of believers that pray for us and will help when we need it. Thank you from the bottom of my heart for the visits and the meals and for sitting with us. I am truly touched by your love, kindness and caring.

Father, there is more to say but perhaps another time? Thank You, Lord, for the gift of caring, loving people in our lives.

165.REFLECT

Ecclesiastes 5:19-20 (NIV) Moreover, when God gives someone wealth and possessions, and the ability to enjoy them, to accept their lot and be happy in their toil—this is a gift of God. They seldom reflect on the days of their life, because God keeps them occupied with gladness of heart.

I have had a couple of difficult days physically. It has caused me to reflect more than usual. I am reflecting on the reality that when I feel worse, I act worse. I just wanted to be left alone. My patience, which is always a challenge, was practically non-existent. I quickly returned to my old nature and I wonder when I will be truly set free from this world of sin?

On the other hand, how wonderful to reflect on the love of my brothers and sisters in Christ who lifted me up in prayer and provided practical expressions of Christian empathy. Despite wanting to be alone, I am incredibly thankful to all of you who were the church to me. Thank you. It is something I will reflect on for a long season.

It has been said (by Socrates, I believe) that "to live a life without reflection is to live a life not worth living." Us introverted types are more inclined to reflect on life but, as this scripture teaches us, when life is good there is no need to reflect on our lives.

In some ways it is good to have so much good that reflection seems superfluous. On the other hand, reflection is good for the soul. It helps us avoid taking life for granted and helps us to understand who we truly are.

As believers, reflection is more important for us than for non-believers. If we do not take the time to reflect on our relationship with the heavenly Father and with one another, we could miss an important element of Christian growth. Reflection is simply thinking deeply about things. Surely this is something that pleases God.

Philippians 4:8 (NIV) Finally, brothers and sisters, whatever is true, whatever is noble, whatever is right, whatever is pure, whatever is lovely, whatever is admirable—if anything is excellent or praiseworthy—think about such things.

Father, incline our hearts to reflect deeply on these things. Please use these one-word devotions to guide us in thoughtful reflection on our lives. Thank You.

166. WEARY

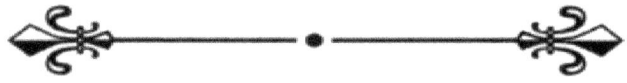

Matthew 11:28-30 (NIV) "Come to me, all you who are weary and burdened, and I will give you rest. Take my yoke upon you and learn from me, for I am gentle and humble in heart, and you will find rest for your souls. 30 For my yoke is easy and my burden is light."

Yesterday I was engaged in the "hustle and bustle" of life. You know the routine. Put dinner leftovers away, wash the dishes, clean the counter, collect the trash for tomorrow's early morning pick up. And then there are the little "extras I get to do. Help May to get settled, take care of my tracheotomy, make sure the plants are OK, get our hot tea and evening snacks ready, get caught up on texts/emails etc., go over my notes for the next day's bible study gathering, put on my night clothes. All the while wondering what the "word for today" is going to be.

In the midst of all this the above verse came to mind along with a common exchange between May and me. She often tells me to "stop and relax." My usual response is "you know a man's work is never done." Invariably she gives me this "look" that says I have something wrong.

I realized I was weary. So much to do, and it never stops. Most days I am OK and just take it all in stride. But last night was different. I felt overwhelmed (a form of weary), and I needed to take May's and Jesus' advice seriously. Stop the hustle and bustle and find my rest in Him.

Lord, thank You for meeting me in the moment and giving me rest. Please keep all of us from becoming overwhelmed and weary from the details of life and instead come to You to find Your rest. Thank You.

167.WANDER

Psalms 119:10-11 (NASB) With all my heart I have sought You; Do not let me wander from Your commandments. Your word I have treasured in my heart, That I may not sin against You.

As I was writing yesterday's devotion (weary), this word, "wander" came to mind. I was reminded of a time when our daughter, Lisa, and her husband, Jerry, treated us to a short stay at a cabin in the Olympic National Forest in Washington State. I remember May and I leisurely wandering down a forest pathway amidst some of the most magnificent trees I had ever seen. Everything was pristine, quiet, restful, peaceful, energizing, and beautiful. The opposite of being weary.

As I suggested yesterday, some of our weariness comes from ourselves. We hustle about attempting to do everything that seems to be in front of us to do. God calls us to be a people at rest in Him and at rest even while being strangers and foreigners upon this earth.

Wandering around my garden is extremely relaxing and invigorating to me when it is leisurely, casual or aimless. Without the anxiousness that comes from noticing the weeds or other things that need attending to. Perhaps the focus makes the difference? I believe that aimless wandering in the presence of those things (or people) that bring us pleasure is useful for our souls. Where do you wander to find refreshment for your soul?

On the other hand, the Psalmist gives us a subtle warning to not let wandering become a life-style. When we live without intention and purpose (which is a kind of wandering through life) we probably do escape some of the hustle and bustle of life. However, too much wandering can cause a break in fellowship with our Creator.

Father God, once again we are faced with the principle of living a life that is balanced. Lead us so that we are refreshed as we attend to your purposes in our lives. Thank You.

168.WILDERNESS

John 1:23 (NIV) John replied in the words of Isaiah the prophet, "I am the voice of one calling in the wilderness, 'Make straight the way for the Lord.'"

Today's verse was my line in a grammar school play. I remember asking the teacher what it meant, and was told something like, "you don't need to know, just say it."

Today's word came to me as I concluded the devotion on "weary." Both wander and wilderness came to my mind simultaneously. It seems like the three go together (weary, wander, and wilderness).

We all know the story about God's people wandering in the wilderness for 40 years because they trusted in their own abilities more than in His. What a weary time that must have been wandering around the wilderness all those years.

I can't help but think that many of us are living in the wilderness. We have become conditioned to the "security" of trusting in ourselves and what is seen, instead of a radical faith in God.

At times I can hear the call. It seems to be getting louder recently, "come, it is time to leave the wilderness."

The problem with the wilderness is that it offers a certain degree of comfort and security. We do not see it as wilderness at all. We are comfortable with the way things are. It is not that we do not love God. We do, but we have become comfortable in what we know and what we see and feel and touch. Despite our years of professing Christ, we still have trouble fully trusting and resting in God.

The wilderness is very seductive. It is especially entrapping when we have abilities or resources at our disposal. Who needs faith when we can handle it ourselves? The great lure of the wilderness is self-sufficiency.

Father, are You calling us out of our own faithless wilderness? Please lead us by Your Spirit to experience the power of the resurrection and not fear the sufferings of Christ. Thank You.

169.WORRY

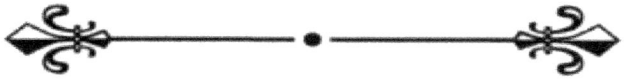

Luke 12:24-26 (NIV) Consider the ravens: They do not sow or reap, they have no storeroom or barn; yet God feeds them. And how much more valuable you are than birds! Who of you by worrying can add a single hour to your life? Since you cannot do this very little thing, why do you worry about the rest?

Is it not amazing how worry can creep into our lives, sometimes when least expected? I cannot tell you how many times I have been concerned about something (worried) and then hear God's gentle voice in my spirit saying, "have I not taken care of you in the past?" It is a most wonderful, always timely, reminder to let go of my fears, anxieties, concerns. Name them whatever you want. Just lean in closer to the King of Kings and the Lord of all comfort.

Jesus understands how our nature can be prone to worry, for some more than others. So, He has given us this wonderful advice. Look to God's creation and see the miracles of provisions, they are everywhere.

How is it that a plant produces a seed that dies and then comes back to produce many more? How is it that the dead plants decay and become compost and offer nourishment so the seeds can flourish? How incredible that the birds will eat the seeds and then spread the plants far and wide. All so the birds of the air can have the nourishment they need.

How much more has He done for us. No, fellow believer, let worry be cursed and die on the cross. Jesus has made provision for life. Do not give no room to worry. He has already provided for everything we need.

Oh Father, I was caught in a place of great worry the other day. Once again, You set me free from the bondage of sin, including needless worry. Thank You.

170.WEAR

Isaiah 51:6 (NIV) Lift up your eyes to the heavens, look at the earth beneath; the heavens will vanish like smoke, the earth will wear out like a garment and its inhabitants die like flies. But my salvation will last forever, my righteousness will never fail

Matthew 6:20-21 (NIV) But store up for yourselves treasures in heaven, where moths and vermin do not destroy, and where thieves do not break in and steal. For where your treasure is, there your heart will be also.

Have you noticed that almost everything in life eventually wears out? Our most treasured possessions, even our cars and homes, will one day be little more than rust and dust. Isn't it remarkable how much effort we invest in pursuing a "good" life? If only we had the eyes to see how fleeting it all truly is.

Even in Jesus' time, people were drawn away by the treasures of this world. Let's be honest—there are many "treasures." Things that can make life comfortable, useful, even meaningful or entertaining. Yet the reality remains: nothing created will last. Everything will return to nothing.

There is only one thing that endures. Only one thing with real meaning, true worth, and lasting value. That is our relationship with our Savior, Jesus Christ.

Matthew 6:33 (NIV)... seek first his kingdom and his righteousness, and all these things will be given to you ....

My dear friends, do not wear yourself out seeking after things that do not have eternal value. Instead, seek a vibrant relationship with Jesus.

Father, thank You for giving us an understanding of what is important and what is not.

171.WISDOM

Proverbs 24:3 - 4 (NIV) 3 By wisdom a house is built, and through understanding it is established; through knowledge its rooms are filled with rare and beautiful treasures.

I often use the "3D" illustration (desire, discipline, and delight) about spiritual maturity for believers. I believe today's proverb illustrates that point.

When we first come to Christ we have come to a place of wisdom. We recognize we cannot save ourselves and that we are hopelessly lost without a Savior. We are like a house under construction. From the outside the house might look pretty good but when we go inside, we will find things incomplete, still a work in progress. No inside walls, no plumbing, no electricity, no appliances etc. The house has potential and so do we. Potential for "greatness" but we start off as just a shell of what we can be in Christ.

Imagine if the builders stopped building once the house was framed in. Yes, it is a house, but it needs a lot of work. Just as the builders want to finish the house, so we also must want to continue on with the work that was started in us.

A lifestyle of consistent time in God's word is required along with obedience to His commands. Over time, our understanding grows and we mature. In time, we find that our spiritual house becomes fully functioning and well established.

But do not stop at just being established. Let us come to the place of perfect delight that comes through KNOWING the Holy One of God.

Just as we discover treasures in a well-built house equipped with every modern convenience, our spiritual lives are enriched with

God's treasures as we grow in intimate knowledge of Him (See Philippians 3:10).

Oh Father, we long for a deeper revelation of Yourself. Lord, fill us with the rare and beautiful treasures that await us in Your presence. Thank You.

172.HARMONY

Romans 12:16 (NIV) 16 Live in harmony with one another. Do not be proud, but be willing to associate with people of low position. Do not be conceited.

The words "harmony" and "low position" caught my attention in this verse. Have you ever listened to an orchestra warming up? It sounds like chaos with everyone playing his or her own tune. Then, as the conductor raises their baton, the orchestra transitions from chaos to harmony

Nowadays there seems to be much more chaos than harmony. Why? Maybe because we are doing "what seems right in our own eyes" instead of keeping our eyes on the Conductor, the Lord Jesus Christ?

Or perhaps because we consider those with different viewpoints from our own to be in a "low position"? I find this to be an interesting question. When I esteem someone, I am inclined to give more consideration to their point of view and am more inclined to seek harmony with them. However, if I have little or no respect for someone, perhaps thinking they are "beneath me," it is very unlikely I will seriously consider their opinions and certainly will not seek to be in harmony with them.

How does one overcome such ingrained prejudices? Simple, do what the orchestra does. They keep their eyes on the conductor and only play the tune he directs, and so must we.

Lord God, may we be done with all our opinions and self-assessments of what is right. Instead, let us look to Jesus and take the position of love, unity and harmony in every relationship we have. Thank You.

173.MISSION

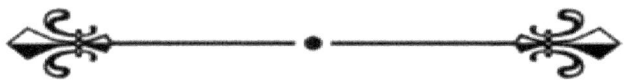

1 Corinthians 10:31 (NIV) 31 So whether you eat or drink or whatever you do, do it all for the glory of God.

Are you familiar with the name Jonathan Edwards? I know the name but not very much about him.

The internet says,

"Jonathan Edwards was an important figure in the Great Awakening. He is credited with starting the Great Awakening in 1734 with his sermon series, "Justification by Faith Alone." He went on to write numerous publications that supported the Great Awakening and critiqued its excesses. He is well known for his sermon "Sinner in the hands of an angry God."

Obviously, he is an important person in the religious history of our country. I wonder why I barely know his name? What got me interested was reading an article that mentioned the "70 resolutions that guided the life of Jonathan Edwards." I have always felt making and keeping resolutions are useful in having a life that is "on mission."

I found the resolutions and I want to share the first one with you:

"Resolved, that I will do whatsoever I think to be most to God's glory, and my own good, profit and pleasure, in the whole of my duration, without any consideration of the time, whether now, or never so many myriads of ages hence. Resolved to do whatever I think to be my duty and most for the good and advantage of mankind in general. Resolved to do this, whatever difficulties I meet with, how many and how great soever."

Did you notice the similarity between his resolution and today's? "Do it all for the glory of God."

In happy times and sad times, in prosperity and when in need, while hungry or full, while energized or tired, that is our mission. To do it all for the glory of God.

Lord God, Creator of the universe, please keep us on mission to bring glory to Your name. Thank You

174.WALK

3 John 1:3-4 (NIV) It gave me great joy when some believers came and testified about your faithfulness to the truth, telling how you continue to walk in it. I have no greater joy than to hear that my children are walking in the truth.

Have you heard the phrase, "to walk the walk" or to "walk the talk"? This phrase implies that one is living with integrity because what they say and what they do are aligned.

I too understand the joy the Apostle John expressed. When a teacher sees that their student not only understands what was taught, but is applying it to their life, it is indeed a special feeling.

However, that is not the kind of walking I am thinking today. I am again reminded of the song we used to sing about that wonderful day, "when Jesus will take me by the hand and walk with me through the promised land. Oh, what a day that will be. No more sickness, no more pain, no more disappointment, no more frustration, no more trouble over there. No more grief nor sadness nor even tears of sorrow. It will be a day when Jesus I will see. A day of being in His presence for all eternity."

Dear Father, in this life we have to discipline ourselves to walk consistently with You. We look forward to that day when we get to naturally walk together in Your kingdom. Thank You.

175.FROZEN

Job 38:29-30 (NIV) From whose womb comes the ice? Who gives birth to the frost from the heavens when the waters become hard as stone, when the surface of the deep is frozen?

The above verses come from a dialogue between God and Job. Job was challenged to see how little he knew compared to the incomparable greatness of our God.

We now know much more about how liquids respond to heat and water and air pressure. But in Job's time, it must have been a mystery. How is it that liquids can also be solids or gaseous? Why does the boiling temperature of water become less as the air pressure decreases? Did you know that water can boil at room temperature if the pressure is low enough?

Simple principles of chemistry (did you fall asleep in your chemistry class like some other people I know?). If you were paying attention this change from liquid to gas or solid is well understood. No mystery at all. Or is it?

How is it that these principles operate not only in our hometown but all over the world? Everywhere in the universe these principles, and so many others, are present. Why? I submit that it is because there is a Great Designer and we call Him God.

The world we live in, even with all its brokenness, still operates within the laws, principles, and boundaries set by the Sovereign God. This is a remarkable gift, one we often take for granted. Imagine living in a world where these laws and principles constantly changed—or worse, in a world of chaos where no rules existed at all.

Some claim that there is "no God." Do not give their arguments even the slightest consideration. Instead, reflect on the incredible universe around us. It is no accident, I assure you. Look closer to home, at the human body, and you will see that we are wonderfully made.

Father, we take so much for granted. Help us to not do that. Open our eyes daily to be able to see and appreciate Your incredible creation. Thank You.

176.HOT

Revelation 3:15-16 (NIV) I know your deeds, that you are neither cold nor hot. I wish you were either one or the other! So, because you are lukewarm—neither hot nor cold—I am about to spit you out of my mouth.

Yesterday's word was "frozen". Today it is "hot." (I wonder if we will be doing a series on temperatures?) But today I am not as inclined to write about temperature as I am about attitude. Our attitude toward Christ

God prefers hot to lukewarm. I do too. I think almost anything is better than being lukewarm. So, what does it mean to be "hot" for Christ?

Some words that could describe a "hot" believer are animated, fierce, lively, intense, passionate, impassioned, spirited, ardent, fervent, strong, powerful, heartfelt, wholehearted, earnest, burning, zealous, and sincere among others. Do any of these words describe you? I hope so.

Select the words that describe you, or the words that you would like to have describe you. Use them in writing a heartfelt prayer to God. Something for your eyes only. Describe your relationship with Him now and how you would like it to be.

I am convinced that the many distractions in our lives, from taking care of home and loved ones to dealing with emergencies or emerging difficulties, are like being doused with cold water. It is a daily struggle to stay focused on God while dealing with the distractions that come from all directions.

Hopefully we are learning to practice the discipline of "stop." Just stopping our ceaseless activity to spend some focus time with our Sovereign God. To some this may seem like a waste of precious time (to all the Martha's out there) but to others they will find this "waste of time" a source of eternal wellbeing (for the Mary's among us).

Lord, please help me and all who read these devotions to cease our constant busyness. Lead us to stop and spend time with You. Lord, please blow Your breath on the flame within us. Give us a passionate energized relationship with You. Thank You.

177.COLD

Matthew 10:42 (NIV) And if anyone gives even a cup of cold water to one of these little ones who is my disciple, truly I tell you, that person will certainly not lose their reward.

I have not enjoyed the cold mornings lately. I always struggle to rise from bed. When it is cold out, the struggle is amplified.

On the other hand, the chilly air is invigorating. It is nice to be do chores outside without breaking into a sweat. It makes me think we can usually find good and not so good in most of our circumstances. Jesus tells us some things are always good and always result in a reward.

The example Jesus used in today's verse is cold water. He is talking about acts of kindness directed toward His disciples. The verse reminds us that even the smallest act of kindness towards others, especially believers, is noticed by God. Jesus wants us to know that no kind deed is ever wasted.

Today's verse comes at the end of instructions Jesus gives to His disciples before they are sent out to minister. It is instructive that Jesus would use acts of kindness to summarize all that has been said before.

Lord God, You called us to represent You as we go about our daily lives. Make acts of kindness as natural as breathing. May the world see and comprehend that we are indeed different because we act with love towards others because we belong to You. Thank You.

178.HOSPITALITY

3 John 1:5-6 (NIV) Dear friend, you are faithful in what you are doing for the brothers and sisters, even though they are strangers to you. They have told the church about your love. Please send them on their way in a manner that honors God.

Some years ago, May and I were members of "Mennonite Your way." It was a network of homes that were available to traveling Mennonites. There was no charge for lodging, but you were expected to compensate the homeowners for any meals that were provided. It was one of the many ways God blessed our lives. We met so many people who came as strangers but often left as new friends. Some became repeat guests year after year.

In the early church, this was an accepted practice. The Apostle John is thanking his readers for welcoming these people even though they are strangers.

I know we live in a different time, and perhaps welcoming strangers into our homes is not always possible or even wise. So, what is the application for us today?

Hospitality is just another way to be kind, friendly, warm and neighborly. It is taking time for the people around us, strangers and friends alike. To listen to them, to get to know them, to spend time with them. It can take place in our homes, coffee shops, grocery stores and even at work. Hospitality is warmly engaging another human being and welcoming them into your presence to the point that when they leave they know that they were with someone who cared.

Lord, please help us to be hospitable - friendly, warm and inviting - to all people but especially to strangers that are truly our brothers and sisters in Christ. Thank You.

179.LOCUST

Psalms 78:46 (NIV) 46 He gave their crops to the grasshopper, their produce to the locust.

Have you ever seen a swarm of locusts? I have only seen them in videos, and I am most thankful it has never been a personal experience. Here in Florida we have a certain type of grasshopper that reminds me of locusts. Its name is Romalea microptera.

These locusts have never swarmed, as far as I know. I sure hope it never happens. But, like clockwork, they appear each spring and start their devastating attack on my plants. They prefer my orchids, but they are not picky. Each spring, as they emerge, I attack them fervently. It is the only time they can be killed with a spray or powder. They grow really fast and in no time, they are a couple of inches long and the only way to bring about their demise is to kill them mechanically. I cut their heads off. I know that sounds a little gross, but it does work.

After a few years of aggressive combat between me and the locusts their numbers seem more manageable and they are not causing nearly as much damage as they used to. That is the point of this devotion.

There are potential locusts all around us, also known as distractions. Distractions, take our time and interests and come between us and God. They have a way of consuming our strength and energy. They keep us busily engaged but are of little or no use to the kingdom of God.

No locusts in your life? Oh, I forgot to mention, they are masters of disguise.

Lord, are there locusts in our lives that we do not see? Please, Father, reveal anything in our lives that hinders our walk with You. Thank You.

180. GENUINE

Philippians 2:19-21 (NIV) I hope in the Lord Jesus to send Timothy to you soon, that I also may be cheered when I receive news about you. I have no one else like him, who will show genuine concern for your welfare. For everyone looks out for their own interests, not those of Jesus Christ.

Apparently, Paul found it difficult to find people who genuinely cared for. I think we have a similar phenomenon today. Although we can be very generous and give freely of our finances and even of our time and energy. That does not necessarily mean that we genuinely care for others.

It has been said, "we can give without loving but we cannot love without giving." I would add that we must give of ourselves, if we genuinely care.

I am convinced that Jesus wants us to give all of ourselves in service to Him and to one another. Remember, we are to love Him and others with all we have, no reservations, no holding back. That sounds pretty genuine to me. This is difficult since it is contrary to our human tendency towards self-centeredness.

Paul addresses the heart of the issue in today's verse: "for everyone looks out for their own interests, not those of Jesus Christ." I am often amazed at how Christians can become so absorbed in social media, gaming, sports, music stars, actors—anything, really. They seem unaware that none of these things serve the interests of Christ. Like the "locusts" mentioned in yesterday's devotion, they pull our attention away from what truly matters.

Lord, please search our hearts and reveal all distractions in our lives that hinder our walk with You. Lead us to be genuine Christians in every sense of the word. Thank You.

181.DEPOSIT

Matthew 25:27 (NIV) Well then, you should have put my money on deposit with the bankers, so that when I returned I would have received it back with interest.

Most financial advisors recommended that you have cash in case of an emergency. Some recommend a month's worth while others think at least a year's worth of savings is best.

If a person is cash-strapped, how do they build an emergency cash fund? The answer is with consistency. Regular deposits, even small ones, can add up to significant savings over time. The key is being consistent in making deposits over time and only touching the money for emergencies.

I propose that the same principle is true in our relationships. When we make small consistent deposits in the lives of our loved ones, we can build a substantial emotional "bank" account. Again, the key is consistency over time.

Why do we need to build an emotional bank account? Because sooner or later, you will have to make a withdrawal. Even the strongest relationships can encounter rocky ground as we navigate life together. A well-stocked emotional bank account gives us the ability to forgive and continue loving despite the withdrawals. It helps prevent emotional bankruptcy.

I know some will say this does not work either with our finances or our relationships. I suggest something is amiss in their financial or relational lives. To never be able to build a cash emergency fund usually means one is living an undisciplined financial life. Living at or beyond one's means instead of under it. To never be able to build and sustain an emotional bank account usually means there is sabotage going on in the relationship.

Why do we need to build an emotional bank account? Because sooner or later, you will have to make a withdrawal. Even the strongest relationships can encounter rocky ground as we navigate life together. A well-stocked emotional bank account gives us the ability to forgive and continue loving despite the withdrawals. It helps prevent emotional bankruptcy.

Dear Father, please lead all of us to build relationships that model Your love for us. Thank You.

182.BUSY

2 Thessalonians 3:10-13 (NIV) For even when we were with you, we gave you this rule: "The one who is unwilling to work shall not eat." We hear that some among you are idle and disruptive. They are not busy; they are busybodies. Such people we command and urge in the Lord Jesus Christ to settle down and earn the food they eat. And as for you, brothers and sisters, never tire of doing what is good.

I am sure you have heard the saying, "if you want to get something done give it to a busy person." Similarly, there is the principle that an object at rest will tend to stay at rest while an object in motion is easier to change course or pick up speed.

I think I have noticed some of that principle playing out in my own life, especially as I get older. Sometimes I see things that need attending to and, for some reason, I procrastinate and do not do what is right in front of me. There is a part of me that wants to take care of things, but there is another part that is overcome, it seems, by gravity.

And then there are the days when I am more motivated. I get myself in gear and accomplish all kinds of things once I get rolling. I think I have been in a slump lately, but the recent visit of our children stirred me to want to "take care of business." They accomplished so much in just a few days and, frankly, I want to be more like them.

I also noticed that there is deep, intrinsic value in doing what needs doing. The reward is in the work itself. Once a task is completed do you notice a certain degree of satisfaction?

So, what is our lesson today? Simply be careful of becoming a couch potato. That is not God's best design for us. The more we do not do the more we do not want to do. On the other hand, once we get going, the more we do the more we will want to do.

Lord, please help us to not blame anything (not even old age) for our procrastination. Instead let us see what needs doing and let us get on with it. Thank You.

183.WANT

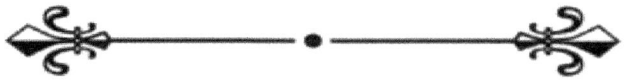

Matthew 20:31-33 (NIV) The crowd rebuked them and told them to be quiet, but they shouted all the louder, "Lord, Son of David, have mercy on us!" Jesus stopped and called them. "What do you want me to do for you?" he asked. "Lord," they answered, "we want our sight."

I ask you, my dear friend, what do you want? Do you want to master that game on your phone? Or do you want to get lots of "likes" on social media? Maybe you want to be like some movie star or sports idol? Or be successful in your career or hobby or ministry? Or maybe you want a winning lottery ticket?

If you are like most people, you only have a vague sense of what you want (happy, carefree, healthy etc). Jesus is interested in hearing us express what we really want.

That requires some thought. What is really important to you? If you write it down and/or share it with a close friend you might get more clarity. What is really high up on the list of what is important to you?

When we get clarity on what is really important, we are better able to focus our lives to move in that direction. It enables us to live with intention and direction and to not be easily distracted.

What if you do not know what you want? That is a common experience. I suggest you ask. The scriptures remind us that if one needs wisdom, God is just a prayer away. (James 1:5 (NIV) If any of you lacks wisdom, you should ask God, who gives generously to all without finding fault, and it will be given to you.)

Father, it seems that we are more inclined to be governed by the circumstances of our lives rather than the deep-seated desires You place in our hearts. Please give us understanding of what is really important and the desire and discipline to live with intention. Thank You.

184.SIMPLE

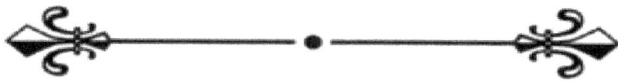

Matthew 11:28 (NIV)28 Come to me, all you who are weary and burdened, and I will give you rest.

Many years ago, I realized that I have a tendency to make things more complicated than they need to be. It is, I assure you, a pervasive personal trait that shows up in just about every aspect of my life, including when I teach. I imagine that over the years I frustrated many students over my ability to dig deep over the simplest things.

Having become conscious of that many years ago, I strive to make my life simpler. It is a regular prayer of mine, and I have enlisted a sort of online coach by the name of Joshua Becker. He is a Christian, former youth pastor and author. He does not know me but I read and reflect on his articles about being a minimalist. I have no desire to become a true minimalist, however, his articles often have useful points. Below, I share part of a recent post by Becker.

"The story is told of a man named Arenius who lived in the fifth century. Determined to lead a holy life, he abandoned the comforts of Egyptian society, choosing instead a simple and solemn existence in the desert. Yet whenever he visited the great city of Alexandria, he would wander through its bustling bazaars and markets. When asked why, he explained, 'My heart rejoices at the sight of all the things I do not need.' I first heard this story more than ten years ago, and since then I have both shared it and returned to it in thought countless times. Consider the meaning and the opportunity behind that final sentence: My heart rejoices at the sight of all the things I do not need. When was the last time you reflected on the joy of not wanting things?" (Joshua Becker)

My dear friend, when was the last time you considered the joy of wanting nothing but Jesus?

Father, what an interesting journey we are on. All of us are like pilgrims on a journey, daily making progress as You conform us to the simple life of Your will. Let us be simply devoted to You. Thank You.

185.CONTEND

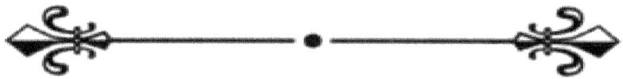

Jude 1:3 (NIV) Dear friends, although I was very eager to write to you about the salvation we share, I felt compelled to write and urge you to contend for the faith that was once for all entrusted to God's holy people.

The word contend is not for the faint-hearted, especially when it comes to standing firm in our faith in Christ. It calls for taking a stand, prepared to face the battle. It means actively engaging in the struggle rather than standing on the sidelines. It is not about being just a "fan" of Christ. It is being fully on the playing field, giving all our strength and energy against the enemy who constantly seeks to undermine us.

In some ways, nothing much has changed in the 2000+ years since Jude penned these words. Despite America being formed under Christian principles, it is imperative that we contend for our faith in this "modern" age. Christianity is snubbed and even ridiculed by many political leaders and activists. It was "normal" to be a Christian in our society 50, 30, even 10 years ago. But, today, if you want to boast of your Christianity you best be prepared to contend for your faith.

How do you prepare to contend for your faith? Now STOP! Give that some thought and consider your answer before you read on.

Good, so you are now clear on how to prepare to contend for your faith? Or are you unsure? Give it a little more thought and we will come back to this point another time.

On the other hand, if you think you really do know how to prepare to contend for your faith, share that with another. And if you couldn't care less about contending for your faith it is time to reconsider your relationship with Jesus. Remember what He said about being lukewarm?

Oh, Lord, as I think of contending for my faith, I have this sense of being drawn into battle for You. In some ways, I prefer to stay on the side lines but that is not Your message to us. Please give us understanding of how to contend for our faith. Thank You.

186.GRUMBLE

Numbers 14:27-28 (NIV) How long will this wicked community grumble against me? I have heard the complaints of these grumbling Israelites. So, tell them, 'As surely as I live, declares the LORD, I will do to you the very thing I heard you say.

To grumble is to complain, whine, mutter, find fault with, bellyache, gripe, etc. I am confident that God must "groan" when we, as followers of Jesus, moan and groan over some aspect of our lives. Yet some folks are inclined to this activity.

I make every effort to not complain outwardly. Whenever I sense a "grumble coming on," I have this little "ditty" that I sing to myself. "I shall not grumble, I shall not complain, just like the tree planted by the water I shall not grumble or complain." (Psalm 1:3 is the inspiration)

The other night, just as May and I were getting ready to settle in for the night, we heard a sharp, urgent knock at the door. I could tell from the sound that something was wrong. I opened the door to find a neighbor, nearly out of breath. She said, "Oh, Paul, there's been an accident. The wind blew your plant cart down the driveway. It overturned, and everything is now in the middle of the street."

In an instant, I was ready to grumble. I could see the damage in my mind's eye. When I really saw it, it was much worse. As I was about to grumble, here came the ditty into my mind. "Paul, do not grumble and complain, be like the tree." I took a deep breath or two (I think that helped) and went back into the house to let May know I would outside for "a while."

As I returned to the scene of the "disaster," my neighbor showed up to help. I do not like to ask for help, but I was so overwhelmed that I felt compelled to answer in the affirmative. After thirty minutes, the debris was cleared off the road, uprooted plants had been retrieved, broken pots tossed etc. Mostly I held the light, and he did all the work. I now have a neighbor that I appreciate so much more.

Yesterday, as I began to restore all the plants that were dumped out of their pots, I had this sense that God is doing something new and not grumbling was just a little push toward resting in Him.

Father, I know we think we have reason to grumble, but if we are in Christ there is never a reason to grumble or complain. Thank You.

187.PURPOSE

Exodus 9:16 (NIV) But I have raised you up for this very purpose, that I might show you my power and that my name might be proclaimed in all the earth.

It seems that most of us live without purpose. We go from day to day, perhaps do the best we can, but our lives are mainly driven by circumstances. What would change if we had a clear understanding of our true purpose in life?

Some 30+ years ago, while attending a training class, the instructor mentioned the usefulness of having a clearly stated purpose for our lives.

I took his advice and after some time/thought decided on mine. I modeled mine on the instructor's because I thought it was potentially very powerful. I do not believe I have ever shared mine with anyone in my current circle of influence. Here is my stated purpose that has guided me (although not perfectly) over the years.

"My purpose in life is to make a positive, meaningful difference in the lives of people for Christ."

This simple statement has helped me make many decisions over the last few decades. Like I said, not perfectly, but I recall when knowing my purpose helped when making some difficult decisions.

We only get this one time around. Soon our lives will be just a memory and even that will fade. In 100 or so years who we are and what we accomplished will be forgotten. But not all. What we do for Christ will remain for all eternity.

Dearest Father, You placed eternity in our hearts. Give us a purpose that guides our lives today and persists for all eternity. Thank You.

188.LESS

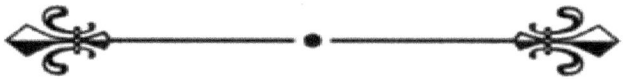

Luke 12:20-21 (NIV) But God said to him, 'You fool! This very night your life will be demanded from you. Then who will get what you have prepared for yourself?' This is how it will be with whoever stores up things for themselves but is not rich toward God.

Living in America, we have "normalized" the god of materialism. You might think this does not apply to you. That is partially my point. We have so normalized having so much that we no longer see how it dominates our lives.

This morning, I want to again share part of a devotion by Joshua Becker:

"There is an unmistakable joy found in living an intentional life. The relentless pursuit of "more" can be exhausting. Stepping off that consumer treadmill would do more than liberate us from the pressure to hurry and chase every new fad. It would empower us to make choices each day that align with our deepest selves.

Not wanting things allows our aspirations to evolve. We begin dreaming bigger dreams for our lives beyond physical possessions. We start to see our one life as more valuable and full of opportunity. Our ambitions can focus entirely on creating a positive impact rather than filling a shopping cart. In doing so, we enrich both our own lives and the lives of others.

As a result, life feels genuinely fulfilling and purposeful. Doesn't that sound worthy of rejoicing and celebration?

—JOSHUA BECKER

Living our lives intentionally with a clear God-given purpose sure beats wandering around aimlessly so we can pass all we have on to someone else. As shared previously, it has been said, "an unexamined life is a life not worth living."

Lord God, please help us that we might see our lives as You see them. Give us hearts that break over the things that are breaking Your heart and rejoices over the things that bring joy to You. Thank You.

189.ATTITUDE

Romans 15:5 (NIV) May the God who gives endurance and encouragement give you the same attitude of mind toward each other that Christ Jesus had.

Have you ever thought about how attitude is such a "governing behavior" in our relationships? Attitude is a viewpoint, perspective, stance, belief, orientation, position we have about a person, place, thing or situation. It acts like a filter. If our attitude is "good" towards a person we tend to not see the bad in that person. On the other hand, if our attitude is "negative" it is almost impossible to see the good.

As followers of Christ, we are commanded to love one another. This is quite difficult when our attitude is critical or judgmental or otherwise prone to nor seeing the good in a person.

When May and I counseling couples with "troubled" marriages we frequently ran into people who had been so hurt that they had closed their spirit to the other person. It did not matter how much the offending person tried to "make it right." Every effort was dismissed for one reason or another.

Over time they acquired an attitude of dislike, bitterness or even hate toward the person they had chosen to spend their life with. It was most difficult to work with couples in this situation. They had formed such an attitude that seemingly no amount of counseling could break through I remember a pastor telling me, "Paul, when you are working harder than the couple, something is wrong."

That is an extreme example, however, our attitude towards others (positive or negative) greatly affects how we see and respond to them. So here is the "rub." As followers of Christ we have little choice about our attitudes towards other believers. We must esteem them with the "same attitude of mind that Christ Jesus has." I understand that may seem impossible at times, but even our attitude can be adjusted when surrendered to the Holy Spirit.

Lord, God, please give us an attitude check. Wherever we might have a wrong attitude please bring it to our attention and may we respond with humble submission to Your will and Your way. Thank You.

190.ENCOURAGE

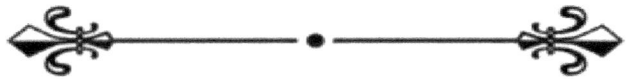

Romans 12:6-8 (NIV) We have different gifts, according to the grace given to each of us. If your gift is prophesying, then prophesy in accordance with your faith; if it is serving, then serve; if it is teaching, then teach; if it is to encourage, then give encouragement; if it is giving, then give generously; if it is to lead, do it diligently; if it is to show mercy, do it cheerfully.

Have you ever gotten to the place where you were so discouraged that you just wanted to "give up"? I think it is a common experience and, if allowed to fester, depression is often not far behind.

As I read the biographies of some well-known Christians, it becomes clear that many experienced discouragement from time to time. We often read about their lives and assume they were some kind of "super Christian." The truth, however, is that they were made of flesh and blood just like us. Yet somehow, they persevered and moved beyond their discouragement to accomplish what we would consider "great" things. It seems that God always placed the right people in their lives to encourage them during difficult times.

The point of today's devotional is NOT for us to do great things, but to encourage one another as we do the work that God has prepared in advance for us to do (Ephesians 2:10).

This life can bring much heartache (grief, poor health, financial failures etc). These are common to all of us in one form or another. As followers of Jesus, we still get to experience these disappointments and trials, but we must not be overcome by them. Jesus has promised to be with us when life gets difficult.

(John 16:33 (NIV) "I have told you these things, so that in me you may have peace. In this world you will have trouble. But take heart! I have overcome the world.")

I believe we have a responsibility to encourage one another. Even the smallest of gestures (a touch, a call, a text, a visit, a note, a small gift, etc) can make a really big difference in people's lives. Who can you encourage today? Will you do it today?

Father, I thank You for the many encouragers you have given to May and me over the years. Please lead us to encourage one another to live lives that reflect our love for You and one another. Thank You.

191.REAL

1 John 2:27 (NIV) 27 As for you, the anointing you received from him remains in you, and you do not need anyone to teach you. But as his anointing teaches you about all things and as that anointing is real, not counterfeit—just as it has taught you, remain in him.

The word anointing refers to the Holy Spirit, which is the gift given to us when we accept Jesus as Lord and Savior. The anointing is given so that we can discern truth from falsehood, to know what is genuine and what is not, and to live according to the truth.

John 14:26 (ASV) But the Comforter, even the Holy Spirit, whom the Father will send in my name, he shall teach you all things, and bring to your remembrance all that I said unto you.

The apostles warned the believers that many false teachers would enter the church and attempt to deceive the elect. Scripture repeatedly urges us to remain vigilant against unscrupulous teachers who seek to mislead believers for their own gain. I believe these deceptive teachers have become widespread in the modern American church. We are told that in the last days, men would have itching ears. Clearly, that day has come.

2 Timothy 4:3 (NIV) For the time will come when people will not put up with sound doctrine. Instead, to suit their own desires, they will gather around them a great number of teachers to say what their itching ears want to hear.

How do we protect ourselves from false teachings? The more we know and apply the word of God, the more we will be able to recognize false teachings. We should continually ask the Holy Spirit to guide us into all understanding so that we are not drawn away by our own inclinations nor the deceit of false teachers.

Oh Lord, lead us to pursue the real thing. Do not let us settle for a Christianity that "looks good" but lacks the power of God and does not really know You. Fill us with discernment and wisdom and understanding. Let our ears yearn for Your truth and intimacy with You. Thank You.

192.BUILDING

Jude 1:20-21 (NIV) But you, dear friends, by building yourselves up in your most holy faith and praying in the Holy Spirit, keep yourselves in God's love as you wait for the mercy of our Lord Jesus Christ to bring you to eternal life.

Matthew 7:24 (NIV) Therefore everyone who hears these words of mine and puts them into practice is like a wise man who built his house on the rock.

We often hear God's word, agree with the word, and then sometimes almost immediately do the opposite. It is an amazing phenomena. I see it in myself and I see it all around me. We sometimes think we are better at doing something than we really are.

Romans 12:3 (NIV) For by the grace given me I say to every one of you: Do not think of yourself more highly than you ought, but rather think of yourself with sober judgment, in accordance with the faith God has distributed to each of you.

I think the key issue is to purposely apply God's words in our lives. To actually practice what the word commands us as children of God (love our enemies, weep with others, care more for others than ourselves, give joyfully and generously, pray for our government leaders, seek His kingdom first, forgive people who offend us, make peace as far as it is possible for us etc.) Do you see what I mean? Although we give mental ascent to these things, few of us practice them with consistency.

It is in the practice of these commands that we realize how inadequate we truly are and need Jesus. The Spirit of God can build in us a faith that will withstand the storms of life.

Father, what can I say? We need help, a lot of help. Please build a strong faith in us by applying Your word to every turn of our lives. Thank You.

193.CONTENT

1 Timothy 6:6-8 (NIV) But godliness with contentment is great gain. For we brought nothing into the world, and we can take nothing out of it. But if we have food and clothing, we will be content with that.

There is something very special about living as contented individuals, satisfied with God's provisions, and not wanting what we do not have.

The other day, as I was doing the dishes and May and her nurse from Vitas health care were talking, I overheard the nurse tell May, "May, you have learned to enjoy the simplicity of life." Such simple words spoken by someone who hardly knows May and yet she expressed such truth about my wife.

May has never yearned for something more. She has never complained in my ears about the tragedies in her life. She has been content to love her husband and her family. She has never to my memory ever complained about a person, place, situation or circumstance. She has accepted everything into her life as coming from the hand of God. She has never tried to "one up" another. She is most content in the role that God has orchestrated for her life.

She is a woman who has earnestly sought the presence of God from an early age. In her heart, she believes she has been created "to know God, to love Him and to serve Him in this world and the next." She not only believes this, she has lived her life being an example of a godly woman. In my opinion, the woman of Proverbs 31 has nothing on my May.

As I write these words, I am overwhelmed with gratitude that God brought such an extraordinary woman into my life. Not only does she endure my many shortcomings, but she loves me despite them.

And now we find ourselves in the winter season of our lives. There are no longer dreams of future adventures, not even for me. We are simply content with what has been, what is, and whatever is yet to come.

What about you? Are you content with the blessings God has given you?

Oh God, thank You for my wife and for a life well lived. Thank You from the depths of my heart.

194 MINISTRY

2 Corinthians 4:1 (NIV) Therefore, since through God's mercy we have this ministry, we do not lose heart.

I have often said, "we are always to be on mission." It is another way of saying we need to be about the ministry God has called us to. Knowing God's ministry for our lives and being consistent in applying it gives us purpose and hope. Having purpose and hope enables us to endure and even to consider it joyful when life goes "south."

James 1:2-4 (NIV) Consider it pure joy, my brothers and sisters, whenever you face trials of many kinds, 3 because you know that the testing of your faith produces perseverance. 4 Let perseverance finish its work so that you may be mature and complete, not lacking anything.

So how does one "consider it joyful" while experiencing grief, loss, pain, frustration, sadness, and the like? It is not an easy task, but here is what I have come to understand. As followers of Jesus, we must not allow our feelings to dictate our lives. This is contrary to what we often hear. We are frequently told to "follow our heart," which is essentially the same as following our emotions or feelings.

As believers, we must follow God's revealed word along with the guidance of God's Spirit. Please understand, I am not suggesting that we should ignore or try to stuff our feelings. On the contrary, feelings can be most useful in getting our attention and helping us. But, and this is a strong "but," we must not be led solely by our feelings.

Staying on task, staying on mission, being faithful to God's call on our lives, continuing to minister even when dealing with difficulties, is all "counting" it joy. We are to live our lives with intention. We are to live with purpose, doing everything for the glory of God.

Colossians 3:17 (NIV) And whatever you do, whether in word or deed, do it all in the name of the Lord Jesus, giving thanks to God the Father through him.

Father, thank You for the calling you have placed on each of our lives. Please keep us faithful "even when the winds are blowing contrary." Thank You.

195.IMITATION

Jude 1:12 (NIV) These people are blemishes at your love feasts, eating with you without the slightest qualm—shepherds who feed only themselves. They are clouds without rain, blown along by the wind; autumn trees, without fruit and uprooted —twice dead.

Matthew 13:30 (NIV) Let both grow together until the harvest. At that time I will tell the harvesters: First collect the weeds and tie them in bundles to be burned; then gather the wheat and bring it into my barn.

Sometimes an imitation resembles the real thing so closely that it is almost impossible to tell the difference between the fake and the real. I believe that is what today's two verses are trying to tell us. In our midst are imitators of Christ, followers who are not really His. They may look like the real thing, and they may even do a lot of the outward things that are signs of a Christ follower but their hearts do not belong to Jesus.

So, what are we to do? We are to continue living genuine Christ-like lives so that they see the real thing in us. You and I are not the harvesters and so we must not judge. Instead, we must consistently love others, true followers of Jesus or not. Only Jesus knows a person's heart (sometimes we even fool ourselves). So, we leave it up to God to decide what is weed and what is wheat.

In the meantime, as we await the time of the harvest, let us continue to do good. The greatest good we can do is to love one another. (Romans 12:21 (NIV) Do not be overcome by evil, but overcome evil with good. - John 13:35 (NIV) 35 By this everyone will know that you are my disciples, if you love one another.")

Lord, You have placed in our hearts the desire to be real, genuine, followers of Jesus Christ of Nazareth. Please let there be nothing fake, no imitation, in our walk with You. Thank You.

196.BLESSING

Psalms 128:1-2 (NIV) Blessed are all who fear the LORD, who walk in obedience to him. You will eat the fruit of your labor; blessings and prosperity will be yours.

Most of us have been abundantly blessed. Even if we do not have as many material comforts as our neighbors we still have a multitude of blessings when compared to much of the world. Beyond material blessings, we have been blessed with the certainty of eternal life in the presence of the Almighty God.

Our days may be filled with joy or sadness and yet we are still abundantly blessed because we are no longer under the bondage of sin and our fleshly nature. We are not only set free from the bondage of sin, but we are also set free from the penalty of sin. Jesus' all sufficient sacrifice paid the price for all our past sins, all of our present sins, and all sins we might commit in the future.

Even with all this there is one more blessing that goes way beyond what we have been set free from. It is what we have been set free "to".

As children of God, we are free to serve Him and in so doing be a blessing to others. It is important to grasp this principle. The blessings we have received give us a certain level of peace and comfort. However, we are not blessed so that we might "feel good." We are blessed so that we can bless others.

Lord, thank You so much for the multitude of blessings we have received. Please Lord incline us to bless others. Lead us mostly to give the blessing of loving others. Thank You.

197.OPPORTUNITY-COST

Galatians 6:10 (NIV) Therefore, as we have opportunity, let us do good to all people, especially to those who belong to the family of believers.

Please pardon me using two words as one. Opportunity cost is often used as a financial concept to help decide if an expenditure is wise when compared with the opportunities that might be lost.

For example, a person might decide to purchase a new car. That would produce some benefit. At the same time, it might limit funds for other opportunities such as travel, food, entertainment etc. The idea is to weigh the future potential cost/opportunity lost against the benefit of the proposed purchase. Is it worth buying a new car and having to scrimp on other desirable things for several years?

This principle applies in all areas of our lives. Since we are finite beings, we have finite limitations. If I decide to participate in one activity, I am at the same moment saying "no" to some other activity. A common example is choosing to participate in sports instead of attending a church service. The opportunity cost is that I will not spend that time in worship.

If I decide to spend time on social media or playing computer games, then that time is not available for other activities that might be more useful. If I decide to spend my money on things that please me, I will have less to give away as the Lord leads me. If I decide to stay angry and upset with someone, I bear the cost of an unreconciled relationship.

We are on a mission to bring glory to God by doing the work He prepared for us to do (Ephesians 2:10). Is the way we spend our money, our time, our resources and our talents creating opportunity costs that prevent us from becoming more like Christ Jesus?

Lord, often we are driven by circumstances and personal preference. Let us see the opportunity costs and purpose to live with the intention of bringing glory to You. Thank You.

198.SEVEN

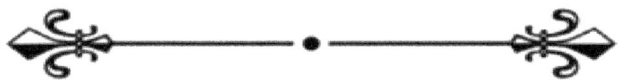

Isaiah 11:2 (NIV) The Spirit of the LORD will rest on him— the Spirit of wisdom and of understanding, the Spirit of counsel and of might, the Spirit of the knowledge and fear of the LORD—

John 14:16-17 (NIV) And I will ask the Father, and he will give you another advocate to help you and be with you forever— the Spirit of truth. The world cannot accept him, because it neither sees him nor knows him. But you know him, for he lives with you and will be in you.

In our natural state we are far from perfect but God has gifted us His Spirit, which is perfect. Why? To live a life that is pleasing to God. When we work from our natural selves, we simply fall short. God is perfect, and we are not. God in His great mercy and compassion has given us a helper, the Spirit of Truth, so that we can live lives that please Him and bring glory to His name.

With the gift of His Spirit, we have access to rest, wisdom, understanding, counsel, might, knowledge and fear of God (See Isaiah 11:2). These seven attributes of God's Spirit are available to us as children of the most high God. The challenge, however, is always before us. Will we seek the guidance of the Spirit of God or will we persist in "doing what is right in our own eyes" (See Judges 21:25)?

My wife, May, has often said that "the Holy Spirit is a perfect Gentleman. He will not force us to do anything against our will." We must come to the place of surrender and submit ourselves to the Lordship of Jesus in order to live the Spirit-led life. How will we know we "have arrived"? Perhaps when Galatians 5:22-23 is persistently obvious to the most casual observer as they see how we love one another (John 13:35).

Father, I am so thankful we do not have to do this walk on our own. Thank You for Your Spirit that leads us into all truth.

199.PRIESTS

Revelation 1:5-6 (NIV) …. from Jesus Christ, who is the faithful witness, the firstborn from the dead, and the ruler of the kings of the earth. To him who loves us and has freed us from our sins by his blood, and has made us to be a kingdom and priests to serve his God and Father —to him be glory and power for ever and ever! Amen.

Today's verses were part of my "praying through the New Testament" time the other morning. We do not refer to ourselves as priests very often, but that is what the scriptures say we are. The following is from the Life Application Bible Commentary:

"Israel had been called to be "[a] kingdom of priests, [a] holy nation" (Exodus 19:6 NLT). This saying describes the Christians as the continuation of the Old Testament people of God—his kingdom and priests (see also Hebrews 13:15; 1 Peter 2:5, 9)".

I know some denominations have the office of priest but I think that is a distortion of the scriptures. The office of priest is not set aside for a few. No, it is a designation given to all believers in Jesus Christ. Yes, that does mean you and I are priests.

The priest is an intermediary between the people and God. Since all believers are priests, I surmise this means born-again Christians are to be intermediaries for all who are not saved and do not know God.

What an incredible privilege and responsibility we have. To intercede for the lost, that they might answer the call and respond to God's love. We must not take this responsibility lightly. The eternal destiny of many may be determined by how faithful we are to this calling of God.

Father, with the privilege of being Your children comes responsibility to respond to Your calling in our lives. Thank You.

200.STEPS

Proverbs 20:24 (NIV) A person's steps are directed by the LORD. How then can anyone understand their own way?

Psalms 119:105 (NIV) Your word is a lamp for my feet, a light on my path.

Have you ever been lost but did not know you were lost until suddenly something clearly lets you know you have lost your way? Some, even after realizing they are lost, refuse to ask for help (I have heard some men are like this).

In most cases, it is not a big deal. Sooner or later, we find our way and reach our destination. But what if we are talking about our lives? What if we reach the end and realize we have been traveling the wrong road? Or, in the words of Stephen Covey, "What if after spending a lifetime climbing, we discover we have climbed the wrong wall"?

God knows that we can get confused and make wrong choices. That is why He has given us His Word, so we can have wisdom for life.

There are two key factors in gaining wisdom for life. First, we must be on the right path. If we are not on the right path, it does not matter how many steps we take—we will never reach where we think we are going. God wants us to follow the narrow path, yet most of us choose the wide, convenient path.

Matthew 7:13-14 (NIV) "Enter through the narrow gate. For wide is the gate and broad is the road that leads to destruction, and many enter through it. 14 But small is the gate and narrow the road that leads to life, and only a few find it.

The other factor is the steps we will take today. Your very next steps, even as you finish reading this sentence. Will you take the steps that lead to fulfillment in Christ?

How can we be sure we are on the right path? The answer is the word of God. Not something we read on occasion but something we live our lives by. And how do we make sure we take the "right" next steps? The answer is seeking the Spirit of God to help us and to lead us, followed by obedience.

Lord, it is easy to get off the path and to take foolish steps. Please lead us on the narrow path through Your word and Your Spirit. Thank You.

201.WITNESS

Acts 22:15 (NIV) You will be his witness to all people of what you have seen and heard.

What makes for a witness incredible? Is it that they have done something great? No, of course not. An incredible witness is one who can accurately report what happened.

Take Paul for example. His "story" was rarely about him. He consistently told the story of what God has done.

People are reluctant to share the good news of Jesus because they feel they have not changed their lives "enough." Guess what? You may never feel you have changed "enough." That is not relevant. What is relevant is what God has done and is doing in your life.

He has set you free from the bondage and penalty of sin. He gives you the freedom to be a witness for Him. That is a privilege we must never take lightly. He has graciously adopted you into the family of God.

Every one of us has a story to tell. It is a story of what God has done and continues to do in our lives. It is a story of victories and failures alike. It is a story of reaching a place where we can find rest in God, even when life feels overwhelmingly difficult. It is a story sometimes spoken with words, but always revealed through how we live and the choices we make.

I understand that we may fear embarrassment, worry about not finding the "right" words, or even dread being ridiculed for our beliefs or decisions. That is natural. Fear is part of being human. But we are not just ordinary people. We are children of God, followers of Christ. God grants us the courage to be His living witness, even when fear is present.

Father, please enable us to speak the truth boldly in love. Thank You.

202 EDIFY

Romans 14:19 (ASV) So then let us follow after things which make for peace, and things whereby we may edify one another.

To edify means to lift someone up (either morally or intellectually) to a higher place. Words like instruct, teach, tutor, coach, guide, enlighten, cultivate, develop all have the sense of edifying.

In a previous devotion, I shared my mission: "to make a positive and meaningful difference in the lives of people for Christ." I could simplify my mission to "edify others for Christ."

I know and fully understand that I am a work in progress. I have not fully attained what I shall be. Yet I want to help others on their journey to the Creator. Is anything more fulfilling than seeing people mature in their relationship with God and knowing you have been part of their journey?

What about you? Where is edification of others on your priority list? Is it near the top or do you rarely think about it? We do not hear the word "edify" too often so I wonder if may have trouble identifying how one edifies another. In its simplest form, to edify others is to put their needs before your own. Is that not the essence of living the Christian life?

1 Corinthians 10:24 (NIV) 24 No one should seek their own good, but the good of others.

Father, we all live busy lives filled with all kinds of activities. Remind us that edifying others is part of our higher calling. Thank You.

203.PREDISPOSITION

Romans 3:23 (NASB) for all have sinned and fall short of the glory of God

I don't come across the word "predisposition" too often. But it is something we all have. Perhaps we do not want to talk about it. It means we tend towards a certain viewpoint and it does not matter much if our viewpoint matches up with the facts or even if it is useful.

I will use myself as an example. I have a predisposition to resist authority. To this day I do not like people telling me what to do. Even when I know they want the best for me or the situation. I have some theories about why I have this predisposition, but they are not relevant. What is relevant is that my predisposition to resist authority has NOT served me well over the years.

Even though I know I am predisposed in this area, and I know it is NOT a useful disposition, it is still my "go to" place when someone wants to exercise their rightful authority over me. I am amazed at how much influence the flesh can have over me.

What does one do with a negative predisposition? We could say, "well, that is just me" and continue down the same path even when it can be destructive. Or I could blame it on the devil and say, "he made me do it." Or I can blame it on my circumstances, or the culture. Any excuse will do, so long as I can continue to do what I am predisposed to do, even when it is sin.

But wait. Are we not Christians? Have we not been set free from the bondage of sin and our sinful nature? The complicated answer is "yes, we have, but, no, not yet." This is the now and not yet dilemma of becoming all we will be in Christ Jesus.

My resistance to authority is another opportunity to "do battle" with my flesh, to yield to what is good, and useful and uplifting and encouraging and not yield to my predisposition.

Here is the point of this devotion. What predispositions do you have that are not aligned with the word of God? Are you engaging them in "battle" or are you yielding territory to the enemy?

Oh, Father, awaken us from our slumbers and give us grace to give you glory, even when faced with predispositions that are not useful. Thank You.

204.INSPIRE

Jeremiah 32:40 (NIV) I will make an everlasting covenant with them: I will never stop doing good to them, and I will inspire them to fear me, so that they will never turn away from me.

This word came to me via my daughter, Lisa. She told me it was one of her favorite words. I wondered why at the time. As I reflected, I came to understand that many of the wonderful, creative, good works of mankind were the result of inspiration.

Where did I get that idea from? Could it be simple inspiration? Not sure, but from time to time thoughts and words seem to "pop" into my head from "out of nowhere." I am confident that this is a common experience. Do you agree?

But that is not the kind of inspiration I want to focus on this morning. Instead of being inspired from "out of nowhere" we have the Word of God to inspire us.

2 Timothy 3:16-17 (NASB) All Scripture is inspired by God and profitable for teaching, for reproof, for correction, for training in righteousness; so that the man of God may be adequate, equipped for every good work.

I am convinced that the early church members lived inspired lives. Despite severe persecution and hardships they literally turned the world "upside down" in just a few hundred years. Why? Could it be that they were inspired to live their faith regardless of their circumstances?

Could it be that they loved one another despite their differences? Could it be that they prayed for their enemies even as they were being killed by them? Could it be that they gave generously to all in need?

Could it be that they were not entrapped by the culture of the time? Could it be that they lived lives inspired by God's Holy Word?

Lord, thank You for Your Inspired word. Do not let us read it without becoming inspired to live it out for You. Thank You.

205.INSPIRE (2)

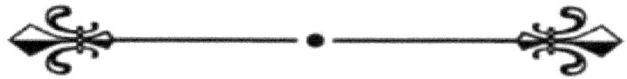

2 Peter 1:13-14 (ASV) And I think it right, as long as I am in this tabernacle, to stir you up by putting you in remembrance; knowing that the putting off of my tabernacle cometh swiftly, even as our Lord Jesus Christ signified unto me.

Yesterday we briefly looked at inspiration that "comes out of no-where" and inspiration that comes from the Word of God. Consider Peter's words in today's verse. It seems reasonable to understand the words, "to stir you" as meaning to inspire you.

God let Peter know that his days remaining on this earth were coming to a close (the putting off of my tabernacle cometh swiftly). Despite facing the end of his life, he still thought it important to "stir them up" or to inspire them.

Yes, we can be inspired by one another. Over the years I have been inspired by a few people. What stands out is that most are believers whom we ministered to while they were at death's door. With no exception, they died with peaceful and grateful hearts. They had settled spirits as they approached the fulfillment of their "number of days."

These experiences inspire me to finish well. With the grace of God, "finishing well" is the normal experience of many followers of Jesus.

I have been greatly inspired by "famous" Christians of years gone by. I have read their biographies and been inspired to live a life that is pleasing to God, regardless of circumstances. Because of their example, I am able to "keep going" even when I want to give up.

For me, I am inspired by watching believers grow in their relationship with God and with one another. As I witness people forgive others, I am reminded that I can do the same. As I see acts of generosity, I know I am capable of giving as well. As I observe people caring for others with great patience, I am encouraged to do likewise. When I see the suffering of Christians around the world, I am strengthened in the knowledge that I can prevail in Christ, regardless of my circumstances. As I watch believers face various physical challenges and yet continue to glorify God, I am motivated to follow their example. And as I witness everyday miracles in the lives of others, I remain hopeful for God's unexpected blessings in my own life.

Father, we are on such an adventure. You inspire us through happenstance, Your Word and one another. Let it be said of us that we encourage and inspire one another. Thank You.

206.INSPIRE (3)

Psalms 65:8 (NLT) Those who live at the ends of the earth stand in awe of your wonders. From where the sun rises to where it sets, you inspire shouts of joy.

Psalms 139:14 (NIV) I praise you because I am fearfully and wonderfully made; your works are wonderful, I know that full well.

Romans 1:20 (NIV) For since the creation of the world God's invisible qualities—his eternal power and divine nature—have been clearly seen, being understood from what has been made, so that people are without excuse.

One of the sad things about human nature is that we become conditioned to see God's wonders as normal. The first time we notice something spectacular we are amazed and maybe even inspired. But, as we encounter the same thing day after day, it becomes routine and normal and no longer a source of amazement or inspiration.

Having been brought up in the Bronx, I hardly knew what a tree was, and I had certainly never grown anything. I remember the first time I was told to, "stick a branch in the ground and it will grow." I thought, "no way." But I stuck it in the ground, and it grew. I have been inspired to grow things ever since.

Over time I was no longer amazed. I just took it for granted, until maybe 20 years ago. I asked God to reveal Himself and His principles through His creation, particularly plants.

As I think back, I am reminded over and over of His faithfulness in answering that prayer. I look at the wonder of a tiny seed, so small it can hardly be seen. Yet it becomes a living thing that brings beauty and pleasure. I am still amazed. Oh, thank You Lord!

Dear God, please open our eyes. Inspire and amaze us as we gaze at the wonders of Your Creation all around us. Please stop us. Let us take time to "smell the roses" and to praise You, the Creator of the universe. Oh, what a day it will be when we see You face to face, and we experience all of Your creation in its wonderful glory. What an amazing thought. Thank You.

207. INSPIRE (4)

Psalms 1:2-3 (NIV) but whose delight is in the law of the LORD, and who meditates on his law day and night. That person is like a tree planted by streams of water, which yields its fruit in season and whose leaf does not wither—whatever they do prospers.

2 Timothy 2:7 (TPT) Carefully consider all that I've taught you, and may our Lord inspire you with wisdom and revelation in everything you say and do.

As wonderful as it is to be inspired and amazed, it is not the goal. Inspiration is like getting in the game, or getting up to bat. You must act on the inspiration or it will become little more than a memory, or a dream, or a wish.

Look back at your own life. Have you ever seen someone do something that amazed you and felt truly inspired? You told yourself, "I can do that." Time passes and it never happens. Perhaps there was an attempt. Maybe you tried, but success slipped away because of—well, you know, life, circumstances, or anything else that got in the way.

What fascinates me is that when we are inspired, we crave the joy of that inspiration. Yet, more often than not, we fall short of the desire—and the discipline required to turn it into reality.

For example, many of us have been inspired by someone who seems to know the scriptures really well. We think, "I could be like that." The reality is that it will take years of study, dedication, discipline and applying God's word. Unless we really desire this deeply, we will not endure the discipline needed to make the inspiration true for ourselves.

Sometimes our difficulty is not in desire or discipline but we become too busy with what is not important.

Matthew 13:22 (NIV) The seed falling among the thorns refers to someone who hears the word, but the worries of this life and the deceitfulness of wealth choke the word, making it unfruitful.

Oh, Father, there is inspiration all around us. Inspire us and give us the desire and discipline to pursue Your presence above everything else. Thank You.

208.FORSAKEN

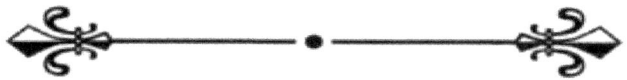

Revelation 2:3-4 (NIV) You have persevered and have endured hardships for my name, and have not grown weary. Yet I hold this against you: You have forsaken the love you had at first.

1 Corinthians 13:1-3 (NIV) If I speak in the tongues of men or of angels, but do not have love, I am only a resounding gong or a clanging cymbal. If I have the gift of prophecy and can fathom all mysteries and all knowledge, and if I have a faith that can move mountains, but do not have love, I am nothing. If I give all I possess to the poor and give over my body to hardship that I may boast, but do not have love, I gain nothing.

My dear brothers and sisters, can you see how important it is to act in love (not just feel love) towards one another? God has placed a calling on your life (and mine) to vertical and horizontal loving relationships. We are called to love God (vertical relationship) with all our hearts. We are also called to love one another (horizontal relationship) as we love ourselves.

This is the cross we bear. We die to self. We prefer to love instead of pleasing our own selves. It is the cross that we have been called to. Nothing else will satisfy the calling God has placed upon our lives.

How does one love God? It begins with intentionally spending time in His presence. Much more than the casual prayers we often utter. Intentional time set aside to be with God is the path for growing in knowledge, understanding, love and intimacy of God.

We must not depend on others to take us there, not even the best of pastors and teachers. You take this journey yourself, going where only you can go in your relationship with God.

How do we love one another? Again, the answer is mostly presence. It is the willingness to be with another and to prefer their needs over your own. Being kind when they are not kind. Generous despite not having enough. Praying and caring for one another. Seeking to do them good whenever we have opportunity.

Unless we come to this place of practicing the presence of God and being present with others, we will never know the intimacy of our calling with Jesus. Let us lay aside our busyness and seek after Him with all our being.

Father, please lead and teach us to love You and one another. Thank You.

209 NICOLAITANS.

Revelation 2:6 (NIV) But you have this in your favor: You hate the practices of the Nicolaitans, which I also hate.

Luke 16:13 (NASB) No servant can serve two masters; for either he will hate the one and love the other, or else he will be devoted to one and despise the other. You cannot serve God and wealth."

I have prayed through the Psalms and am now praying through the New Testament. I highly recommend this practice. There is no schedule. I do as little as a verse or two a day. It is very meaningful to take God's word and pray it back to Him.

I write out my prayers because otherwise my mind tends to wander. By writing, I am forced to slow down and give serious thought to what I am praying about. The other day, I came to Revelations 2:6 and realized I did not know what the "practice of the Nicolaitans" was. I looked it up and here is what I found.

It is having one foot in the world and one foot out. It is trying to follow Jesus while also following our worldly desires. It is viewing sexual and other sins as nothing more than simple pleasures, mere expressions of our humanity and certainly not sin.

We may have many professing Christians who are Nicolaitans in the church in America today. Even some "main line" denominations are ordaining, approving and "blessing" relationships that are clearly outside of scriptures. We often find ourselves seeking after the good things of this life, to please ourselves. Frequently they become our idols. We worship the idols of success, materialism, wealth, social status, sports, hobbies, celebrities, social media, etc.

Father, please purify our hearts and minds. Let us not be double minded and try to worship You and the pleasures of this world. Lead us to be singularly devoted to You. Thank You.

210.RICH

Revelation 2:9 (NIV) I know your afflictions and your poverty—yet you are rich! I know about the slander of those who say they are Jews and are not, but arc a synagogue of Satan.

John 14:27 (NIV) Peace I leave with you; my peace I give you. I do not give to you as the world gives. Do not let your hearts be troubled and do not be afraid.

The pursuit of success, riches, fame, and fortune is "drummed" into us from very early in our lives. Frequently our parents want us to be more successful than they have been. Our schools are mostly designed to give us skills that promote success in the marketplace. We are reminded repeatedly of how important it is to get an education or a marketable skill.

Our institutions, including the church, often give more honor to those who have "made it." Members with nicer homes, cars, or furniture are sometimes seen as more important or valuable.

Jesus challenged the social norms of His time, including the pursuit of wealth. Consider His command in Matthew 6 to seek Him first. He promises to provide what we need, though not always what we want, when we place Him at the center of our priorities. The religious leaders of His day scoffed at Him. Do we not do the same when we offer God only lip service?

The pursuit of wealth does not satisfy. When was the last time you met a wealthy person who thought they had "enough"? It is a relentless search to get more, be more successful, be more powerful, be more esteemed etc. There is no end unless we stop the pursuit of what this world has to offer and instead pursue the true giver of all blessings.

Father, Your word makes it clear, afflictions and poverty do not make us poor. Our riches come from our relationship with You. We are rich in You. Thank You.

211.REGENERATIVE

1 Peter 1:3 (NIV) Praise be to the God and Father of our Lord Jesus Christ! In his great mercy he has given us new birth into a living hope through the resurrection of Jesus Christ from the dead

I recently read articles about regenerative farming/gardening. I am intrigued. It is a concept for growing plants, food, trees and even forests by replenishing the soil instead of taking life out of the soil. It goes a bit past organic gardening by reviving the soil so that it can produce all that it was originally meant to produce. I am not a practitioner yet but I am dabbling.

But today's devotion is not about the soil of the earth but rather the soil of our souls. The Greek word ἀναγεννάω (anagennaō) is translated as "new birth," and it means to regenerate or to bring life back to what it was originally intended to be.

Is that not what happens to us when we yield our lives to Christ? The old is gone. Our old ways, our old desires, our old ambitions, our old pleasures all done away with. In their place are new ways, desires, ambitions, and pleasures. Regeneration releases us to be truly human in Jesus Christ. We express ourselves in self-giving rather than with self-assertion.

From what I have read (and observed in old growth forests) regenerated soil provides a more abundant life than most of us have experienced. The same should be true for us who have experienced the regeneration of the new birth. The roots of our spiritual lives are now deeply set into the rich soil of Jesus Christ. It is this new life that enables us to endure and even to prosper in this life, even when it is difficult.

The regenerative process is not an overnight fix. It can take years and even generations to restore lost forests and farmlands. So it is with us. If we persist in Christ and do not lose heart, we too will experience regeneration in this world and the next.

Father, thank You for the quiet work You are doing in our lives, for being the regenerative force that gives us a new life in You.

212.DEATH

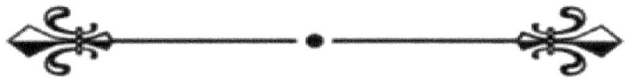

Revelation 2:11 (NIV) Whoever has ears, let them hear what the Spirit says to the churches. The one who is victorious will not be hurt at all by the second death.

Today's word came as a surprise to me. Yesterday we talked about the New Birth and regeneration. Today we talk about death. Of course, the regenerative life requires death. The death of self.

The "secret" of regenerative soil is the death of living things so they can be transformed into new soil that is alive and teeming with life. The "secret" to the new birth is the death of ourselves and submission to the Lordship of Jesus.

When soil is regenerated there is no sign of what it used to be. Even the hard stuff like eggshells, small branches, and oak leaves are no longer recognizable. And so it should be with us. When we are fully regenerated there should be no sign of what we were, only what we have become.

1 Corinthians 6:11 (NIV) And that is what some of you were. But you were washed, you were sanctified, you were justified in the name of the Lord Jesus Christ and by the Spirit of our God.

You and I are still in the compost pile of our lives. We are works in progress (Phil 1:6) and we are not yet what we shall become (now and not yet). But do not give up or be discouraged. The hard things in our lives will die and be regenerated. The old will be no more and in its place will be a new living being. Oh, what a day that will be.

Lord, I thank You so much for the promise of eternal life in Your presence. Let me not in any way be afraid of dying to my old self. Let it be gone and replaced by the new me in Christ.

213.CROWN

Revelation 2:10 (NIV) Do not be afraid of what you are about to suffer. I tell you, the devil will put some of you in prison to test you, and you will suffer persecution for ten days. Be faithful, even to the point of death, and I will give you life as your victor's crown.

1 Corinthians 9:24-27 (NIV) Do you not know that in a race all the runners run, but only one gets the prize? Run in such a way as to get the prize. Everyone who competes in the games goes into strict training. They do it to get a crown that will not last, but we do it to get a crown that will last forever. Therefore I do not run like someone running aimlessly; I do not fight like a boxer beating the air. No, I strike a blow to my body and make it my slave so that after I have preached to others, I myself will not be disqualified for the prize.

We do not often hear of people seeking to get a crown. In the ancient world it was a very understandable and visible symbol of distinction gained by a victory or achievement.

The Life Application Bible Commentary states, "in ancient Rome this was the most sought-after prize. To have gained this wreath meant that one had done special acts for Rome and would be considered a patron of the Empire. This can be compared to being knighted in England."

Today crowns are difficult to come by and few have achieved them. In the spiritual world, however, all of us can have one or more. If you consider today's verses, to get a crown in God's kingdom may mean suffering loss, even your life. To receive a crown may require great discipline, i.e. not living aimlessly or without intention.

Are you interested in a crown? Are you willing to discipline yourself to receive the crown(s) God has prepared for you? Or will you arrive at God's kingdom with nothing to offer?

Revelation 4:10 (NIV) the twenty-four elders fall down before him who sits on the throne and worship him who lives for ever and ever. They lay their crowns before the throne.

Father, I find this life to be full, full of mundane tasks, struggles and difficulties. In all of this let me keep my eyes on You and the crown. Thank You.

214.INTERRUPTIONS

Mark 6:34 (NIV) When Jesus landed and saw a large crowd, he had compassion on them, because they were like sheep without a shepherd. So he began teaching them many things.

James 5:8-9 (NIV) You too, be patient and stand firm, because the Lord's coming is near. Don't grumble against one another, brothers and sisters, or you will be judged. The Judge is standing at the door!

How do you handle interruptions? I am much better now than I used to be, but I can still find them annoying. The other day I went to start the car and I got the message, "cannot find key." I thought, "what is your problem? The key is in my pocket." But the key battery decided it was time to go "moi moi" (sleep). I was annoyed because taking care of the battery was not part of my plans.

Yes, it was a small thing. I have a readily available back-up. This could have been much worse, but was I thankful? No, I was annoyed and grumbling under my breath.

Here is the questions. Can the interruptions in our lives, no matter how trivial or unimportant, be part of God's plans for our lives? If He is sovereign and nothing enters my life except through His permission, then what is my problem? A little bit of my old selfish nature is apparently still alive in me.

I am confident that when Jesus was "interrupted" to Him it was not an interruption at all. As in today's scriptures, He took advantage of the situation and used it to advance God's kingdom. And that is where I am setting my heart and mind today.

I suspect I will be annoyed again but I intend to see it as God's sovereign will for me. I can take a deep breath, accept His will and use the interruption for His glory. Regardless of the interruption, people or circumstances, I will yield without grumbling or complaining to God's plan for my day.

Jesus, I call you Lord, let it be so, even in the interruptions of my life. Thank You.

215.DUPLICITY

Proverbs 11:3 (NIV) The integrity of the upright guides them, but the unfaithful are destroyed by their duplicity.

Psalms 119:113 (NIV) I hate double-minded people, but I love your law.

Duplicity means to say one thing and do another. It is being deceitful, false and dishonest. It is hiding behind a cloak of virtue while living a lie. It is acting one way with one group of people and another way with another.

I think it borders on being hypocritical or double-minded. The example that comes to mind is the many smiling faces in our churches that turn into chaos at home.

Or when people say, "I love you," but offer no tangible evidence. Or when someone is a model child at home yet a troublemaker at school—or the other way around. What you see is not always what you get.

None of us would consider ourselves masters of duplicity, would we? But is it possible? Could we be living lives of hidden contradiction when we fail to put Jesus first?

Are we living lives of duplicity when we attend to our own affairs before the needs of our loved ones or fellow believers in Christ? Could we be living lives of duplicity when we hear of Christians around the world suffering, and we do little to be of help? Could it be when we see the stranger in need and we ignore him or her? Or maybe when there are strangers in our church and we do not greet them?

I do not like what I am writing. It is getting a little too close to home. But I ask you, can you see it in your own life? We can talk a really good story but sometimes our actions are very far behind.

Lord God, I confess my duplicity. Please allow me and all who read this to see ourselves as You see us. Thank You.

216.WORK

1 Corinthians 15:58 (NIV) Therefore, my dear brothers and sisters, stand firm. Let nothing move you. Always give yourselves fully to the work of the Lord, because you know that your labor in the Lord is not in vain.

Colossians 3:23-24 (NIV) Whatever you do, work at it with all your heart, as working for the Lord, not for human masters, since you know that you will receive an inheritance from the Lord as a reward. It is the Lord Christ you are serving.

NO WORK PERMITTED:

These words suddenly sprang into my mind as I cleaned up after breakfast. I asked myself, "is this work?" My immediate reaction was, "it looks like work but it does not feel like work." I wondered, "why is that?"

My dictionary defines work as something that is done to achieve a goal. In that case, my cleaning up should count as work, right? So why does it not feel like work? The dictionary lists all kinds of work scenarios and activities, often involving pay of one form or another. It also refers to an accomplishment or an attempt at an accomplishment. Yet, as I read, I realized something seems to be missing.

When is work not really work? It is not work when the missing ingredients are present. Oh, you want to know what those ingredients are? Surely, you know. Think back to the last time you worked and didn't feel like you were working. Was it when there was joy in your heart as you did the work?

There are at least three things that can give us joy in our work. First is when we do something that we naturally like to do. Perhaps we are somewhat accomplished at doing the work. The second is when we are doing something intentionally for the Lord. The third is when we have found the place of service that the Lord has called us to. When all three are present there is sure to be no work.

It is not work (in my opinion) when we are in the center of the Lord's will, joyfully doing what He has called us to do.

Father, I thank You for the works that have been prepared for us to do. Make us into faithful, joy-filled people doing Your will. Thank You.

217 FINISH

1 Corinthians 9:24 (NIV) Do you not know that in a race all the runners run, but only one gets the prize? Run in such a way as to get the prize.

Do you know that the finish line approaches and that sometimes the very end of the race is the most difficult? That is especially true in longer races when physical energy and strength is all but depleted at the end. Hopefully we have kept our eyes on the prize and not wandered off onto a side road in the race of life.

I encountered an old friend in a grocery store the other day. It must have been ten years since we last saw each other. I recognized him immediately but could not remember his name. I am somewhat pleased that I admitted my memory lapse (I have been known to pretend). We chatted for a few moments and then he said something that really touched my heart.

He said, "Paul, one thing you said that has stuck in my mind all these years, and that is 'my goal is to finish well', and it has helped me a lot." This has been my goal for a long time, but I had no inkling I had ever spoken it in his presence. It warmed my heart to know something I said 10+ years ago had an impact on another person's life.

Having that "end goal" in mind has helped me to stay the course and not become overly distracted or overly discouraged. Yes, at times I do get knocked to the sidelines but having my eyes on the prize helps me to get back in the game of life and living for the Creator of the universe.

How about you? Do you have an end goal in mind? What do you want God to say about you when this life is over and you stand at the finish line?

Lord, I am deeply aware of the many distractions in life. Thank you for this reminder to keep the high calling of life in You as my focus.

218.GEESE

1 Kings 4:22-23 (NASB 2020) Solomon's provision for one day was thirty kors of fine flour and sixty kors of meal, ten fat oxen, twenty pasture-fed oxen, and a hundred sheep, besides deer, gazelles, roebucks, and fattened geese.

Although Solomon's dinner table included fattened geese, today's devotion is about another kind of geese. It is about the kind of geese that are out and about doing what geese (and us) are meant to be doing.

A week or two ago, May and I picked up breakfast at one of our favorite places (McDonalds) and we were sitting in our car enjoying our gourmet breakfast along with the view of the beautiful ocean and sky. Suddenly we noticed a very large V formation in the sky making its way from South to North. It was by far the largest geese formation we had ever seen. I would guess that there were close to 100 birds. It was an amazing sight even though they were way up in the sky, honking to one another as they were headed home for the summer.

Geese are good at supporting and encouraging one another as they make their long journey. We could learn a few things from them, I am sure. They work together as a team and achieve what would otherwise not be possible. They have shared goals and know where they are going.

There are not many references to geese in the scriptures but I did come across the following:

(Preacher's Commentary Series) "I love the famous story told by the nineteenth-century Danish theologian Søren Kierkegaard about the state of the church in his time. It remains just as powerful today in reminding us of what we are called to be together. He tells of a barnyard full of big, fat, sleek geese who had long since lost the ability to fly. Every seventh day, they would waddle over to a corner of the barnyard, and the biggest and fattest goose—probably wearing a black robe—would stand on a stump and proclaim the glory of being geese. Occasionally, while this goose was speaking, a honking would sound overhead, the call of a wild goose flying so high it could not even be seen. For a brief moment, the barnyard geese would stop, look, and listen in hushed silence. Then the sermon would continue, celebrating the joys of being geese."

Father, please make us "flying geese" and awaken us from our complacency. Thank You.

219.PROCLAIM

Psalms 9:11 (NIV) Sing the praises of the LORD, enthroned in Zion; proclaim among the nations what he has done.

Psalms 35:28 (NIV) My tongue will proclaim your righteousness, your praises all day long.

Luke 9:60 (NIV) Jesus said to him, "Let the dead bury their own dead, but you go and proclaim the kingdom of God."

If we are children of God, then one of our callings is to proclaim Jesus as Lord of the universe. To proclaim means to announce publicly. It is a sort of manifesto of whom we have become in Christ.

It has also been said that, if necessary, we should use words. The implication is that the way we live as Christians should be so reflective of God's transformation that non- believers become somewhat puzzled over us and curious enough to ask us "why are you different?"

1 Peter 3:15 (NIV) But in your hearts revere Christ as Lord. Always be prepared to give an answer to everyone who asks you to give the reason for the hope that you have. But do this with gentleness and respect,

Perhaps both are true. We should live our lives in such a way that people will ask us for the reason for our hope. We should also be prepared to tell them, always in love and with gentleness and respect.

It is a wonderful privilege to be a child of God. May we live quiet lives that reflect the peace God gives to us, yet be so bold and full of God's grace that the unbelieving world can't resist asking "what is going on with you?"

As I have said many times over the years, 'if people are not asking about your relationship with God something is amiss."

Dear Lord God, reign sovereignly in our hearts and minds so that we always reflect You. Thank You.

220.REPUTATION

Revelation 3:1-2 (NIV) "To the angel of the church in Sardis write: These are the words of him who holds the seven spirits of God and the seven stars. I know your deeds; you have a reputation of being alive, but you are dead. Wake up! Strengthen what remains and is about to die, for I have found your deeds unfinished in the sight of my God.

Is it possible to have a good reputation and be spiritually dead? Jesus thinks so. I am reminded of Jesus' words at the end of the Sermon on the Mount:

Matthew 7:21-23 (NIV) "Not everyone who says to me, 'Lord, Lord,' will enter the kingdom of heaven, but only the one who does the will of my Father who is in heaven. Many will say to me on that day, 'Lord, Lord, did we not prophesy in your name and in your name drive out demons and in your name perform many miracles?' Then I will tell them plainly, 'I never knew you. Away from me, you evildoers!'

Yes, it is relatively easy to earn a good reputation with outsiders. It is even easier to gain a favorable reputation within our own circles. We might even consider ourselves to have a good reputation because of the "good works" we perform. Yet Jesus looks beyond all of that. He examines the heart and our true motives.

Notice what Jesus says in Matthew 7:21: "It is not what is done that is important; rather, it is doing the Father's will." What is the Father's will? That we love Him and love one another. Whenever we act with motives other than love, we risk making much noise but gaining no true "spiritual points."

1 Corinthians 13:1 (NIV) reminds us: "If I speak in the tongues of men or of angels, but do not have love, I am only a resounding gong or a clanging cymbal."

Lord, may we frequently return to David's prayer in Psalm 139:23-24. Search our hearts and reveal any offensive way within us. Thank You.

221.FAIL

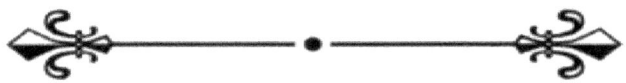

Luke 22:32 (NIV) But I have prayed for you, Simon, that your faith may not fail. And when you have turned back, strengthen your brothers."

Have you noticed that you are not perfect yet? Of course you have. If you are uncertain just think back to this past week. I am sure you can find an imperfection or two. Even the apostle Paul had his difficulties:

Philippians 3:12-14 (NIV) Not that I have already obtained all this, or have already arrived at my goal, but I press on to take hold of that for which Christ Jesus took hold of me. Brothers and sisters, I do not consider myself yet to have taken hold of it. But one thing I do: Forgetting what is behind and straining toward what is ahead, I press on toward the goal to win the prize for which God has called me heavenward in Christ Jesus.

I have often said that the Christian life involves a lot of falling down AND getting back up. C.S. Lewis put it this way:

"No amount of falls will really undo us if we keep picking ourselves up each time. We shall of course be very muddy and tattered children by the time we reach home. But the bathrooms are all ready, the towels put out, and the clean clothes in the airing cupboard. The only fatal thing is to lose one's temper and give up. It is when we notice the dirt that God is most present in us; it is the very sign of His presence" (C.S. Lewis).

Yes, we will fail, sometimes a lot. We must get back up (the sooner the better) and stay in pursuit of the prize of being IN CHRIST. Dead to ourselves and alive in Him.

Father, thank You for redemption of all who come to You and accept the saving sacrifice of Your Son Jesus. Give us strength, encourage us daily. You are there when we stumble. You are there when we fall. We are never alone because You are there. Thank You.

222.DRESSED

Revelation 3:5 (NIV) The one who is victorious will, like them, be dressed in white. I will never blot out the name of that person from the book of life, but will acknowledge that name before my Father and his angels.

Some of us like to "dress to kill," others couldn't care less about their outer appearance. Some like to coordinate what they wear, prefer to wear contrasting colors. We have all kinds of preferences when it comes to what we wear. It probably does not matter at all, in most cases.

Our clothes are just an outer covering and does not reflect who we really are. But is it important to God? In pagan times it was an insult to approach a deity with soiled clothes. Jesus describes what happens when people show up dressed inappropriately at a wedding.

Matthew 22:11-12 (NIV) But when the king came in to see the guests, he noticed a man there who was not wearing wedding clothes. He asked, 'How did you get in here without wedding clothes, friend?' The man was speechless.

Jesus is referring to the inner clothing of righteousness, but are there implications for how we dress? Long ago I formed the habit of asking God "what should I wear today," as I was about to get dressed. Sometimes I got a clear answer. That became my choice for the day. No clear answer? I wore whatever I wanted.

A simple thing, yes? Really necessary? Probably not, unless we truly desire Jesus to be Lord with no exceptions, not even what we choose to wear as our outer covering for the day.

For those of you who might be thinking, "Paul is off his rocker," I challenge you to try this for 30 days. See if God speaks to you about

His preferences for what you wear. I hope you will not stop at clothing. After all, if He is Lord, should He not be Lord of all?

Father, we are fully capable of making these simple choices on our own. Yet if I have died to self and am IN CHRIST, then my personal preferences no longer matter. I desire only to do what is pleasing to You. Guide us to seek You even in the ordinary, everyday moments of life. Thank You.

223.WHITE

Revelation 4:4 (NIV) Surrounding the throne were twenty-four other thrones, and seated on them were twenty-four elders. They were dressed in white and had crowns of gold on their heads.

Revelation 4:10-11 (NIV) the twenty-four elders fall down before him who sits on the throne and worship him who lives for ever and ever. They lay their crowns before the throne and say: "You are worthy, our Lord and God, to receive glory and honor and power, for you created all things, and by your will they were created and have their being."

I am not particularly fond of the color white for my clothing. Especially as I have gotten older and seem to be a bit messier. Working in the garden does not help at all. White shows all the imperfections. Perhaps that is why white is so prevalent in the kingdom we are headed for?

(Life Application Bible Commentary New Testament) To be "clothed in white" signifies being set apart for God, cleansed from sin, and made morally and spiritually pure. Revelation mentions white robes repeatedly. The believers in Laodicea are urged to buy white robes to cover their shame (3:18). The martyrs awaiting justice are described as wearing white robes (6:11). The twenty-four elders in heaven also wear white robes (4:4), as do the great multitude who have washed their robes in the blood of the Lamb, making them white (7:9, 13). Even the armies of heaven are clothed in white (19:14). The whiteness of these garments symbolizes the purity that comes from being washed in Christ's blood. Evil deeds stain garments, yet Christ can cleanse those sins completely. As Isaiah proclaimed, "Though your sins are like scarlet, I will make them as white as snow. Though they are red like crimson, I will make them as white as wool" (Isaiah

1:18 NLT). Only those who allow Christ to cleanse them from sin and clothe them in white will be able to reign with him (2:27).

I might have to rethink my thinking about wearing white.

Lord, we thank You for doing only what You can do. You cleansed us from our sin and prepared garments of white for us to wear in Your kingdom. Thank You.

224.MARROW

Galatians 2:20 (NIV) I have been crucified with Christ and I no longer live, but Christ lives in me. The life I now live in the body, I live by faith in the Son of God, who loved me and gave himself for me.

Now here is a word that I seldom hear or use. Marrow is the substance in the cavities of bones that produce blood cells. It is also often used to symbolize strength and vitality. In a spiritual sense, marrow is the essence of the innermost being. In other words, our core, heart, center, soul of who we are.

When I read Paul's passage in today's verse, it seems that he is referring to the marrow, the new inner self that He has become. He is no longer just flesh and blood and his own spirit. Rather, he is regenerated with the marrow of the Holy Spirit that now lives inside of Him. The old inner self is dead to Paul. It has been replaced by the life blood of the "new marrow," the Spirit of the living God.

How does one live so that the old self is dead and stays dead? This is difficult, as proven by our many failures. We try but no one has succeeded by their own power. It is not even remotely possible. So, what can we do?

Look again at today's. The answer is simple. The way that we die to self and live for Christ is the same way that came to salvation. Simply by faith.

You are probably thinking, "that has not worked for me." That may seem to be true, but have you truly surrendered all of yourself? Have you come to the place of total submission to the King of the universe?

Our old person is resilient and persistent. It does not want to die. For many of us, we state emphatically that we belong to Christ when the reality is we do not want to die. We are comfortable in our old "skin." Sometimes we are even fond of our "little" foibles. Yet all of that must die and stay dead if we are to live In Christ. That takes total and complete surrender.

Father, it is perplexing how we often want to do good and do not. Our old self is still alive. Please, Lord, lead us to live by Faith in You alone. Thank You.

225.OPEN

Isaiah 22:22 (NIV) I will place on his shoulder the key to the house of David; what he opens no one can shut, and what he shuts no one can open.

Revelation 3:7 (NIV) To the angel of the church in Philadelphia write: These are the words of him who is holy and true, who holds the key of David. What he opens no one can shut, and what he shuts no one can open.

We no longer live in the time of uncertainty between the death of Jesus and His resurrection. Now we know with absolute certainty that we can live our lives confident that we are in "good hands." Not like the old insurance commercial, but in the Good Hands that sustain us and bring us home into our heavenly kingdom.

It can be difficult to grasp that God is absolutely sovereign. Even when it seems as though He has lost control, rest assured that God is fully in command. Yes, the ruler of this world, Satan, is running amok, but just as God sets boundaries for the oceans, He has placed limits on the ruler of this age.

Do not fear, my friend, for our full redemption is drawing near. Right now, we live in the age of "now and not yet," but the day is coming when only the "now" will remain. Oh, what a glorious day that will be when the sovereignty of God is fully revealed!

(Life Application Bible Commentary New Testament) "Christ holds absolute power and authority over entrance into his future kingdom. After the door is opened, no one can shut it—salvation is assured. Once it is shut, no one can open it—judgment is certain."

Let us live lives that are utterly devoted to serving God and one another. While the door is still open may we be inspired to reach out to the lost and hurting in this world. Let God conform us so that the world sees Jesus in us.

Lord, thank You that we do not have to wonder "who is really in charge." We bow down to You. Reign over all of us Lord, let Your kingdom come, let Your will be done on earth as it is in heaven. Thank You.

226.SOON (SUDDENLY?)

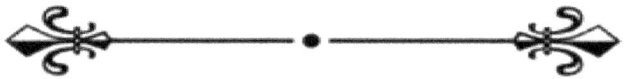

Revelation 1:3 (NASB) Blessed is he who reads and those who hear the words of the prophecy, and heed the things which are written in it; for the time is near

Revelation 3:11 (NIV). I am coming soon. Hold on to what you have, so that no one will take your crown.

When we hear or use the phrases "time is near" or "coming soon," we naturally expect that whatever is promised will happen within a short period. By that logic, it would seem that Jesus should have returned long ago, based on today's two verses. Yet even after more than two thousand years, we are still waiting.

It can be difficult to grasp that we and God experience time very differently. We are bound by seconds, minutes, hours, and years, while God is not. He exists beyond the confines of time, a reality that is hard for us to truly comprehend. Consider what Peter had to say:

2 Peter 3:8-9 (NASB 2020) But do not let this one fact escape your notice, beloved, that with the Lord one day is like a thousand years, and a thousand years like one day. The Lord is not slow about His promise, as some count slowness, but is patient toward you, not willing for any to perish, but for all to come to repentance.

So, it has only been a little more than two days since Jesus promised His "soon" return. I wonder if there is an element of surprise in His return? Not only will it be "soon," but it will be suddenly. When few are expecting Him, there He is! Oh, what a day!

In Matthew 24-25, Jesus and His disciples discussed the end times. Take a few moments to read through these chapters, and you will see that the exact timing is not as important as being ready.

Lord Jesus, our Messiah, I long for Your soon return. Please establish Your kingdom at any moment. Until that day, help us to be vigilant and prepared. Maranatha—come, Lord Jesus, come. Thank You.

227.PILLAR

Revelation 3:12 (NIV) The one who is victorious I will make a pillar in the temple of my God. Never again will they leave it. I will write on them the name of my God and the name of the city of my God, the new Jerusalem, which is coming down out of heaven from my God; and I will also write on them my new name.

Have you ever thought about what it means to be a pillar? A pillar is a strong, vertical structure that supports something, like a building or even a monument. But how can a person be like a pillar?

People can be like pillars when they are a mainstay in their community or churches. When they exhibit strength in times of difficulty or adverse circumstances. When they provide support to others who are championing what is good and useful. They are examples to others, particularly when life is difficult. Some might even say they are the backbone or patron of any given organization.

Consider this: 1 Corinthians 3:16 (NIV) Don't you know that you yourselves are God's temple and that God's Spirit dwells in your midst?

If we are the temple and God dwells within us, then being a pillar in His temple becomes deeply personal. If I am God's temple, then being a pillar in His temple is truly a place of honor.

How do we become pillars in God's temple? The answer is found in today's verse, Revelation 3:12. When we are victorious, God establishes us as pillars in His temple. But how do we achieve victory? The answer is both simple and challenging. The simple part is that God accomplishes it for us. The challenging part is that we must genuinely place Him first in every aspect of our lives.

Matthew 6:33 (NIV) ... seek first his kingdom and his righteousness, and all these things will be given to you as well.

My dear friends in Christ, please remember that we live in a culture and a time full of distractions. These distractions are not inherently evil, but they can draw us away from our primary mission of seeking God first and, in doing so, bringing glory to Him. I wonder if we can truly be pillars in God's temple when we allow ourselves to be consumed by what this world offers.

Father, the work within us is Yours to accomplish. Please guide us toward full and complete surrender. Thank You.

228.LUKEWARM

Revelation 3:15-16 (NIV) I know your deeds, that you are neither cold nor hot. I wish you were either one or the other! So, because you are lukewarm—neither hot nor cold—I am about to spit you out of my mouth.

For many years I was puzzled that Jesus preferred the spiritually indifferent people (cold). I think I misunderstood the context. You see, lukewarmness relates to the water supply in Laodicea. It was always lukewarm and not pleasing at all. To be hot or cold was a good thing. Either was much preferred to being lukewarm.

(LABC) "Many have thought that this cold and hot refers to spirituality—and that Christ would rather have "cold" people (without faith at all, or without any sort of growth) than "lukewarm" believers (who believe some). They take the word "cold" to be negative and "hot" to be positive, with "lukewarm" in between. Instead, both "cold" and "hot" should be taken as positive. Christ wished that the church had cold, refreshing purity or hot, therapeutic value, but it had neither. They were lukewarm."

The point is that God is displeased when His people lose their zeal for Him. Laodicea resembled America today—wealthy, self-sufficient, and convinced that we can live without God's presence in our daily lives. They may call themselves Christians, but in reality, their god is the pursuit of the pleasures of this world.

I think the words spoken here and in Matthew 7:23 ((NIV) "…. I will tell them plainly, 'I never knew you. Away from me, you evildoers!'" Should give all of us modern day Christians pause. Are we truly hot or cold? Are we on fire for God and a refreshing fragrance to the people around us? Or have we adopted the priorities and ways of our culture so much that we are lukewarm?

(LABC) "There is nothing more disgusting than a halfhearted, in-name- only Christian who is self-sufficient. Don't settle for following God halfway. Let Christ fire up your faith and get you into the action."

Yes, Lord, please do not let us be hearers only. Let us be about the work You have prepared for us to do with passionate joy. Rekindle the fire in our spirits to bring glory to You. Thank You.

229.REMEMBER

Hebrews 10:15-17 (NIV) The Holy Spirit also testifies to us about this. First he says: "This is the covenant I will make with them after that time, says the Lord. I will put my laws in their hearts, and I will write them on their minds." Then he adds: "Their sins and lawless acts I will remember no more."

There is a saying to "let bygones be bygones," or, in other words, do not dwell on the past. In general, I think this is good advice. After all, we have enough to deal with here and now.

Matthew 6:34 (NIV) Therefore do not worry about tomorrow, for tomorrow will worry about itself. Each day has enough trouble of its own.

On the other hand, lessons from the past can guide us in avoiding the same mistakes in the future. Surely, it is only the foolish who continue to fall into the same spiritual traps. The past should not be a source of worry, but a place of learning. If our past mistakes are keeping us down, we are the ones being foolish.

"Let your memory have its way with you. It is a minister of God bringing its rebuke and sorrow to you. God will turn what might have been into a wonderful lesson of growth for the future." (Excerpt From My Utmost for His Highest Oswald Chambers).

On the other hand, God has a "memory problem" when it comes to our past sins, transgressions and foolishness. He doesn't remember them. Oh, my dear friends in Christ, let us rejoice in these words. All our past foolishness, all the times we went our own way and did what we wanted to do, are buried deep in the pit of God's forgetfulness, never to rise against us again.

Dear Father, thank You for the gift of forgiveness and justification through Your Son Jesus Christ.

230.PURSUE

Proverbs 15:9 (NIV) The LORD detests the way of the wicked, but he loves those who pursue righteousness.

1 Timothy 6:11 (NIV) But you, man of God, flee from all this, and pursue righteousness, godliness, faith, love, endurance and gentleness.

Philippians 4:12 (NIV) I know what it is to be in need, and I know what it is to have plenty. I have learned the secret of being content in any and every situation, whether well fed or hungry, whether living in plenty or in want.

My dear friend, what is it to be? Am I to be content in all circumstances? Should I pursue righteousness? The answer is yes.

One of the greatest difficulties we face in America is that we are not content with our outward circumstances (finances, health, relationships, where we live, how successful we are, etc). We are prone to "want more." I know it is easy to blame this on our culture. Every advertisement encourages us to want more and we easily fall into the trap. I sometimes wonder why we Christians expose ourselves to propaganda that is contrary to God's direction for us. You do understand that it is our own fault, not our culture, right?

But pursue? What are we to be pursuing? It is not material things, or success, or even better relationships. We want to thrive, but we cannot thrive when we pursue the "wrong" things. The pursuit after things is endless. We are never satisfied, and we always want more. It is simply our flesh, the desires of the old man, that tries to find satisfaction in things that can never satisfy.

So, yes, we must learn to be content with all of life's circumstances, whether they are "good" or "not so good." At the same time, we should pursue righteousness that can only come through our relationship with God. My dear friends, I beg you to seek to know God intimately so that you are familiar with all His ways. Do that and you will find that righteousness (and contentment) that comes from being IN CHRIST.

Lord, you have given us much. Please let us hold it all loosely in open hands as we pursue KNOWING You intimately. Thank You.

231.WANT

Matthew 20:21 (NIV) "What is it you want?" he asked. She said, "Grant that one of these two sons of mine may sit at your right and the other at your left in your kingdom."

May and I sometimes watch "House Hunters" and the one theme that seems to be present in almost every show is "I want." I want "bigger", "grander", "more modern", "more vintage", "newer", "older", "closer", "farther". There is no end. Often the couple making the purchase have different desire and expect the agent to resolve their differences.

An interesting thing often happens when a "financially responsible" person looks at a house that lacks most of their "wants" and the price is high. Yet when a house satisfies most of their wants, the cost hardly seems to matter. Clearly, our desires often govern many of our decisions.

Benjamin Franklin wrote in his autobiography, "It is more difficult for a man in want to act always honestly." The problem is that when we want what we do not have, then we are not content with God's provisions and are prone to "bend the rules." Often getting what we want becomes more important than doing what is "right." Consider the following:

"A constant need for more, while seemingly innocent, can subtly coax us into compromising our character, integrity, and values. ….the greater the pull of want, the greater the temptation to compromise virtue. Think about it, a man or woman who is never satisfied with the amount of money in their bank account, who constantly wants more and more of it, is more tempted to be dishonest in their pursuit of it than the man or woman who is satisfied with what they have. The man or woman who is always wanting a bigger house, a grander vacation, a larger wardrobe, or a more luxurious car is often tempted by greed, selfishness, manipulation, impatience, and jealousy, to name just a few. When we live in a state of constant desire, it becomes far more difficult to lead an honest and virtuous life. (Joshua Becker)

Lord, please lead us to want only You and what You want for us. Nothing more Lord. Thank You.

232.HONOR

Revelation 4:11 (NIV) "You are worthy, our Lord and God, to receive glory and honor and power, For you created all things, and by your will they were created and have their being."

Today's word takes me back to a marriage workshop May and I attended over 45 years ago. It was led by Gary Smalley, who emphasized how crucial it is to honor our spouses if we want a relationship that is peaceful and full of joy.

What does it mean to honor a spouse? It starts with accepting them as they are, foibles and all. Think about it—don't you want to be loved exactly as you are, without having to change in order to be loved?

But acceptance is just the first step. Honor begins with acceptance but must move quickly on to holding your spouse high esteem. Why? Because they are God's gift to you. You spouse is not there just to make you happy but to help you become the mature man or woman in Christ that God wants you to be. When we honor our spouses, we put their desires ahead of our own. Their needs and even their wants become our priorities. Not because they deserve it but because it is right in the eyes of God.

We honor our spouses when we have short memories after they offend us. We honor them when we put aside our own desires to meet theirs. We honor them when we want to be with them more than with any other person. We honor them when we place few, if any, demands upon them. We honor them when we take care of them, when we comfort them, when we sit quietly with them.

There is so much more, but you get my drift. Let me encourage you to honor your spouse, even with all their foibles. God will guide you in honoring the gift He has chosen for you, if you ask. Do not be selfish—give yourself fully to the one God has chosen for you.

If you are not married, no problem. Look around you. Who can You honor? Do it intentionally and meaningfully. I believe that is what God wants us to do. Do you think our culture needs a "make over"? Do your part today by honoring the people God has placed in Your life.

Father, I know at times even acceptance is difficult but You said we can do all things in You. Make that true in our lives. Thank You.

233.WELL

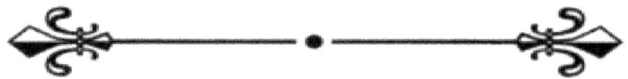

Matthew 17:5 (NIV) While he was still speaking, a bright cloud covered them, and a voice from the cloud said, "This is my Son, whom I love; with him I am well pleased. Listen to him!"

My dear friends in Christ, I assume that all of us would welcome God saying, "I am well pleased with you," when we stand before the judgment seat of Christ. (2 Corinthians 5:10 (NIV) We must all appear before the judgment seat of Christ, in order to receive what is due for the things done while in the body, whether good or bad).

Please understand that this verse does not refer to our eternal destiny, which can only be secured through the redeeming work of Jesus Christ. However, it is still important to understand that we have an incredible responsibility to live our lives well. Not just to secure heavenly rewards (though that is true), but because we are children of the eternal King of the universe and carry royal responsibilities, which can be summed up in the simple phrase: "live life well."

But what does it mean to live well? Today's devotional was inspired by a recent post by Joshua Becker. He offers wonderful ideas, including knowing your purpose in life, living according to your priorities, loving deeply, and giving generously. A lot of good stuff. But, as I was writing, I had the sense that we know all that already. We know it very well. And yet, like the "wretched man of Romans 7," we still ignore what is truly important in life.

How sad it will be when Jesus wipes away our tears because of a life wasted doing the inconsequential while the truly important things were left undone. Instead of hearing the words "well done" we are liable to hear "why did you waste your life on what is not important?"

Please let me come back to what I have said many times about the three "D"s (DESIRE - DISCIPLINE - DELIGHT). We must, in the core of our being, DESIRE to hear the words "well done," as we enter the kingdom of God. We must DISCIPLINE our lives (beginning right now) to let go of the unimportant and focus on seeking God with all of our being. If we do just these two things, I am pretty sure we will experience the DELIGHT of Jesus saying, "Well done." Oh, what a day that will be!

Father, let us turn our eyes upon You and seek You and Your kingdom with all of our being. To live this life well, as a pleasing offering to You. Thank You.

234.SEEN

John 9:25 (NIV) He replied, "Whether he is a sinner or not, I don't know. One thing I do know. I was blind but now I see!"

Hebrews 11:27 (NIV) By faith he left Egypt, not fearing the king's anger; he persevered because he saw him who is invisible.

Are you blind or can you see? Have you seen Him who is invisible? Have you seen Jesus? That was the focus of a devotion I recently read by Oswald Chambers. As Oswald might put it, "we are enamored with His gifts but not really with Him - for we have yet to see Jesus."

Ephesians 1:18 (NIV) I pray that the eyes of your heart may be enlightened in order that you may know the hope to which he has called you, the riches of his glorious inheritance in his holy people.

As I have said many times, we live in a culture that has many, many distractions. We like to put our minds on idle, forgetting that we are children of God and that our purpose is to give glory to God. I strongly doubt that playing games on our computers, scrolling through social media, watching TV, etc. contribute much to our maturity as Christians.

On the other hand, there are lots of mundane tasks in our lives that have great potential. Things like washing dishes, cleaning our homes, putting things away, washing the car, making dinner, etc. All are potentially useful when/if we do them with thanksgiving and offer them to God as simple sacrifices.

And then there are the not so mundane things such as comforting those in pain, helping those who in need, being a friend, honoring your spouse, resting, relaxing, traveling, waiting on God, enjoying life, etc. All have great promise in helping us fulfill our calling when done with the right heart and mind. And then there are the truly important things: spending quality time in God's Word, loving those who are difficult, giving from our need and not just our abundance, and persevering in prayer for those who struggle.

My dear friends, we will never know God intimately nor His power if we fail to attend to what is most important. We are called to be living sacrifices and to know Him with all our hearts (Romans 12:1-2; Philippians 3:10). How are you doing?

Dear Father, many distractions can be turned into worship, but there are also those that waste the gift of time You give to us. Please, Lord, let us purpose to live intentional lives for You. Thank You.

235.JUSTICE

James 1:27 (NIV) Religion that God our Father accepts as pure and faultless is this: to look after orphans and widows in their distress and to keep oneself from being polluted by the world.

There are many opportunities placed before us to represent our Savior. Perhaps one of the most important is to be concerned for fellow believers who are suffering persecution and/or other distress. Along with that, we have a responsibility to help relieve the suffering of our fellow believers, near and far. This world is not fair but we have a responsibility to uphold justice and do good whenever we have the opportunity. Is this not "true" religion?

(Life Application Bible Commentary New Testament) "Injustice, then, attacks God's children. When we do nothing to help the oppressed, we are in fact joining with the oppressor."

There are many Christian ministries that uphold the name of Christ and intentionally seek to relieve the suffering of both believers and non-believers. I hope that all who read this are supporting one or more of these ministries in some way. We can help address injustices through our prayers, financial contributions, and acts of service. No gift is too small. Even the simplest offering can provide encouragement and meet the needs of many. What do we call it when we recognize a need but choose not to help?

The heart of James 1:27 is to ask God for compassion for those who are treated unjustly, whether near or far, and to take action as He leads us to advance His kingdom.

Lord God, there is so much suffering among so many. Please, Father, deal with our hearts that our "religion" might be true and not just empty words. Thank You.

236.FULLNESS

Ephesians 3:16-19 (NIV). I pray that out of his glorious riches he may strengthen you with power through his Spirit in your inner being, so that Christ may dwell in your hearts through faith. And I pray that you, being rooted and established in love may have power, together with all the Lord's holy people, to grasp how wide and long and high and deep is the love of Christ and to know this love that surpasses knowledge —that you may be filled to the measure of all the fullness of God.

Are you full yet? I mean, do you have all of God? Are you experiencing His power through the Holy Spirit in your inner person? Are you rooted in love so that, despite being hurt, your normal response is kindness and gentleness? Do you understand and comprehend that God's love for you and me far surpasses anything this world can offer? Do you understand that all the knowledge of this world cannot even begin to approach the wonder of God? Are you so filled to overflowing with God that others notice that You have been with Jesus?

Yes? No? Work in progress? For me, all is true. There are times I have clearly wandered away from the fullness of God and there are times I can see God working to conform me into the image of His Son. Every now and then there is the fullness of God. The presence that is overwhelming and does what only God can do.

As Paul prayed for the Ephesian church, so I pray for you, dear reader, and for myself. I ask God to fill us with His power that we dwell consistently in Christ. I pray life's circumstances will deepen the love in our hearts for Him and that He will increasingly reveal His love for us. I pray people will notice we have been with Him, because we have.

Dear Lord, may the fullness of Your power and love encompass all we are. Thank You.

237.LIKENESS

James 3:9-10 (NIV) With the tongue we praise our Lord and Father, and with it we curse human beings, who have been made in God's likeness. Out of the same mouth come praise and cursing. My brothers and sisters, this should not be.

What do you "look like"? I mean, do you look like your old self to your friends and family? Or, have you taken on the likeness of Jesus?

"The proof that I have experienced crucifixion with Jesus is that I have a definite likeness to Him. The Spirit of Jesus entering me rearranges my personal life before God. ...The idea all through the apostle Paul's writings is that after the decision to be identified with Jesus in His death has been made, the resurrection life of Jesus penetrates every bit of my human nature" (Excerpt From My Utmost for His Highest Oswald Chambers)

We are works in progress. That is because part of us is not dead, i.e. crucified to the cross of Jesus. Somehow, we manage to "crawl off the cross" from time to time, acting more like our selves than like Jesus.

This must be confusing to those who are looking for something real. They see us sometimes "looking like Jesus" and at other times more like His adversary. Just as James says in today's verse, "this should not be."

Have you asked God to reveal ways or habits that are not useful for your maturity in Him? (Psalms 139:23-24(NIV) Search me, God, and know my heart; test me and know my anxious thoughts. 24 See if there is any offensive way in me, and lead me in the way everlasting.)?

Lord God, to take on the likeness of Jesus seems impossible at times, but nothing is too difficult for You, not even our stubborn flesh. Help us to die to Jesus Christ and to stay dead. Thank You.

238.TEMPLE

1 Corinthians 6:19 (NIV) Do you not know that your bodies are temples of the Holy Spirit, who is in you, whom you have received from God? You are not your own.

Paul refers to believers as "temples of the Holy Spirit." This might have been perfectly clear to the early believers, but I am not sure I really understand. Part of the answer though is in the sentence, "you are not your own."

The temple was a special place. In many ways, it resembled our churches today. We went there to focus on God, and our behavior often changed while we were inside. We smiled more, spoke softly, and even greeted people we did not know.

We understand that we have entered a "special" place and we try to "act the part." I have even seen people that I know are upset with each other who become all smiles when they enter the church.

If we are walking, talking temples that must mean we are

always in the presence of God because of God's Spirit in us. In other words, we need to STOP doing anything that might be offensive in the presence of God because that is where we are.

I know you are not a "gross sinner," but what about the small stuff? Are you wasting your time, energy and resources as a temple because you think you are in charge of yourself? If you are a born-again believer, that is foolish thinking. You are not your own. You were redeemed at a great price and all of you belongs to Your Redeemer, Jesus Christ.

(Life Application Bible Commentary New Testament) Just as the temple was a place for worship, sacrifice, prayer, and communion with God, so should our bodies be used to implement these high purposes.

Lord God, just as we behave differently when we enter a place of worship, I pray we will always "act whom we have become." May our practice match our position. Let it be that people nearby sense they are in the presence of God. Thank You.

239.WAITING

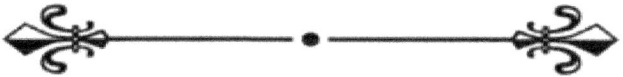

Isaiah 40:31 (NASB) Yet those who wait (hope in NIV) for the LORD will gain new strength; They will mount up with wings like eagles, They will run and not get tired, They will walk and not become weary.

Waiting is one of my least favorite things to do. But not all waiting is the same. Waiting in a doctor's office or at the department of motor vehicles can be frustrating, and all I want is for the wait to be over.

Then there are the waits that come with great anticipation, like a child graduating or getting married. The purchase of our first car/home or waiting to take a trip.

We can put situations like the above to good use simply by looking toward and trusting God in the process. Even waiting at the doctor's office can be useful if we practice patience, and who knows, perhaps God is bringing about an encounter especially arranged for you?

I am convinced that every situation in life has the potential to be an act of worship, even waiting when we do not want to; (1 Corinthians 10:31 (NIV) 31 So whether you eat or drink or whatever you do, do it all for the glory of God.)

But there is another kind of waiting. The waiting for God to give directions, for healing, for relationships, for peace. In other words, waiting for God to make a move. At times, He seems very slow.

He may seem slow to us, but He is never really slow. He is giving us the opportunity to practice patience and trust in Him. Maybe waiting has intrinsic value? Is it one of our teachers? Potentially, yes.

Lord, lead me to not wait with the attitude of "get it over with." Put in me the delight of waitingon You, to notice what You are doing. Lead all of us to get "on board" with the work You are doing all around us. Thank You.

240.PRESENCE

Job 2:13 (NIV) Then they sat on the ground with him for seven days and seven nights. No one said a word to him, because they saw how great his suffering was.

Over the years I read many commentaries and heard many preachers give Job's three friends a bad rap. I know much of it is deserved, however, they were speaking out of ignorance. What about us?

I wonder what it was like to spend seven days sitting in silence with Job, mourning with him over his loss. I have never done that. Have you? Do you know anyone who has?

From chapter three of the book of Job onward, we see the foolishness of Job's friends. They thought they had all the answers and were ever ready to give advice. It reminds me so much of myself. I always seem to have an answer for nearly everything. I hope God is making progress on keeping me silent more often.

But let us return for a moment to Job 2:11-13. Is there a profound lesson here for you and me? It is the lesson of presence. Sometimes we may not know what to say, or we may think we do, yet there are moments when silent presence is exactly what is needed.

Yes, there is a time for words, but not words that come merely from our own understanding. The words that bring healing are those that come from the Spirit of God. From Him flow wholesome words that can truly help those in need.

Ephesians 4:29 (NIV) Do not let any unwholesome talk come out of your mouths, but only what is helpful for building others up according to their needs, that it may benefit those who listen.

As we encounter sorrow, tragedy, grief and loss, let us truly mourn with others but be slow to give words of advice.

Father, please give us empathy for those who are suffering. Lead us to be a comforting presence as they mourn. Thank You.

241.BURDEN

Psalms 55:22 (NIV) Cast your cares on the LORD and he will sustain you; he will never let the righteous be shaken.

I find that getting older is fascinating in many ways. One of the biggest differences is that what once felt exciting now often feels like a burden.

For example, I used to relish the challenge of an unresolved problem, especially when others were stumped. God would give me the assurance that there was an answer, and He would provide it. These days, I tend to avoid problems. I used to embrace change, but now I find it burdensome. I prefer things to remain constant. Oh well, such is life.

What are we to do with such "burdens"? The short answer is in today's verse. I assure you that casting our cares on the Lord is not a virtue that many of us have mastered. How does one do such a thing and then not turn around and pick the burden right back up?

I realize that God must do this for me. Simply presenting my burdens before God in prayer continually, every day, every hour if necessary, and allowing Him to bring me to that place of rest in Him.

Matthew 11:28-30 (NIV) Come to me, all you who are weary and burdened, and I will give you rest. Take my yoke upon you and learn from me, for I am gentle and humble in heart, and you will find rest for your souls. For my yoke is easy and my burden is light.

Please understand that casting our burdens upon the Lord does not mean casting them away. Any burden placed on us by the Lord is a burden we need to willingly engage.

Burdens like helping the needy, resolving relational difficulties, loving a difficult person, being consistently kind, forgiving repeated offenses, etc. These are burdens we must come face-to-face with and deal with them in the strength of the Spirit (never alone).

Father, please give us discernment over which burdens need to be just cast away and the wisdom, strength and willingness to stay the course, walking in Your strength, for all the burdens that come from You. Thank You.

242.MARKED

Revelation 7:3 (NIV) Do not harm the land or the sea or the trees until we put a seal on the foreheads of the servants of our God.

Ephesians 1:13-14 (NIV) And you also were included in Christ when you heard the message of truth, the gospel of your salvation. When you believed, you were marked in him with a seal, the promised Holy Spirit, who is a deposit guaranteeing our inheritance until the redemption of those who are God's possession—to the praise of his glory.

Are marked with the seal of the Holy Spirit? As I read chapter 7 of Revelations I wondered how the end will come. Christians have many different theories about the end times. Many hope and expect to be raptured before things get really bad.

I lean that way because it is my preference. Then I consider the suffering church today. I wonder if this is not a great tribulation for them right now?

What is clear is that we do not need to know the times and the unfolding of events. We must, however, be assured that we are marked, sealed by the Holy Spirit. God extends His assurance of eternal life to those who are sealed. Destiny secured!

So, please, let me ask you again. Are you been marked by the Holy Spirit? If you say "yes, then what is the evidence? Is your life transformed day-by-day as the Spirit of God takes control of your life, all of your life? Or are you a pretender, pretending all is well when it is not?

(Life Application Bible Commentary New Testament) Having believed, we were marked in him with a seal, the promised Holy Spirit. In our daily lives, we bear this mark now, although others can't see it directly. Does your life reveal that you are God's possession? Do your words and actions convey that you are a marked person?

Father, even as I sit here and write in safety, many believers are suffering beyond my capacity to understand. Please, dear God, by Your Spirit lead us to full submission to Your Lordship. Thank You.

243.PENDING

Matthew 5:23-25 (NIV) Therefore, if you are offering your gift at the altar and there remember that your brother or sister has something against you, leave your gift there in front of the altar. First go and be reconciled to them; then come and offer your gift. Settle matters quickly with your adversary who is taking you to court. Do it while you are still together on the way, or your adversary may hand you over to the judge, and the judge may hand you over to the officer, and you may be thrown into prison.

Things left undone, things pending, steal our strength and energy. I have written about this before, perhaps because I see it in my life. Perhaps in yours also?

There are things I know I should do, yet remain undone. Even with full awareness, I do not act. It seems that Romans 7 lives strongly within me. Perhaps it does in you as well?

Let me use a common example. Suppose there is some "big" thing you know you need to attend to (like cleaning the garage, clearing the clutter off the table/desk, washing the pile of dishes in the sink, cleaning the mildew spreading on the house, cleaning the siding, pulling the weeds etc.).

You can make your own list. For some it can be very long. And that is part of the problem, the list is too long. We would rather hide ourselves in computer games, social media, sports, all kinds of distractions. Such is the way of the world. But should it be that way for followers of Jesus? After all, can you find even one thing that Jesus left pending?

Let us suppose you decide to tackle one of these pending projects. At first, it may feel overwhelming, and you might be tempted to quit before finishing. If you persevere, however, you will likely experience a deep sense of pleasure and satisfaction, along with a renewed energy that comes from a job well done.

My dear friends in Christ, let us attack our "pendings." Let us leave nothing undone. As we cross from this earth into the presence of the Father may it be said of God and man, "here was a faithful servant who left nothing pending."

Father, please lead us by Your spirit. Where You have given us something to do let us be faithful to do it. If we have stuff to do that is not from You, lead us to discard it so that we might attend to what is important to You. In all things Lord lead us. Please do not let our flesh control us. Thank You.

244 COMPENSATE

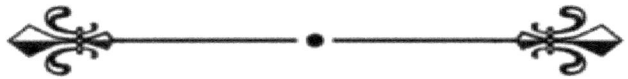

Exodus 21:26-27 (NIV) An owner who hits a male or female slave in the eye and destroys it must let the slave go free to compensate for the eye. And an owner who knocks out the tooth of a male or female slave must let the slave go free to compensate for the tooth.

This word came to me by way of a friend and, I must say, I had difficulty writing today's devotion. Compensation is paying for what is owed or making people whole again when they have suffered a loss.

This was a "standard" in the Old Testament. If someone suffered loss and if I contributed to that loss, then I was obligated to make that person "whole" again, as much as it was possible to do so.

In the New Testament we are reminded that the "great compensation" is to love one another. It is one of the distinguishing marks of a true born-again follower of Jesus Christ (See John 13:34-35). Love is not just a nice feeling (although feelings may be present). Rather, love is giving of ourselves, of whatever is needed, to another.

Romans 13:7-8 (NIV) Give to everyone what you owe them: If you owe taxes, pay taxes; if revenue, then revenue; if respect, then respect; if honor, then honor. Let no debt remain outstanding, except the continuing debt to love one another, for whoever loves others has fulfilled the law.

I often tell people that if there is a hurt out there with your name on it, you are responsible for addressing it. It does not matter whether you caused the hurt intentionally or by accident. If someone is suffering and your actions contributed to it, you must first take steps to make things right and offer amends. Only then can you return to worshiping God fully.

What happens when the compensation you deserve falls short? The best thing is to find a way to love them even more. If we are in Christ then surely this, too, is possible.

Father, in the simple mundane things of life and in the areas that are not so mundane let us be the first to willingly "step up" and compensate (love) others and help bring healing to their lives. Thank You.

245.MOUNTAIN-TOP

Revelation 21:10 (NIV) And he carried me away in the Spirit to a mountain great and high, and showed me the Holy City, Jerusalem, coming down out of heaven from God.

Technically, this is two words, but they belong together. Wouldn't it be wonderful to live on the mountaintop? No troubles reach that high. The air is fresh and clear, and the view stretches for miles.

The gentle breezes are cooling even on the hottest of days and there are few things more beautiful than seeing snowcapped mountains in the distance and a sun blazed forest in all its glory beneath your feet.

Being on the mountain top, physically or metaphorically, is a unique experience. Unfortunately, it is rare to find a person who lives on the mountain top. Yes, many of us visit from time to time. However, it is the special person that can honestly say, "I live my life on the mountain top."

Why is that? Why is it that the mountain top and the deep valley are part of the lives of even the most dedicated followers of Jesus? From great joy and splendor to sorrow and dreadful, awful and horrible circumstances.

I do not fully understand why, but I have seen time and again that it is life's difficulties that shape us into strong, courageous, and faithful individuals, able to complete the tasks set before us.

There is a purpose for the mountain top. It is not just to rejoice when we are in it but to encourage us when we are in the valley.

"Those moments are moments of insight which we have to live up to even when we do not feel like it. "Many of us are no good for the everyday world when we are not on the mountaintop. Yet we must bring our everyday life up to the standard revealed to us on the mountaintop when we were there." (Excerpt From My Utmost for His Highest Oswald Chambers).

So, yes, by all means enjoy the mountain top experiences in life, but make them more than just a memory. Let God's spirit use those experiences to lead and guide us while in the valley.

Father, thank You for all of life. Let us not grumble or complain while in the valley. Let us refresh our memories of the mountain top and be useful to You in the here and now. Thank You.

246.INTERCESSOR

Job 16:20-21 (NIV) My intercessor is my friend as my eyes pour out tears to God; on behalf of a man he pleads with God as one pleads for a friend.

There was a time when I believed that people could and should "pull themselves up by their bootstraps" and get on with life. I had no empathy whatsoever. That was me. Until God put me in that place where, similar to Job, I could not even pray as my soul was so downcast. It was a very difficult time, but I am thankful for the experience. I am still not an empathetic person like my May, but I have a much clearer understanding of how someone can reach a state where they are unable to even pray.

I still believe that many of our troubles are self-inflicted and we can and should do something about them. However, some crosses, even when self-inflicted, require outside help. Not all of us can always "pull ourselves up by our bootstraps."

An intercessor is one who stands in the gap for another, sort of like a "go between", between the friend and God. Sometimes, when we are in a mess, we cannot see clearly. But an intercessory friend might see more clearly and can be a more honest petitioner before God.

In these times, there are people all around us who are stuck in their troubles. I believe that we Christians have a responsibility to intercede for these people, and to not grow weary in our prayers.

I understand that we might believe their troubles are of their own making. Be careful of judging, lest you find yourself in similar circumstances. It is much better to intercede for others than to need interceding yourself.

In many of Paul's letters he asked the people to pray for him. In this letter I am asking you to be faithful to pray for the people in your lives that are stuck in their troubles. Be a friend. Encourage them if they will let you. Help them physically and financially if you can. Regardless of whatever else you might do, be an intercessor between your friend and God.

Father, we are all family in You. Please use us to intercede for one another. Thank You.

247. THINKING

Philippians 4:8-9 (NIV) Finally, brothers and sisters, whatever is true, whatever is noble, whatever is right, whatever is pure, whatever is lovely, whatever is admirable—if anything is excellent or praiseworthy—think about such things. Whatever you have learned or received or heard from me, or seen in me—put it into practice. And the God of peace will be with you.

As I reflect on thinking, several observations come to mind. First, every action, whether good, bad, or indifferent, begins with a thought. Second, every emotion is preceded by a thought. Third, our thoughts can be uplifting or discouraging. Fourth, while thoughts may seem random, we have the power to choose which to entertain and which to dismiss. Fifth, our thoughts shape not only our day but, ultimately, our life. Sixth, thinking itself is a precious gift of being human. I am not certain, but I do not believe animals engage in much thinking. Seventh, our ability to think is evidence that we are wonderfully made. Eighth, I am responsible for my thoughts. Ninth, I am responsible for the effects my thoughts produce. Tenth, I choose to stop thinking about all I am thinking about thinking—right now.

Sorry for what may seem like rambling. I often have no idea what I am going to write about until I put pen to paper and the above is one of those cases. What am we to think about what we are thinking? If I am going to have a good day (week, month, year, life) then it begins with what I think (what are you thinking right now?).

If you think your life is the "pits," I expect your thinking will prove to be so. If you think you have a lousy memory you probably do. If you think you are depressed, I bet you are. If you think you kill plants, you probable do. If you think you can't do something it is almost certain to be so. If you think you can do all things in Jesus everything becomes a possibility. If you think you are filled with joy and peace, I am pretty certain that is what will turn up. If you think this is a foolish devotion, so it is, to you.

Please do not take this to extremes. I am not suggesting that we can ordain everything that happens in our days by our thinking. But I am saying that we can have one heck of an influence over our lives simply by deciding to think about things that are positive and avoiding the negative. It truly is your choice, you know.

Father, You have given us so much, including the ability to think on what is good. Lead us to stop our "stinking thinking" and think the "thoughts of God." Thank You.

248. READY

2 Timothy 4:2 (NIV) Preach the word; be prepared in season and out of season; correct, rebuke and encourage —with great patience and careful instruction.

Are you ready for today? I hope you are. I know I am. We never truly know what our days will bring. We make our plans—and I believe we should—and we prepare in advance for what the day might hold, which is also something I think we should do.

Sometimes life takes unexpected turns, both wonderful and challenging. If you are alive, you already know this. But the question remains: are you ready? Are you ready for whatever completely unexpected moment might come your way today?

In Matthew 24:3 Jesus' disciples asked Him when they should expect His return and the end of the world. His response? Matthew 24:4 (NIV) Jesus answered: "Watch out that no one deceives you." In other words, be ready, be prepared, for a surprise. The rest of Mathew 24-25 gives us clues about the end of this age but the real theme of both chapters is to be ready, be prepared, because we do not know the day or the hour.

How does a Christian make sure they are ready? The disciplines (such as prayer and bible reading/study, acts of service, etc,) are helpful. However, the Christian is ready when they settle it in their hearts that they are fully committed to God. They are dead to self. What Jesus wants is what they want, no exceptions. Whenever or whatever God may ask of them, the answer is already "yes." Is that you?

"Be ready for the sudden surprise visits of God. A ready person never needs to get ready—he is ready" In other words, we should "be ready" whether we feel like it or not." (Excerpt From My Utmost for His Highest Oswald Chambers)

As we begin this day, ask God to give us a "readiness check." Are we truly ready for whatever He may allow into our lives?

Father, make us a "ready people" to serve You unreservedly regardless of the surprises. Thank You.

249.STRENGTH

2 Corinthians 12:10 (NIV) That is why, for Christ's sake, I delight in weaknesses, in insults, in hardships, in persecutions, in difficulties. For when I am weak, then I am strong.

Do you take delight in your weaknesses? Do you truly believe you are strong when you are weak? Today's statement from Paul challenges everything our culture teaches us.

It does not seem to make sense. Why should I be delighted when I see a weakness in me? Our culture teaches us to be strong, to fake it if we must, to show the world how tough we are. Never, never, show the world your weaknesses.

The Christian life is "upside down" in many ways compared to the world around us. This may be one of the most important truths to grasp if we want to be truly useful to God. When we excel at something, we are in serious danger of believing that it is our own ability, rather than God working through us. We tend to think it is our strength, knowledge, wisdom, understanding, and skills that allow us to succeed, rather than His.

It is easy to subtly shift reliance from God to ourselves. We might think, "oh, how good I am," but God knows better. (Jeremiah 17:9 (NIV) The heart is deceitful above all things and beyond cure. Who can understand it? - Isaiah 64:6 (NIV) All of us have become like one who is unclean, and all our righteous acts are like filthy rags; we all shrivel up like a leaf, and like the wind our sins sweep us away.)

Today, right now, is a good time to do a survey. What are your weaknesses? Name them one by one. Acknowledge to God how much You need Him in every area of Your life.

Let us also reflect on the areas where we are strong, surrender them to the Lord, and humbly thank Him for the remarkable gifts He has entrusted to us.

"Unguarded strength is actually a double weakness, because that is where the least likely temptations can most effectively sap our power. The Bible characters stumbled over their strong points, never their weak ones." (Excerpt from My Utmost for His Highest, Oswald Chambers)

Lord, please take all our weaknesses and use them mightily for You and Your kingdom. Thank You.

250.CAN'T

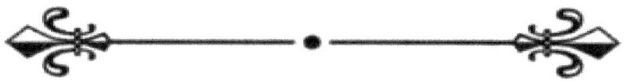

Philippians 4:13 (NASB) I can do all things through Him who strengthens me.

I am not fond of the word "try" as I think it is a substitute for not really doing what needs to be done even though we are able to do it. "Can't" is another word we use to excuse ourselves from doing something difficult because we really do not want to do it.

I cannot tell you how many times I have heard Christians say word along the lines of "I can't do that." And then moments before or after they proclaim the truth of Philippians 4:13. So which is it? Either you can or you cannot. Both cannot be true at the same time, can they? Maybe they can.

Today's verse has one of those "now and not yet" principles that show up all over the New Testament. From a human perspective, there are many things we cannot do, so "I can't" might be a useful and truthful term.

However, if I have died to self and am alive in Christ how could we ever think to utter the word "can't" if Jesus has told us we can? It is "through Him" (being dead in Christ) that "all things" are possible, meaning that there is nothing we cannot do IF we are in Him and He has given it to us to do. Got it?

In other words, every time we utter the words "can't" we are actually saying, "I am not in Christ, so I cannot." The next time we are tempted to say, "I can't" we really should say "I can't because I don't believe I can do it through Jesus."

"When it is a question of God's Almighty Spirit, never say, "I can't." Never allow the limitation of your own natural ability to enter into the matter. If we have received the Holy Spirit, God expects the work of the Holy Spirit to be exhibited in us." Excerpt From My Utmost for His Highest Oswald Chambers

Father, I know that some things in life feel like "I can't," but if they come from You, then I can—through You. Please help us discern the difference. Thank You.

251.TIME

Luke 21:7 (NIV) Teacher," they asked, "when will these things happen? And what will be the sign that they are about to take place?

My dear friends, for most of my Christian life, I have tried to avoid concerning myself with the "signs of the times." Over the years, I have noticed that many faithful Christians, far wiser than I am, often miss the mark as they try to declare, "surely now is the time." I wonder, however, if this might begin to change in the coming week or so.

Recently, during my devotion time, God gave me a series of words that all relate to the end of the ages. I am clueless right now about what He wants me to say. Perhaps it won't be about the end times at all, but I am confident He will give me His words to write.

Despite my confidence that I will hear from God, I also know my flesh can easily enter in and, instead of writing what God gives me, I end up writing my own thoughts. So, I have a request for all who are reading this. Would you please text me privately and let me know you are praying for me? Pray for discernment and that I write with clarity and under the anointing of the Holy Spirit?

Please pray that the Spirit will have access to all of me and that there is nothing in me to hinder His work.

Lord, there is much evil in this world today but we are told to "overcome evil with good." I ask for the anointing that I write only good words that flow from You. Thank You.

252.WHEN

Luke 21:9 (NIV) When you hear of wars and uprisings, do not be frightened. These things must happen first, but the end will not come right away.

The disciples were like many of us. We want to know the future. We want to know what will happen and when. I find it interesting that Jesus rarely answers people directly. Often there is a story to puzzle over as if He wants us to give it some thought. Maybe a lot of thought.

If you go to the gospel of Matthew, chapters 24 & 25, you will find a similar dialog between Jesus and His disciples (Matthew 24:3 (NIV). "As Jesus was sitting on the Mount of Olives, the disciples came to him privately. 'Tell us,' they said, 'when will this happen, and what will be the sign of your coming and of the end of the age?')

The disciples (unlike most of us) were very familiar with what we call the Old Testament. It was not old to them. For many, it was the essence of their spiritual lives. They knew that things were not right in the world, and they understood that a time was coming when the Lord God Almighty would make all things right.

Psalms 2:1-6 (NIV) Why do the nations conspire and the peoples plot in vain? The kings of the earth rise up and the rulers band together against the LORD and against his anointed, saying, "Let us break their chains and throw off their shackles." The One enthroned in heaven laughs; the Lord scoffs at them. He rebukes them in his anger and terrifies them in his wrath, saying, "I have installed my king on Zion, my holy mountain.

Christians are waiting for the King of Kings to laugh at the rulers of this world. How many world rulers govern with the fear of the

Lord? Not many it seems to me. A day is coming when the Lord will reign again in full authority and every knee will bow in complete submission to Him.

We do not know the "when," but we can be assured it will be. The emphasis in Matthew chapters 24 & 25 is to be ready (because we do not know the when). Are you ready? What is the evidence?

Lord, I was reminded by a friend that 1,000 years is like a day to you. So, in your time Jesus died just 2 days ago. Your return might be today or in 1,000 years or more. It matters not. Let us be faithful today, to serve You, to be about the work You have given us to do. Thank You.

253.WATCH

Luke 21:8 (NIV) He replied: Watch out that you are not deceived. For many will come in my name, claiming, 'I am he,' and, 'The time is near.' Do not follow them.

In the following verses of Luke, Jesus describes what we should watch for. It is my opinion that most Christians in America are unaware or unconcerned about these events that are happening outside of our immediate lives. What about you? Are you watching?

There are 16 events between verses 8 and 18 that Jesus tells us to be watching for. In the upcoming days we will look at some of these. Perhaps all. I hope that we see that the vast majority of these events are happening right now all around the world. I also hope that we will gain greater clarity in recognizing that many of these events are happening here in America as well.

However, we must keep all of this in context — "not yet." Jesus tells us that these events will occur before the end (Luke 21:9, NIV): "When you hear of wars and uprisings, do not be frightened. These things must happen first, but the end will not come right away."

In other words, this is simply part of life. There is no need to be overly excited, dismayed, worried, or fearful. It is just the course of "normal life" as evil plays out its hand across the earth and in our lives.

We belong to the King of Glory so there is no need to be perplexed or worried (Luke 21:14-15 (NIV) But make up your mind not to worry beforehand how you will defend yourselves. For I will give you words and wisdom that none of your adversaries will be able to resist or contradict.) "No worry," I like the sound of that.

So, I think that Jesus is telling His disciples (and us) that there will continue to be a season when things are just simply not right in this world. These events are just examples of life on this planet when the evil one is in control.

The disciples were perhaps mostly concerned with the when, but Jesus is concerned with our awareness. There is much evil in the world, and suffering will come—even for believers. He calls us to watch and trust that He will protect and care for us, so we do not lose heart (2 Corinthians 4:1, NIV: "Therefore, since through God's mercy we have this ministry, we do not lose heart").

Lord God, please awaken us from our slumber so that we may rightly discern the times we are living in. Thank You.

254. DECEPTION

Luke 21:8 (NIV) He replied: "Watch out that you are not deceived. For many will come in my name, claiming, 'I am he,' and, 'The time is near.' Do not follow them.

The first clue Jesus tells us to watch for is deception. As I see it, the church has been plagued by deception from the earliest of times. Paul fought against those who sought to compromise the gospel, and by around 350 AD, secular influences had begun to creep into church traditions. By the Middle Ages, corruption within the church was more common than integrity. The Reformation was desperately needed, and perhaps our world is in need of another one today.

If we look around, it is clear that deception continues to prevail across the land of Christendom. A spiritual battle rages on, yet many remain unaware.

The Bible teaches that the devil is real and that he controls the affairs of this evil world. His great objective is to defeat the will and program of God in the world, in the church, and in the Christian.

I would say that the church in America, with some exceptions, is greatly deceived. Am I being overly harsh? Consider the following news from 5/2/24:

"The legislative body of the United Methodist Church voted to repeal a 40-year ban on the ordination of gay clergy yesterday, one of several rule changes around sexuality adopted at their General Conference." (World News) If you read further, you will find that all kinds of "loving relationships" are no longer taboo, not even adultery.

The really sad thing is that this is just one of many examples of the modern-day church in America doing what they see fit regardless of what the Bible teaches.

Consider 2 Timothy 4:3-4 (NIV) For the time will come when people will not put up with sound doctrine. Instead, to suit their own desires, they will gather around them a great number of teachers to say what their itching ears want to hear. They will turn their ears away from the truth and turn aside to myths.

Jesus, You warned us to not be deceived. Please open our eyes, give us discernment and reveal Your truth to us. Thank You.

255.DECEPTION (2)

Revelation 2:4 (NIV) Yet I hold this against you: You have forsaken the love you had at first.

In yesterday's devotion, the deception I spoke of was rather radical. i.e. the abandonment of classical Christian orthodoxy by some main-line denominations and the acceptance of that by literally millions of people who are more devoted to their church organization than they are to the word of God. But I sense that you and I are more likely to get into trouble with subtler deceptions, perhaps without even realizing it.

The first that comes to mind is materialism or, as some call it, the "prosperity gospel," It is the distortion of the gospel that says Christians are entitled to all the good things in life. Even if it means getting into debt, devoting ourselves to acquiring more as we neglect loved ones and family. It is the deception that results in a spirit of dissatisfaction and continuously chasing after the next thing we "need."

Then there is the deception of thinking we can be "fans" instead of "players" in God's kingdom. It shows up when we go to church and pretend to worship but we are really only there for fellowship or to satisfy a sense of obligation.

Or, when we see needs that we could meet but we say no. Or, when we say we will pray and we do not. When we tell a person we offended, "we are sorry," but we do it again and again. Or, when we do not give generously to the advancement of the Kingdom. Or, when we fail to consider the needs of the persecuted church around the world.

There is also the subtle deception of conforming to cultural norms. Things like living together without marriage, spending beyond our means, or seeking so much entertainment that our sins begin to feel less serious.

We know we should not, yet we continue to watch our favorite shows and movies filled with behavior that we know Jesus would not approve of. We spend hours on social media or playing video games, leaving little time for God's Word. We make idols out of sports figures, musicians, movie stars, and others.

And then there is perhaps the most subtle deception of all, thinking we are really something when we are not.

Father, surely many of us are living lives where we are deceived to some degree in one area or another. Pretending to live a godly life in this culture is relatively easy. Please do not let us be pretenders. Thank You.

256.DECEPTION (3)

Matthew 7:22-23 (NIV) Many will say to me on that day, 'Lord, Lord, did we not prophesy in your name and in your name drive out demons and in your name perform many miracles?' Then I will tell them plainly, 'I never knew you. Away from me, you evildoers!

2 Thessalonians 2:9-12 (NIV) The coming of the lawless one will be in accordance with how Satan works. He will use all sorts of displays of power through signs and wonders that serve the lie, and all the ways that wickedness deceives those who are perishing. They perish because they refused to love the truth and so be saved. For this reason God sends them a powerful delusion so that they will believe the lie and so that all will be condemned who have not believed the truth but have delighted in wickedness.

I honestly thought we were done with the word "deception," but in the middle of the night, I woke up with a clear impression that there was more to say. I felt a bit resistant since I had already started the first draft on the next clue to the end times, and, besides, I had no idea what I should write.

However, early yesterday morning, two thoughts came strongly into my mind. The first is that we deceive ourselves when we think all is well with our souls because we do "good stuff." Good stuff like going to church, caring for people, being merciful and thankful and kind.

All the "good stuff" that we, as followers of Christ, are called to do. But is something missing? Have we lost our first love (Rev 2:4)? Could that be us? Are we so busy doing "all the right things" that our devotion to God has grown cold and routine? We do them because we feel we ought to, not because we love Him above all else.

The second thought that came to me is that we deceive ourselves when we want to see signs. We are frequently warned in scriptures to beware of signs. Why? Because Satan is a great counterfeit and is able to easily fool us. (Note: in today's verse, we learn that Satan uses all sorts of displays of power.)

Our reliance upon signs is evidence that our faith is weak. Instead of "trust and obey" we are more like "show me." A time is coming, and I personally believe it is here, when even the elect will be fooled. Why? Because we lost our true love for God and refuse to live by faith alone.

(Life Application Bible Commentary New Testament) "Pray each day for discernment to tell the difference between good and evil, so you will be immune to counterfeits. Saturate your life with God's love and serve him."

Father, please, God, we ask for discernment in all areas of our lives.

257.DECEPTION (4)

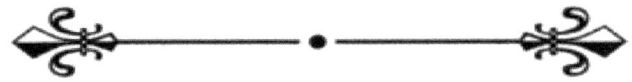

Revelation 13:12 (NIV) It exercised all the authority of the first beast on its behalf, and made the earth and its inhabitants worship the first beast, whose fatal wound had been healed.

Revelation 13:14 (NIV) Because of the signs it was given power to perform on behalf of the first beast, it deceived the inhabitants of the earth. It ordered them to set up an image in honor of the beast who was wounded by the sword and yet lived.

Surely, I thought (and I expect you did also) that we were done with deception as our topic. Yet, as I was praying, God brought one more thought about deception to my mind. The deception of miracles.

I think this can happen at any time but it particularly applies to those who are on the earth during the tribulation period. I know many (most) of us do not plan to be here during those times. However, just in case we do not have it right, it will be a time when many will be completely deceived into worshipping satan and the anti-Christ.

Don't think this could happen to you? You are probably right if you are His. On the other hand, if you are play-acting as a professing Christian while all the while being a practicing atheist in your heart, you could be in big trouble. And you will most likely be completely unaware.

(Life Application Bible Commentary New Testament (comments on the above verses)) The Bible repeats many miracles performed as proofs of God's power, love, and authority. But here counterfeit miracles are performed to deceive. This is similar to Pharaoh's magicians, who duplicated Moses' signs in Egypt. True signs and miracles point to Jesus Christ, but miracles alone can be deceptive. That is why we must ask with respect to each miracle we see: Is this consistent with what God says in the Bible? The second beast gained influence through the signs and wonders that he performed on behalf of the first Beast. ....Allowing the Bible to guide our faith and practice will keep us from being deceived by false signs, however convincing they appear to be. Any teaching that contradicts God's Word is false.

Lord, please give us the desire to know You intimately and to diligently seek Your presence so that we are not deceived.

258.WARS & UPRISINGS

Luke 21:9 (NIV) When you hear of wars and uprisings, do not be frightened. These things must happen first, but the end will not come right away.

I ask you, when have there not been wars upon this earth? No one really knows, but "Time Line for Wars" lists information on 1,500 wars since just the 1800's. Going to war has been happening since the earliest of time.

2 Samuel 11:1a (NIV) In the spring, at the time when kings go off to war.

Apparently "going to war" is the normal way of resolving conflict in a world ruled by evil. Unlike God's plan of reconciliation and mutual submission, we humans seem determined to war with one another and to force submission. Surely this is the "domination" theory in full sway.

We are not content until we dominate others, whether it be nations, governing authorities, bosses at work, or even family members. The concept of mutual submission is rarely practiced, even in countries considered "Christian".

This human tendency, very sadly, carries over into many relationships. Have you experienced the temptation in your own life? When we do not get our own way we often resort to "battling" our opponents.

Sometimes it is with nagging words, sometimes with threats, sometimes with withdrawal, sometimes even with force. We all have our own "club" that we find useful in getting compliance and submission from others. We may not call it "war," but it is an "uprising" against God's plan of mutual submission and reconciliation.

Back to discerning the times. Noticing that many are at war is not a very good clue that the end is near since wars and uprisings have been happening since the beginning and is not likely to stop any time soon.

The important thing is to ensure we do not contribute to conflict in our homes, churches, communities etc. We are in a war, but it is not against flesh and blood. Let us, as followers of Jesus, be the peacemakers whenever and wherever we can.

Matthew 5:9 (NIV) Blessed are the peacemakers, for they will be called children of God.

Yes, Lord, despite the conflicts "out there," let us be the peace makers who are Your children. Thank You.

259.AGAINST

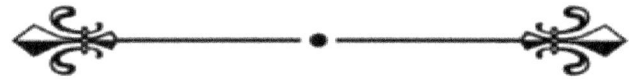

Luke 21:10 (NIV) 10 Then he said to them: Nation will rise against nation, and kingdom against kingdom.

As Jesus continues His dialog, He repeats the previous emphasis on wars and uprisings. We do not know the details, but we can be assured that this world will undergo much suffering before the end comes.

Consider the suffering of so many during the great wars, or the holocaust, or the ongoing suffering in Gaza and Ukraine and many other parts of the world even today. So much suffering. How can it end? Surely not by human endeavor. Was not WWI supposed to be the war to end all wars?

My dear friends, as Christians we must understand that when we respond to violence with violence we become just like those we are fighting against. We try to achieve peace by dominating others. When that does not happen voluntarily, we often resort to all kinds of pressures, including violence.

When Russia invaded Ukraine a couple of years ago, I was very angry in my spirit. I wanted the Russians to be crushed. The anger I had was palatable, until God reminded me that the anger of man can never work the righteousness of God. My desire for the Russians to be violently crushed made me morally just as guilty as they are.

This is a hard pill for me to swallow. I am learning that if I want to do evil to the one who is doing evil to me, then I am just as guilty (evil) as they are.

On the other hand, we are called to be peace makers in whatever capacity we can. With the suffering going on in the world today there is much we can do.

Pray for the individuals on both sides of the conflict who are suffering loss. Support organizations that are involved in humanitarian efforts. Pray for God to bring the warring parties to a place of reconciliation. Support efforts to bring about peace. Oppose all expressions of hate and anger, instead seek to be a balm to the suffering. Let us join no side seeking conflict and expressing hate. Rather let us practice learning how to love, even our enemies.

Matthew 5:44 (NIV) 44 But I tell you, love your enemies and pray for those who persecute you.

Lord, this is very difficult. Teach us to love even those who hate us. Thank You.

260.EARTHQUAKES

Luke 21:11 (NIV) 11 There will be great earthquakes, famines and pestilences in various places, and fearful events and great signs from heaven.

According to the National Earthquake Information Center, there are about 55 earthquakes every day, about 20,000 per year. That is a lot of earthquakes. Most are minor and we do not even hear about them. Then there are those where thousands of lives are lost, and destruction is extensive. Again, this is "normal." Jesus tells us we can expect these things.

According to some reports, as many as 20 countries around the world are currently experiencing famine. Each year, millions of people die from starvation—up to 16 million, according to The Powers That Be by Walter Wink.

Few of us alive today remember the dust bowls and the Great Depression in America during the 1930s. For the vast majority of Americans, hunger is something we only read about.

According to Wikipedia, in 2023 there were "swarms of locusts in Somalia, Kenya, Democratic Republic of the Congo, Djibouti, Eritrea, Ethiopia, Saudi Arabia, South Sudan, Sudan, Uganda, Yemen, India, Pakistan, Iran, Nepal[2,] and Burundi. There was also a major outbreak of locusts in Mexico last year. We, in the US, have not seen a major outbreak since 1877. Have you seen the locusts common to this area of Florida? Imagine hundreds of millions of them all over the place?

But once again, Jesus is telling us what will be considered "normal" before the end comes. He is saying, "Do not be concerned about these things. This is the ordinary state of life on a planet where the evil one holds sway." In America, we are especially blessed, having faced far fewer hardships than many other parts of the world. We also have more resources to respond when disasters occur. That is not the case for countless suffering communities around the globe.

So, what is the message in today's devotion? First, do not be concerned about the "when." Second, be concerned about suffering people and do what you can to relieve their pain.

Matthew 25:37b-40 (NIV) ... 'Lord, when did we see you hungry and feed you, or thirsty and give you something to drink? ......40 "The King will reply, 'Truly I tell you, whatever you did for one of the least of these brothers and sisters of mine, you did for me.'

Father, as we await Your return, let us watch and attend to helping people in need, here at home and around the world. Thank You.

261.FAMINES

1 John 3:17 (NIV) 17 If anyone has material possessions and sees a brother or sister in need but has no pity on them, how can the love of God be in that person?

It was not my intention to write a separate devotion on famines but, apparently, God has different intentions. As I mentioned in the devotion on earthquakes (May 11th, 2024), close to 16 million people die every year from starvation (The Powers that Be - Walter Wink). That is an incredible number that should make us shake our heads in disbelief. Then we do nothing tangible to make a difference. Starvation is such a remote issue for most of us in America that we have little sense of its effect on people.

A few years ago, I read about a World Vision worker who spent two weeks living with a family in a country experiencing famine. I do not remember many details, but I remember that in just a few days she was too weak to do anything, much less forage for scrapes to eat. Would it be useful for us to have such experiences? How else can we empathize with the suffering if we have not experienced similar suffering?

Although we may not have empathy for those who are starving, we can still reflect on their suffering and, with the Holy Spirit's guidance, do something to relieve their suffering. We in America have been given much. Are we not required to help those who are dying because of a simple lack of food? There are many Christian organizations on the "front lines" of helping these people. It is our responsibility to be part of the "team" and support their efforts financially as well as with prayer and advocacy. Let me know if you need help identifying such an organization and I will be glad to help.

The point of today's devotion is that we need to be concerned about people who are suffering (from lack of food or otherwise) and to not stop at just being concerned. Being concerned and doing nothing is callous at best. As followers of Christ, we have a responsibility to help others, especially our brothers and sisters in Christ.

Father, please speak to us, both individually and together, about how we can ease the suffering of others. Thank you.

262.PESTILENCE

Psalms 91:5-6 (NIV) You will not fear the terror of night, nor the arrow that flies by day, nor the pestilence that stalks in the darkness, nor the plague that destroys at midday.

Today's word is one I have heard but do not think I have ever used in conversation. I did not have a clear understanding of the word, so I looked it up and found it really means a total epidemic disease, like the bubonic plague. I immediately thought of COVID-19 and the flu epidemic of the early 1900s. If you look further, you will see that the world has endured many plagues throughout its history.

This is another form of evil that visits the earth repeatedly. It is not a sign that the end of the world is near. It is simply the way things are—ordinary, everyday evil, as long as the great liar holds sway over this earth.

Look again. What does scripture command? "Do not fear." Yet we know that fear still takes root in our hearts when we face the unknown and worry for our lives. Perhaps we do not take the word of God seriously when it tells us not to be anxious?

Philippians 4:6-7 (NIV) Do not be anxious about anything, but in every situation, by prayer and petition, with thanksgiving, present your requests to God. And the peace of God, which transcends all understanding, will guard your hearts and your minds in Christ Jesus.

I know anxiousness is a feeling that can come out of seemingly nowhere The above scripture is not telling us to never feel anxious. Rather, when we feel anxious, we must immediately turn to God in prayer and petition and not giving our anxiety any power over us. Instead, we crush it into defeat at the presence of Jesus.

This world is filled with all kinds of "pestilence" that can steal our peace, but the One who has overcome the troubles of this world is but a prayer away.

Again, the reminder. These things do not mean the end is near. It is just the condition of life on this planet.

Lord, if we spend too much time paying attention to world events, we can easily become anxious. Instead, lead us to focus on You and those things that are good and wholesome. Keep us in perfect peace in You. Thank You.

263.FEARFUL

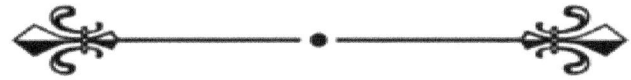

Luke 21:11 (NIV)11 There will be great earthquakes, famines and pestilences in various places, and fearful events and great signs from heaven.

Do you remember the 1962 Cuban missile crisis or the Indian Ocean Tsunami of 2004? And, of course, we all remember COVID 19 and the planes crashing into the World Trade Center Towers and the Pentagon. All fearful events. How about the floods and storms and fires that we read about in today's news? Not to mention the political chaos in our government and the confusion of religious leaders in some denominations. Or how about the mass shootings in America or the mass looting in some cities?

Gee, I better stop. That's a lots of stuff to consider as fearful, or at least worth our worry. On the other hand, that is just a lie from the old deceiver himself. We need not fear. Even though the world, at least in America, often seems determined to promote evil and reject what is good, do not lose heart. As we witness these events, we can take comfort in knowing that our redemption is drawing near.

(Life Application Bible Commentary New Testament) First, much suffering would occur as a part of life on earth, including wars, fighting among nations and kingdoms, and many natural disasters. These, along with fearful events and great signs from heaven, will mean only that history is moving toward a single, final, God-planned goal—the creation of a new earth and a new kingdom (Revelation 21:1-3).

We must guard against preoccupation with signs such as the frequency of earthquakes, etc. Instead, we must focus on doing God's will. Let us be purposeful in doing good. That is how we overcome evil.

Romans 12:21 (NIV) 21 Do not be overcome by evil, but overcome evil with good.

God, do not let us give in to the hate, anger, dissension, revenge etc. that is common today. If we do, then we become just like what we hate. We become who they are. We are to do good, to treat the people who oppose us with respect and kindness. We are to speak truth into a dark and dying world. We will if we keep our eyes on our Savior, Jesus the Messiah. Thank You.

264 PERSECUTION

Luke 21:12 (NIV) But before all this, they will seize you and persecute you. They will hand you over to synagogues and put you in prison, and you will be brought before kings and governors, and all on account of my name.

For quite a few days, these devotions have been about natural disasters and calamities that do not predict the end of the world. Rather, they describe the ordinary events of life in a world corrupted by evil. We accept these things as normal, and they are, whenever evil is at work. Yet in the kingdom of God, evil will exist no more.

As you read the above verse did you catch the word "before"? In other words, even before all these normal disasters we can expect something else. The persecution of the followers of Christ. They persecuted Jesus. Can we expect anything less? Followers of Jesus were persecuted from the earliest times. The persecution continues with apparent vengeance around the world. Perhaps the evil one realizes he is on a "short string"? Oh, what a day that will be when evil is firmly and finally defeated.

Matthew 5:10-12 (NIV) Blessed are those who are persecuted because of righteousness, for theirs is the kingdom of heaven. "Blessed are you when people insult you, persecute you and falsely say all kinds of evil against you because of me. Rejoice and be glad, because great is your reward in heaven, for in the same way they persecuted the prophets who were before you.

So, we have another "norm." The persecution of true followers of Jesus. Societies tend to persecute people who do not conform to societal norms. As America becomes increasingly immoral, can we expect anything less than enormous pressure for Christians to conform to society's immoral norms? As previously mentioned, some Christian denominations have decided to conform to our culture by accepting the world's practices as their own. Beware my brothers and sisters in Christ. Do not be deceived. Conforming to the standards of the world may allow us to escape persecution today but our future is bleak indeed.

Romans 12:2 (NIV) 2 Do not conform to the pattern of this world, but be transformed by the renewing of your mind. Then you will be able to test and approve what God's will is —his good, pleasing and perfect will.

Father, thank You for transforming us and enabling us to "stay the course" in the face of persecution. Thank You.

265.PERSECUTION (2)

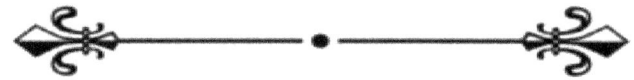

Luke 21:12 (NIV) But before all this, they will seize you and persecute you. They will hand you over to synagogues and put you in prison, and you will be brought before kings and governors, and all on account of my name.

"The antagonism directed against the church has its origin in the hatred of Satan for Christ." (Robert H. Mounce)

Are you aware that Christians in some Western nations have been charged with hate crimes because they quoted and endorsed the scriptures? Just recently, the speaker of the house (Mike Johnson) was severely criticized for His comments about using the scriptures to help make decisions. It is no longer popular to be a professing Christian in many parts of the Western world - including America. In a way, this is good. Perhaps those who are pretending to be followers of Jesus will stop pretending and make a decision to follow Jesus or not.

Persecution in America is mild at best when compared to other parts of the world. Consider this recent report:

"They are burning the church buildings, targeting the pastors, kidnapping church members. Choir members and groups have been attacked and others kidnapped … An estimated 45,000 Christians have been killed in Nigeria since 2009" - (Barnabas prayer guide for May 2024)

And that is just one of many examples of Christians being martyred for their faith. Or being put in prison, or kidnapped, or beaten or refused jobs or social services simply because they are followers of Christ.

I am often amazed at us in America. We are so obsessed with our sports, entertainment, social media etc. that we seem completely oblivious to the torture and killing of Christians all around the world. Why can't we hear the cry of the saints around the world? Have we become like the Laodicean church? Are we lukewarm towards the things of God while we diligently seek after what our culture has to offer?

Revelation 3:17 (NIV) 17 You say, 'I am rich; I have acquired wealth and do not need a thing.' But you do not realize that you are wretched, pitiful, poor, blind and naked.

Father, please enable us to stand firm when persecution comes. Make us mindful of the current suffering of our brothers and sisters in Christ. Thank You.

266.WHEN

Luke 21:20-21 (NIV) When you see Jerusalem being surrounded by armies, you will know that its desolation is near. Then let those who are in Judea flee to the mountains, let those in the city get out, and let those in the country not enter the city.

Is "when" the word we have been waiting for? Despite being repeatedly told not to worry about the "when," isn't that exactly what we want to know?

For many Christians, it seems their primary interest in prophecy is not "How can I be prepared?" but rather "When will this happen?"

In any case here we are. The "when" has arrived but let us look at the previous verses:

Luke 21:16-19 (NIV) You will be betrayed even by parents, brothers and sisters, relatives and friends, and they will put some of you to death. Everyone will hate you because of me. But not a hair of your head will perish. Stand firm, and you will win life.

We know that part of this prophecy was fulfilled around 70AD when the Romans destroyed Jerusalem and its temple. Have you noticed the current animosity against the Jews today? We are not far off from the rulers of the world uniting once again against Israel to crush it. Of course, that is just my thinking. In reality, it may still be a very long wait.

Nevertheless, we have signs that the end may be close. Persecution has greatly increased against the followers of Jesus even to the point of Christians being betrayed by their loved ones (actually happening today in places like North Korea), Christians hated and put in jail simply because they are followers of Jesus (also happening today in countries like Eritrea). Perhaps the rulers of the world will unite soon to war against the nation of Israel and to destroy it.

Consider what Jesus has to say, "stand firm, you will win life." If we are not preparing now, there is no way we will be able to "stand firm" when the "when" comes (if it comes in our life time). It is comforting but very foolish to think I can get ready "later." We do not know when the hour will arrive. Are you ready? Can you stand today against severe persecution by even your family members and the culture at large? If you are not prepared today, you will probably not be prepared tomorrow.

Lord, prepare our hearts to be willing to suffer for You (Philippians 3:10 (NIV) "I want to know Christ….and (participate) in his sufferings, becoming like him in his death." Thank You.

267.STAND

Luke 21:19 (NIV) Stand firm, and you will win life.

One of the great "tricks" of the evil one is to convince us that "all is OK" and that do not need to be concerned with what is happening "out there." However, what is "out there" impacts us and the church if we fall asleep. The church is supposed to be the bearer of God's blessings on this earth. In America, a large portion of the church has become so immersed in the culture that it now exerts very little influence.

If you are reading this, you probably believe that you would stand when evil arises. But what if you are asleep and fail to notice? Little by little, we have compromised with our culture, until there is barely any difference between the professing Christian and the society in which we live.

But that is not totally true. At least one study on Christian divorce points to a major difference between professing Christians and devoted Christians. The study seemed to indicate that those who said they were Christians but had little or no evidence of devotion to God were just as likely to get divorced, lie, get addicted, etc. as the general population. However, those who seemed devoted to God did "much better" than the general population. (Sorry, this is from memory, and I cannot quote the source.)

What is the point? We must not be Christians in "name only." We must actively seek God and His righteousness if we are to have any hope of standing firm when the time of testing comes.

(Life Application Bible Commentary New Testament) Sometimes we have to step back from the involvements of our daily lives to see the patterns of evil and all the complicities of sin around us. Retreats, conferences, and days of prayer and fasting can help us extricate ourselves from jobs, newspapers, and television and bring us to new spiritual heights. Take time to evaluate your life's directions and activities. Do they glorify God and renew you to serve others?

Oh Lord, if any of us are "play acting" as Christians please convict us of our sin. Help us Lord, enable us, to be genuinely devoted followers of Jesus of Nazareth. Thank You.

268.SIGNS

Luke 21:25-26 (NIV) "There will be signs in the sun, moon and stars. On the earth, nations will be in anguish and perplexity at the roaring and tossing of the sea. People will faint from terror, apprehensive of what is coming on the world, for the heavenly bodies will be shaken.

Joel 2:10-11 (NASB) Before them the earth quakes, The heavens tremble, The sun and the moon grow dark And the stars lose their brightness. The LORD utters His voice before His army; Surely His camp is very great, For strong is he who carries out His word. The day of the LORD is indeed great and very awesome, And who can endure it?

Have you ever been so scared that you fainted? That is what it will be like for many who face the wrath of God. So many fearful events happening one after another. Who can stand in such a time? If we are not well-rooted in God, surely, we will be in trouble. Perhaps fainting is a blessing? What do you think? Of course, in time we wake up and then we must deal with the reality of not being ready.

I know many of us are "banking" on the rapture happening before the great tribulation (me included). Then I look at the suffering persecuted church around the world today. Are they not suffering terribly today? Have not Christians suffered terribly over the past 2,000 years? Those of us living in America are living in an anomaly and I suspect that is changing.

So, my dear friend, look around. Awake from your slumber. The time is already here, knocking at your door. Are you ready?

(Life Application Bible Commentary New Testament) Persecutions and natural disasters will cause great sorrow in the world—people will faint from fear and foreboding. When believers see these events happening, they should realize that the return of their Messiah is near and that they can look forward to his reign of justice and peace. Rather than being terrified by what is happening in the world, believers should confidently await the Lord's return, an event that will shake the very heavens.

Father, we await the return of Your Son Jesus. Let us look with anticipation toward the eastern sky. Come, Lord Jesus, come. Maranatha! Thank You.

269.SHAKEN

Luke 21:26-27 (NIV) People will faint from terror, apprehensive of what is coming on the world, for the heavenly bodies will be shaken. At that time, they will see the Son of Man coming in a cloud with power and great glory.

Can we even begin to imagine what it will for like to look to the east and there He is, the Son of Man coming in a cloud with power and great glory. Shaken is not a strong enough word. Oh, what a day that will be!

He will not come as a child in a manger, born to a "nobody." Instead, He will come as Sovereign King and Lord of all. Every knee will bow and everyone (even the ones that do not want to) will confess "Jesus is Lord." The end of the reign of evil will be upon the earth and there will be a new heaven and a new earth. Yes, Lord, please hasten that day.

Revelation 21:1-4 (NIV) Then I saw "a new heaven and a new earth," for the first heaven and the first earth had passed away, and there was no longer any sea. I saw the Holy City, the new Jerusalem, coming down out of heaven from God, prepared as a bride beautifully dressed for her husband. And I heard a loud voice from the throne saying, "Look! God's dwelling place is now among the people, and he will dwell with them. They will be his people, and God himself will be with them and be their God. 'He will wipe every tear from their eyes. There will be no more death' or mourning or crying or pain, for the old order of things has passed away."

So, my dear friends, we await the Lord's return. Let us not wait, cowering from the evil around us. Let us proclaim, by how we live, and by the words of our mouth, that "Jesus is Lord." Let us consistently oppose evil by doing good and proclaim His kingdom until that day when all will be shaken and the King of Kings settles on His throne.

Father, we look forward to the awesome day. May the hope of the return of Jesus prompt us to be living walking breathing examples of children of God. Thank You.

270.STAND

Luke 21:28 (NIV) When these things begin to take place, stand up and lift up your heads, because your redemption is drawing near.

Ephesians 6:14 (NIV) Stand firm then, with the belt of truth buckled around your waist, with the breastplate of righteousness in place.

Revelation 18:4 (NIV) Then I heard another voice from heaven say: "'Come out of her, my people,' so that you will not share in her sins, so that you will not receive any of her plagues.

As we look at our culture and the abandonment of Christian principals across our nation, do not be fooled. God is not mocked. He warned us that these days would come. Days when evil is considered good and good considered evil. That day has arrived in America and even our courts are upholding evil principles over what is good. It seems to be a difficult time to be a Christian, but I would say just the opposite. As the world turns toward evil and becomes darker and darker, surely "our little light" shines brighter as we stand firm in the principles laid out for us in Scripture.

The evils of our culture are enticing, and I suspect many of you have already been drawn in, as shown by how you spend your money and your time—through the TV shows and movies you watch, the books you read, and the company you keep. God is calling us to "come out," to separate ourselves from the allure of wickedness and to stand firm in our faith. This is not always easy, and I understand the challenges, yet we act foolishly if we ignore these warnings. We live in a society that is increasingly godless, and we must not compromise.

According to the Life Application Bible Commentary New Testament, believers must always recognize when compromise with a godless society is unacceptable, for yielding can lead to serious consequences. While "come out" can indicate a physical separation from places of evil, it primarily calls for a spiritual, mental, and emotional distancing from the sins that dominate our society. The church must remain steadfast on the foundations of the faith, never wavering under the pressures of societal trends.

Lord, help us to stand strong for You and to come out of anything in our lives that is hindering our walk with You. Thank You.

271.CAREFUL

Luke 21:34-36 (NIV) Be careful, or your hearts will be weighed down with carousing, drunkenness and the anxieties of life, and that day will close on you suddenly like a trap. For it will come on all those who live on the face of the whole earth. Be always on the watch, and pray that you may be able to escape all that is about to happen, and that you may be able to stand before the Son of Man.

We have come to the final word and devotion that deals with the end of this age. I hope it was helpful to you. It was for me. I cannot help but wonder if we are getting close to the end. But, again, that is speculation and leads to nothing useful.

What is useful is being careful and not conforming to our culture. Instead, live in a state of readiness. To be ready means we do not have to get ready. It has long been my contention that people who plan on getting ready "later" are going to find themselves in trouble.

Please take a moment and re-read the above scripture. Consider how much of your life revolves around the issues of life and how much is focused on being ready should the day arrive and you are still here on this earth. I am deeply concerned that many are asleep, already conformed to our culture.

Romans 12:2 (NIV) Do not conform to the pattern of this world, but be transformed by the renewing of your mind. Then you will be able to test and approve what God's will is —his good, pleasing and perfect will.

I hope none of us take our salvation for granted and just hang out thinking, "by and by I'll get my wings." Our salvation brings forth a new creation. One of the greatest privileges is being a servant to our Lord Jesus while we await His sure return.

Please, my dear friends, do not be anxious or burdened by life's worries. Instead, let us remain vigilant, steadfast in our mission, attentive in all we do, and pray for the strength to stand firm, no matter what the future may bring.

Lord God, guide us to be the "little light" that shines brightly for You. Thank You.

272.WOE

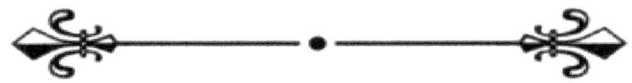

Matthew 23:23 (NASB) Woe to you, scribes and Pharisees, hypocrites! For you tithe mint and dill and cumin, and have neglected the weightier provisions of the law: justice and mercy and faithfulness; but these are the things you should have done without neglecting the others

I am not fond of today's word. It brings to mind thoughts like, "trouble ahead," "you should have known better," and "you reap what you sow." In other words, there is a reckoning ahead and the responsibility is yours because you knew what was right and you did not do it.

I am often reminded of David's prayer in Psalms 139:23-24 (NIV) "Search me, God, and know my heart; test me and know my anxious thoughts. See if there is any offensive way in me, and lead me in the way everlasting".

I think we are a lot like the scribes and Pharisees in Matthew 23:23. We have our "pet" things that we like to do (acting religious) while at the same time ignoring what is important.

A glaring example is our seeming inability to love people who are offensive to us. We treat people we like pretty good. But Jesus says we get "no points" for that kind of behavior. Matthew 5:46 (NIV) "If you love those who love you, what reward will you get? Are not even the tax collectors doing that?"

But let us be practical. If you are a Republican, how do you love the Democrat? If you lean Democrat, how do you love the Republican in your life? If you are conservative, how do you love the liberal? If you are liberal, how are you loving the conservative? If you are reserved, how do you love those who are not? If you like to be alone, how do you love those who are "in your face"?

If you are outgoing, how do you love those who are not? If you are an introvert, how do you love the extrovert? If you are poor, how do you love the rich? If you are rich, how do you love the poor? If you are sick, how do you love the healthy? If you are healthy, how do you love the chronically ill?

These are not necessarily "enemies" but they are good places for us to practice being the people God wants us to be. This is what God desires.

Matthew 5:48 (NIV) Be perfect, therefore, as your heavenly Father is perfect.

Father, please search our hearts. Conform us to You. Thank You.

273.WORKER

2 Timothy 2:15 (NIV) Do your best to present yourself to God as one approved, a worker who does not need to be ashamed and who correctly handles the word of truth.

Even when we are "retired" we are still always "on mission." We are still workers in the kingdom of God. This is one of those areas where we must be careful not to be fooled by our culture, which teaches us to "take it easy," "enjoy the golden years," and "get all we can out of life." We were called into service. We are workers for His kingdom and that does not change just because we have reached a certain age or experienced one of life's difficulties.

Believe me, I understand our bodies age and we experience great physical and emotional difficulties (death of a loved one, financial losses, major health issues, unresponsive loved one etc.). But that does not mean our work is done. Yes, the evil one tells us we are being put out to pasture, or that we are too old or feeble to continue working for Christ. Or grief and depression breaks into our emotional well-being and we sit and complain (woe is me).

Oh, my dear fellow worker in Christ, please do not let your age, health, emotional distress, financial difficulties or anything else keep you from being used by God. You see, whatever you are experiencing can be useful to you if you do not let it destroy you.

Our difficulties can be our greatest assets as we are forced to call out to Jesus for His strength. I am frequently reminded of Charles Spurgeon who suffered greatly from health (gout) and emotional (depression) issues and yet he became perhaps the greatest preacher in the past 500 years. What difficulty are you dealing with? God can use it to serve Him if you will get on with the business of being His worker.

Father, we are merely flesh and can be very weak but it is in that very weakness that we can be strong for You. Let us rise above our circumstances and get on with the work You have called for us to do. Thank You.

274 REGRET

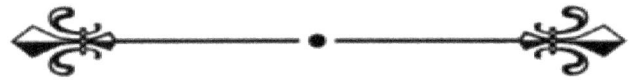

2 Corinthians 7:10 (NIV) Godly sorrow brings repentance that leads to salvation and leaves no regret, but worldly sorrow brings death.

When it is said and done, and all your days have been numbered, will you be one of the many who say, "Oh, I wish I had"?

Over the years, May and I heard these words many times. Our culture tells us that "we need to complete all the items on our "bucket list." That is not what I am talking about.

When we leave something undone that we have dreamt about doing, that is sad, but it rarely leads to true regret. It is more like an "oh well." What leads to true regret is failing to do what truly matters in life, arriving at a point where it is no longer possible to act.

One of the most common examples is not forgiving a loved one or friend who has passed away. Often, the specific memory of what needs forgiveness has faded, yet the opportunity to make amends was still missed. Sometimes, people recognize the need to set things right, but procrastination takes over, leaving them to live with lingering regret.

Is regret quietly building in your life? Is there someone you have distanced yourself from, and the Spirit is urging you to reach out, yet so far you have not taken that step?Is there someone who has made a big difference in your life? Have you told them? Is there a pastor or spiritual leader that helped you get back on the "straight and narrow"? Have you let them know you are still "walking the talk"?

Is your busy life keeping you from what is really important? Are there people in your life that would welcome your company, but you are too busy to visit, call or reach out in some way? Do it before it is too late.

Even more serious than all the above, have you really devoted yourself to God? Are you more of Jesus fan than a disciple? It will be very sad to stand before the Judgment seat of Christ with regrets.

Lord, there are many things that take up our time, energies and talents. Give us discernment to take care of what is important to You, so that when we stand before Your throne there will be no regrets. Thank You.

275.CAPTIVE

2 Corinthians 10:5 (NIV) We demolish arguments and every pretension that sets itself up against the knowledge of God, and we take captive every thought to make it obedient to Christ.

As I shared in a recent devotion, I had a deep anger when the Russians invaded Ukraine. It was an awakening. My thoughts were clearly not God's thoughts. I wanted revenge but God tells us revenge belongs to Him alone. It was a challenge and still is today. Then and now I need to take such thoughts captive and toss them into the bin of nothingness.

Easy, right? Of course not. If your mind is anything like mine, then it is a bit unruly and tends to wander far afield. Sometimes I am amazed at how I can be thinking about one thing and suddenly realize that I am thinking about something completely different. How I got from one to another is a complete mystery.

You can put this devotion "on the shelf" and forget it, but for those of us who have been "blessed" with wandering minds we must take this scripture seriously. You see, most (maybe all) spiritual attacks begin in the mind. The thought suddenly appears; we give it energy, and soon we are following it down a path of destruction.

This applies to all kinds of "ungodly" thoughts such as anger, un-forgiveness, revenge, social/racial prejudice, cheating, being mean or unfriendly, sexual perversion, laziness, unkindness, etc. All kinds of thoughts can enter our minds. The thoughts themselves are not sin but when we give them energy and allow them to take up residence in our minds, they can control us.

The challenge is to cast these unruly thoughts far away as soon as you recognize that they are not of God. Do not give them the slightest bit of energy. If you do, they will grow strong and control you. Begin by acknowledging to God that this is wrong (stinking) thinking. Then ask the Holy Spirit to cast these thoughts from your mind. At the same time, focus on something that is good for you to think about. Turn every negative thought into a virtue.

Philippians 4:8 (NIV) Finally, brothers and sisters, whatever is true, whatever is noble, whatever is right, whatever is pure, whatever is lovely, whatever is admirable—if anything is excellent or praiseworthy—think about such things.

Father, please grant us the willingness to bring every thought into captivity to Jesus. Thank You.

276.ABANDON

Galatians 2:20 (NIV) I have been crucified with Christ and I no longer live, but Christ lives in me. The life I now live in the body, I live by faith in the Son of God, who loved me and gave himself for me.

Luke 9:25 (NIV) What good is it for someone to gain the whole world, and yet lose or forfeit their very self?

Over the last 1500 years or so the Body of Christ in the Western world has lost something that was very dear to followers of Jesus in the early church. The early believers understood that they were called to abandon everything they held precious and to dedicate themselves to Jesus with abandon.

We still see this in Muslim dominated nations when a person converts to Christianity because they know they are also abandoning everything they had before, including homes, jobs, families, friends, respect, etc. They know and understand that the only viable option is to abandon themselves to Jesus. To trust Him for their future, both now and in the future kingdom.

Have we in the modern Western church lost sight of our calling to abandon all for Christ? Jesus said it is difficult for a wealthy person to enter the kingdom of heaven. The more we have, the more difficult it is to abandon it.

"Abandonment means to refuse yourself the luxury of asking any questions. If you totally abandon yourself to God, He immediately says to you, "I will give your life to you as a prize." The reason people are tired of life is that God has not given them anything—they have not been given their life "as a prize." The way to get out of that condition is to abandon yourself to God." (Excerpt From My Utmost for His Highest Oswald Chambers)

Do you see your life as a "prize" from God? Have you abandoned yourself to God?

Father, once again we face many distractions. When we surrender ourselves to You, all questions fade away. We belong to You—end of story. Thank You.

277.RELATIONSHIPS

1 Peter 3:8-9 (NIV) Finally, all of you, be like-minded, be sympathetic, love one another, be compassionate and humble. Do not repay evil with evil or insult with insult. On the contrary, repay evil with blessing, because to this you were called so that you may inherit a blessing.

If you have been in a long-term relationship, you know that it takes work on both sides to make it a good union over time. We are all different in so many ways. Why can't women be more like men? Why can't men be more like women? Perhaps it is because the great Designer of the Universe saw that it was better for us to be different?

We must realize that relationships are not about making us happy. (Yes, I know they can do that, but they can also make us miserable.) Are relationships supposed to help us grow and mature spiritually? To make us more resilient than ever as we depend on God?

When we look to our loved ones to make us happy then we place impossible burdens on them. In time, the relationship suffers and sometimes even collapses.

"When I acknowledge that none of us are perfect in this life, I can enjoy that which is beautiful in a relationship, without expecting it to be perfect." (True Spirituality, Francis Schaeffer)

My dear friends, rejoice in the relationships God has given to you. Expect little but give generously, over the top, so that you find the great pearl that is hidden within. When you give all of yourself to another you will find that your return is multiplied many times over. If you feel "short changed" in your relationship it may be because, instead of giving, you are being stingy.

Father, lead us to give all of ourselves through the empowering of Your Holy Spirit. Thank You.

278.COMMON-SENSE

Ecclesiastes 9:10 (NIV) Whatever your hand finds to do, do it with all your might, for in the realm of the dead, where you are going, there is neither working nor planning nor knowledge nor wisdom.

Sometimes I think "common sense" is not so common any more. Despite knowing better, many of us are prone to do things that are not useful or good, although generally "approved" by our culture. I mean things like getting into debt, eating unhealthy foods, working too much, resting too much, entertaining too much, being too busy, buying what we do not need, etc. Our "common sense" about these things seems to have "fled the coop".

Common sense is necessary for navigating through the world. However, having common sense and using it are two very different things. Our common sense helps us know what is good and useful to do. If we pay attention, it will keep us from falling into the "deep end" when we do not have to. But consider the following for a different view of common sense.

"Certainty is the mark of the commonsense life—gracious uncertainty is the mark of the spiritual life. To be certain of God means that we are uncertain in all our ways, not knowing what tomorrow may bring. This is generally expressed with a sigh of sadness, but it should be an expression of breathless expectation. We are uncertain of the next step, but we are certain of God. As soon as we abandon ourselves to God and do the task He has placed closest to us, He begins to fill our lives with surprises....... when we have the right relationship with God, life is full of spontaneous, joyful uncertainty and expectancy." (Excerpt From My Utmost for His Highest Oswald Chambers)

So perhaps common sense is not so important after all? What do you think? Is it better to be certain of our relationship with God and let Him guide our lives? To the unbeliever we may "look the fool," but I have this sense that God smiles on those who are led by the Spirit, even and especially when it defies common sense.

Lord God, lead us where You want us to go. To do what You want us to do, even when it makes no sense. Thank You .

279.DECISIONS

Hebrews 12:16-17 (NIV) See that no one is sexually immoral, or is godless like Esau, who for a single meal sold his inheritance rights as the oldest son. Afterward, as you know, when he wanted to inherit this blessing, he was rejected. Even though he sought the blessing with tears, he could not change what he had done.

Esau really messed up. Despite his repentant sorrow, it was too late. The blessing that could have been his was forever gone. We, too, are offered tremendous blessings. What fools we are when we forsake the blessings of God for what the world has to offer. The following is from Joshua Becker and it speaks to the importance of every decision we make.

"We are faced every day with decisions to choose the things of God or the things of this world. In many circumstances, those decisions cannot be undone. Once they are chosen, they are chosen. And if we choose incorrectly, we miss the greatest blessings of God in our life.

"When we choose to build up our personal wealth rather than support missions around the world, we reject a blessing from God that cannot be undone.

When we choose to spend money on a vacation rather than tithe, we reject a blessing from God that cannot be undone. When we choose to buy more stuff we don't need rather than aid the poor, we reject a blessing from God that cannot be undone. When we choose to spend time entertained by the world rather than in communion with God, we reject a blessing from God that cannot be undone.

Each time we choose ungodliness with our actions rather than righteousness, we reject a blessing from God that cannot be undone. Every day, in countless ways, we face the same decision that Esau encountered. Will we choose the things of this world or the things of God? Take this warning from the Holy Spirit deep into your decision-making process. Though we may desire to take hold of the blessing we rejected, even with tears, we cannot change what was done." (JOSHUA BECKER)

Lord God if we are truly Yours why would we choose to reject Your blessings by doing "as we see fit to do" (Judges 21:25)? Please, Lord, move deeply in our hearts to pursue You and Your righteousness. Thank You.

280.VICARIOUS

Romans 8:26-27 (NASB) In the same way, the Spirit also helps our weakness; for we do not know how to pray as we should, but the Spirit Himself intercedes for us with groanings too deep for words; and He who searches the hearts knows what the mind of the Spirit is, because He intercedes for the saints according to the will of God

Every now and then I run into someone trying to live their lives vicariously through another person. An example is a father who wanted to be a professional baseball player but never really had the opportunity, yet still pushes baseball on his son. Wanting his son to be the pro he was not. Or the mother who wanted to be a model but gets married and has children instead and who tries to live vicariously through her daughter. Pressing the daughter to be the model the mother never was.

I think it is never good to try to live vicariously through another. We each have our own God-given gifts, talents, resources, interests etc. and they should be used primarily for God's purposes. To bring Him honor and to glorify Him.

When we try to live vicariously through another we are in danger of trying to live out our own selfish interests.

We can even live variously in our prayer life. In other words, our prayers of intercession are prayers for what we really want, not necessarily what God wants. Consider the following:

"Vicarious intercession means that we deliberately substitute God's interests in others for our natural sympathy with them." (Excerpt From My Utmost for His Highest Oswald Chambers).

Typical examples are when we know someone is sick, we usually pray for healing. If someone is having difficulty with finances, we often ask God to provide the finances needed. If someone is sad, we pray they will be happy. But what if the health, financial, emotional, etc issues are just symptoms of the real problem? What if God wants to use the difficult circumstances to draw that person into a deeper walk with Him?

Lord, we do not always know how to pray, but You sure do. Please give us spiritual wisdom and insight as we intercede for one another. Thank You.

281.VIOLENCE

Jeremiah 22:3 (NIV) This is what the LORD says: Do what is just and right. Rescue from the hand of the oppressor the one who has been robbed. Do no wrong or violence to the foreigner, the fatherless or the widow, and do not shed innocent blood in this place.

Luke 6:27-29 (NIV) But to you who are listening I say: Love your enemies, do good to those who hate you, bless those who curse you, pray for those who mistreat you. If someone slaps you on one cheek, turn to them the other also. If someone takes your coat, do not withhold your shirt from them.

Matthew 5:9 (NIV) Blessed are the peacemakers, for they will be called children of God.

Considering today's scriptures, we should conclude that violence (using force to get what we want or to dominate another) is contrary to God's desires for His people. Many say the only way to counter violence is with more violence. Consider the Israel/Hamas war. Is this an explicit example of using violence to get what they want, on both sides?

We have an exhibition for the world to see what hate and attempts to dominate others through violence can lead to. Surely acts of violence upon another group of people makes us no better than they are. Even if they started it.

I know there is a "built in compulsion" among humans to "make things right" or to "just get even." Does not vengeance belong to God and not to you and me? Many of us (especially nations) operate from the perspective that "might makes right."

There is great danger in using violence to fight injustice or evil. It has been said, "when we resort to violence to fight injustice we become like what we oppose. Social injustice can never be changed by resorting to social injustice through violence." I am coming to understand that this is true at every level of society.

I am in no position to tell governments what they should or should not do. The scriptures, however, are very clear for us as individuals. Violence will not work the righteousness of God. Jesus told us another way is a better way. To "reform" those who do injustice we must learn to act with love, caring and kindness and never return violence with violence.

Lord God, my heart can quickly turn to revenge when I am offended. Please kill that desire within me and lead me in a more perfect way. Thank You.

282.UNDEFILED

James 1:27 (NASB) Pure and undefiled religion in the sight of our God and Father is this: to visit orphans and widows in their distress, and to keep oneself unstained by the world.

"Undefiled" is a word we seldom use in our everyday speech. I cannot even remember hearing it in church, although I must have. How about you? When was the last time you were encouraged to keep yourself "undefiled"?

To be "undefiled" is to be unsullied, unmarred or unspoiled. The NIV version translates this word as "faultless." This is a tough one for Christians living in America today. The culture has so deeply penetrated the church that at times it feels as though the culture is shaping the church rather than the church shaping the culture. On a personal level, we are called to be undefiled and blameless. But how do we accomplish this?

The seductions we see in movies and many TV shows should be "off limits" to us. The same goes for seeking after the things the world sees as good (power, wealth, worldly success, etc,).

To remain spiritually undefiled, we must apply God's word to every aspect of our lives. No more doing what we want, even if it seems good to us. Instead, we present ourselves and all our needs and desires before the Lord God, seeking what He wants in every situation.

It takes courage to take a strong stand for the things of God. There will often seem to be negative consequences for choosing God's way. But when you know the end of the story you know God's way is always better.

For some that may mean facing persecution and even death. We have visible examples in many nations today where Christians are being actively persecuted.

If we desire to be undefiled and are seeking after God, He will lead us. Do not neglect the practical part of the above scriptures. Be of meaningful help to those who cannot help themselves.

Lord, by nature we are defiled. But in Jesus we are Your undefiled children. Thank You.

283.SOON

Revelation 22:7 (NIV) "Look, I am coming soon! Blessed is the one who keeps the words of the prophecy written in this scroll."

Almost every time I hear the word "soon" my mind takes off and starts singing this song;

" 🎵 Soon and very soon we are going to see the King - Soon and very soon we are going to see the King - Hallelujah, Hallelujah - we are going to see the King 🎵 "

That is all I remember from the song. This morning, during my prayer time, I came across the verse above and prayed, "Lord, surely You jest." He could not mean "soon" as we commonly understand it.

The Greek word used here is "tachy," which can mean without delay, soon, by surprise, suddenly, or quickly. Considering that it has been two thousand years since Jesus spoke these words, I do not believe He meant "soon" in the sense of any moment.

Rather, the emphasis must be suddenly, quickly, or with little warning. When we least expect it. That is one reason I usually discount any of the prophecies about the soon return of Jesus. If we expect it to be a certain time we are assured it will not be then. Perhaps God smiles at our focus on time. Maybe He likes surprises? Oh, what a day that will be!

Meantime, we await the return of Jesus the King. It could be today or in one thousand years. It is not for us to know. it is for us to be ready and to be faithful until that day when we will look to the Eastern sky and there He is. Oh, what a Day!!!!

(Life Application Bible Commentary New Testament) "REMAIN FAITHFUL ….. What is the Christian's work? … We are to be faithful to Christ. God commended the Philippians for keeping Christ's words and not denying his name (3:8). We are to be morally clean and prepared for his return (7:14; 22:14). We are to endure patiently (14:12). …. … Serving God begins with our faithful service to him now."

Lord, thank You for today and every day You give us. Lead us to faithful service for You. Thank You.

284.INITIATIVE

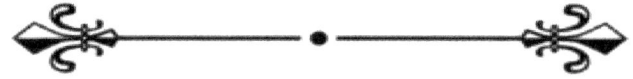

2 Peter 1:5-7 (NIV) For this very reason, make every effort to add to your faith goodness; and to goodness, knowledge; and to knowledge, self-control; and to self-control, perseverance; and to perseverance, godliness; and to godliness, mutual affection; and to mutual affection, love.

As Christians, we must trust our Savior for our salvation and never trust in our works, even when they are wonderful works to behold. At the same time, we should work very hard for the kingdom as if our salvation truly depends on our good works.

We are responsible for what we are responsible for, and we are not responsible for what God is responsible for. We must never attempt to do what only God can do (save us) and we must never expect God to do what He has given us to do (good works) (see Ephesians 2:8-10).

Our life as Christians must be in partnership with God. He has His part to do, and we have ours. Getting the two mixed up causes confusion. When you consider the above scripture, there is something for us to do. We must realize this is ours to do and we must take the initiative to get them done. We do not operate without the guidance of the Spirit, nor are we to sit on our couches waiting for something to happen to us (like magic).

"Take the initiative yourself, make a decision of your will right now, and make it impossible to go back. Burn your bridges behind you, saying, "I will write that letter," or "I will pay that debt"; and then do it! Make it irrevocable......We have to get into the habit of carefully listening to God about everything, forming the habit of finding out what He says and heeding it. If, when a crisis comes, we instinctively turn to God, we will know that the habit has been formed in us. We have to take the initiative where we are, not where we have not yet been". (Excerpt From My Utmost for His Highest Oswald Chambers)

Are you struggling with some aspect of life right now (health, finances, depression, relationships, grief, etc.) and have become discouraged? Take the initiative today to do something about it. We often know what we need to do and do not do it. Don't be like that. Get up, get going, take the initiative.

Lord, how often have we said, "tomorrow I will" and it is still undone? lease Lord, even as we read these words speak to our hearts about what we need to do - today - even right now. Thank You.

285.PARTAKERS

2 Peter 1:4 (NIV) Through these he has given us his very great and precious promises, so that through them you may participate in the divine nature, having escaped the corruption in the world caused by evil desires.

Are we truly partakers of the "divine nature"? Are we living the "divine nature" or are we under the domination of the powers that be? Are we living in the light of God's precious promises to us or are we living under the power and influence of our culture?

Have we escaped the corruption of this world, or are we still giving in to its influences in our lives? Are we still bound to the chains that bind us to our old man or have we come to the place of living a "hidden life" in Christ? Is there enough evidence in our daily lives to convict us of being fully dedicated followers of Jesus Christ?

"If the majesty, grace, and power of God are not being exhibited in us, God holds us responsible. 'God is able to make all grace abound toward you, that you . . . may have an abundance' (2 Corinthians 9:8)...then learn to lavish the grace of God on others, generously giving of yourself. Be marked and identified with God's nature, and His blessing will flow through you all the time." (Excerpt From My Utmost for His Highest Oswald Chambers)

Do not be foolish Christians who live lives that "have the form of godliness but lack the power of God." We follow a Savior who sacrificed Himself and died for us. We must do the same. Unless we die to ourselves, we will find ourselves constantly conflicted, trying to serve God and man at the same time.

We can fool one another. We can even fool ourselves, but we cannot fool God. He sees our hearts and our intentions. What are yours? Have you signed up for the "religion of the cross," daily taking up your cross regardless of what it might be?

(Life Application Bible Commentary New Testament) "Man does not like the religion of the cross, of faith, of self-denial, and each age has witnessed some false system from which all these objectionable elements are eliminated.". (F. B. Meyer)

Lord, give us discernment that we are not fooled into trying to keep one foot in the world and the other in paradise. Thank You.

286.ACCESS

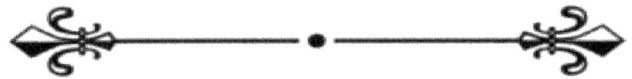

Matthew 27:51 (NIV) At that moment the curtain of the temple was torn in two from top to bottom. The earth shook, the rocks split

Luke 24:50-52 (NIV) When he had led them out to the vicinity of Bethany, he lifted up his hands and blessed them. While he was blessing them, he left them and was taken up into heaven. Then they worshiped him and returned to Jerusalem with great joy.

The tearing of the temple's curtain symbolizes the end of man's separation from God. Because of Jesus' atoning sacrifice we have free access to God. Clearly this is something we learned a long time ago, but should it not be fresh and new in our thoughts every day?

"His Cross is the door by which every member of the human race can enter into the life of God; by His resurrection He has the right to give eternal life to anyone, and by His ascension our Lord entered heaven, keeping the door open for humanity....... From His ascension forward He is the King of kings and Lord of lords." (Excerpt From My Utmost for His Highest Oswald Chambers)

On this hot day in June, we might have reason to grumble about the heat and the humidity, or we can reflect on the wonder of the King who came to earth to save and redeem us through His life-giving blood. I am reminded of the song "there is power, power, power - wonder working power - in the precious blood of the Lamb." Let these words take up residence in our minds as we gratefully thank God for each day.

I understand that some days are difficult. Jesus never promised a "rose garden." What He did promise is so much better. Eternal life in the presence of the King of kings.

Lord, help us to keep life in perspective. You are Father, the King and Lord of the Universe. We are Your children. How incredibly wonderful. Thank You.

287.SIMPLE

Matthew 6:26-28 (NIV) Look at the birds of the air; they do not sow or reap or store away in barns, and yet your heavenly Father feeds them. Are you not much more valuable than they? Can any one of you by worrying add a single hour to your life? "And why do you worry about clothes? See how the flowers of the field grow. They do not labor or spin.

How often have we read these verses, perhaps smiled, and moved on? We do not realize that these words contain the "secret" and the "mystery" of lives that are lived well. Many years ago I felt God speak to my spirit, "Paul, you need to simplify your life." At first, I was clueless about what He meant, but over time I gained insight as I continually asked Him to guide me by His Spirit.

I tend to overcomplicate things, which used to drive May "bananas." Hopefully, not so much anymore. She hasn't mentioned it in a while, so perhaps I've improved a bit. Over the years, I have also learned that living a simple life is often far from simple.

I, and I guess many readers, tend to keep adding to our lives. A little bit here, a little bit there and over time we accumulate many distractors in our lives. Don't believe me? Just move your residence. I bet you will find a lot of things you probably did not even know you had.

But simple does not just mean having less stuff, or less clutter, or a less complicated thought life. Simple also means letting go of all our worldly distractions to be fully devoted to God. Our lives are overly full with all kinds of activities. Much of what we do is just "busy stuff".

"Those who live their lives like the stars in the sky and 'the lilies of the field', simply and unaffectedly. Those are the lives that mold and shape us....If you want to be of use to God, maintain the proper relationship with Jesus Christ by staying focused on Him, and He will make use of you every minute you live. Yet you will be unaware, on the conscious level of your life, that you are being used of Him." (Excerpt From My Utmost for His Highest Oswald Chambers)

Lord, simple is probably different for each one of us. Lead us to live simple lives trusting You for life and for all eternity. Thank You.

288.TARGET

Matthew 6:33 (NIV) But seek first his kingdom and his righteousness, and all these things will be given to you as well.

"Keep your eye on the target." I can still hear those words that my drill sergeant yelled in basic training all those many years ago (about 65). Gee, how the years have flown by.

Apparently, I have wandering eyes. "Keep your eyes on the ball" were words I heard often as I swung and missed once again. I never did too good at shooting a gun or playing baseball. That does not seem so important all these years later. This principle in life, however, is really important. If we do not keep our eyes on the "target" we are almost certainly going to miss it.

In our culture and in this time, it can be very difficult for Christians to even recognize the target. Our lives are filled with so many distractions, so much clutter from endless activities and plans for the future. The world constantly tells us, "You can be anything you want to be," and before long, our eyes and hearts drift away from the true goal—living a life fully devoted to our Father, the Lord of the Universe.

(Life Application Bible Commentary New Testament) "AN EASY TARGET …. As Christians, have we become infatuated with the worldly power of movie stars and sports celebrities, political coalitions, and world economic forces? Are you craving the power and prestige that position, wealth, and connections offer? If so, you are an easy target for Satan's great deception. Worldly power is Satan's trap; the desire for it can turn us away from God. Worship only God and make it your strongest desire to serve him."

So, my dear friend, you profess Christ but have you lost sight of the "target"? Perhaps instead you have become the target?

Can it be that you are no longer seeking after God's kingdom but are pursuing some other "kingdom" created by your desires for the comforts and pleasures of life? In other words, are you deceived and do not know it? Have you taken your eyes off the true "target" and placed them on something else?

Seek God first. That is what Jesus tells us to do. Are you? Really?

Lord God, put it into our hearts to seek You first in all things. Thank You.

289.MOODY

Psalms 42:11 (NIV) Why, my soul, are you downcast? Why so disturbed within me? Put your hope in God, for I will yet praise him, my Savior and my God.

This devotion serves as a reminder to me and to all of you who are now, or may one day become, downcast in spirit. It does not matter why you feel this way. It could be grief, poor health, strained relationships, financial struggles, or even a vague uneasiness about "something." When we are downcast, our eyes are truly cast down—focused on the circumstances of our lives rather than on the God of the universe who calls us His children.

Many of you are aware that I am prone to melancholy. I first became conscious of it over fifty years ago. I suddenly feel "out of sorts" without the slightest clue as to why. Sometimes it would be just a few hours, other times it might go on for days. I asked God, "what is going on?" There was no immediate answer but over time I learned that my feelings of melancholy could only last if I gave them energy.

We give our negative feelings energy by continually yielding to them. We think about them, we talk about them, we write about them, we moan about them, we act like them and maybe even grumble about them. Every time we do these things we give them a little more power, control, and influence over us.

"It is a continual struggle not to listen to the moods which arise as a result of our physical condition (or some emotional distress), We must never surrender to them… We have to pick ourselves up by the back of the neck and shake ourselves; then we will find that we can do what we believed we were unable to do. The problem that most of us are cursed with is simply that we won't. The Christian life is one of spiritual courage and determination lived out in our flesh." (Excerpt From My Utmost for His Highest Oswald Chambers).

Please understand that I have experienced being so downcast that it was almost impossible to "pick myself up by the back of the neck and shake myself." I get that this is not easy. But we are children of the King. Are not all things possible through the power and strength of God? Does not the Spirit who raised Jesus from the dead also live inside of us?

I am not suggesting that you deny how you feel or suppress how you feel. I am saying that you do not have to stay under the power of your feelings. Start acting like who you are, a child of God. Your feelings will soon line up with your position in Christ.

Father, I surrender all of me, even my feelings, to You. Lead us to live lives victorious in You. Thank You.

290.BALANCE

Matthew 6:33-34 (NIV) But seek first his kingdom and his righteousness, and all these things will be given to you as well. Therefore do not worry about tomorrow, for tomorrow will worry about itself. Each day has enough trouble of its own.

As I get older and as my role and responsibilities evolve, I find that maintaining balance can be challenging. I have often thought about how easy it has been over the years to tell caregivers, "Make sure you take care of yourself." Now that I am one, I understand why it is so much harder than it sounds. There is an old Indian saying, "You must walk a mile in someone's moccasins before you can understand their life" (that may not be the exact wording, but you get the idea).

Those of you who know me well are aware that I tend to give advice, even when it is unsolicited. I am truly sorry for that. I want to wait until I am asked. Sometimes what I have to say may be practical, and it may even be right, but if I have not lived through the experience, it is unlikely to be exactly what is needed in the moment.

Ephesians 4:29 (NIV) 29 Do not let any unwholesome talk come out of your mouths, but only what is helpful for building others up according to their needs, that it may benefit those who listen.

Having said all that, here I am writing devotionals as if I had something useful to say. If I may, let me give myself some unsolicited advice (you can listen if you want). "Paul, if you want to stay in balance as life changes around you make sure God stays at the center. Let go of your worries - focus on Jesus. Toss anxious thoughts into the sea of forgetfulness."

"The great concern of our lives is not the kingdom of God but how we are going to take care of ourselves to live. Jesus reversed the order by telling us to get the right relationship with God first, maintaining it as the primary concern of our lives, and never to place our concern on taking care of the other things of life. (Excerpt From My Utmost for His Highest Oswald Chambers)

Lord, another reminder to abide in You. Thank You.

291.VALUES

Luke 16:15 (NIV) He said to them, "You are the ones who justify yourselves in the eyes of others, but God knows your hearts. What people value highly is detestable in God's sight.

Galatians 5:6 (NIV) For in Christ Jesus neither circumcision nor uncircumcision has any value. The only thing that counts is faith expressing itself through love.

We have become so much like the world. We value the same things the world values. Most of us agree that we should not conform to the values of our world (Romans 12:1-2) but many have long given ourselves over to being conformed to our culture.

Our culture values success. Many have aligned themselves to achieving worldly success, fame or recognition. Our culture encourages us to get in debt to get what we want. The scriptures admonish us not to be in debt. Yet we accumulate debts for cars and homes, and appliances, vacations etc. The scriptures teach us to love and pray for those who want to harm us and yet we nurture anger and revenge or withdraw from those who hurt us.

I could go on, but I choose not to. We could come up with a pretty long list. The point being is that we say we value one thing (God and the scriptures) but are living something else.

Perhaps we are walking, talking hypocrites and I do not even know it. We are so well indoctrinated by the culture, the powers that be, our families and even some churches that we no longer truly value what God values.

(Life Application Bible Commentary New Testament) "VALUED VALUES Roman merchants often grew rich by exploiting the sinful pleasures of their society. Many business people today do the same thing. Businesses and governments are often based on greed, money, and power. Many bright individuals are tempted to take advantage of an evil system to enrich themselves. Christians are warned to stay free from the lure of money, status, and the good life. We are to live according to the values that Christ exemplified: service, giving, self-sacrifice, obedience, and truth."

Father, please awaken us. Give us eyes to see and hearts that yearn for You. Put it in our hearts to love what You love and to hate what You hate. Thank You.

292.VALUES (2)

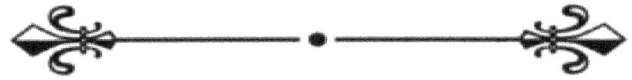

Proverbs 22:6 (The Passion Translation) Dedicate your children to God. and point them in the way that they should go, and the values they've learned from you will be with them for life.

What is truly most important to you? Take a moment to clarify this in your mind and in your heart. If you do not, I assure you that the day will come, on your death bed or perhaps before the Judgment Seat of Christ, when you will say, "Oh, I wish I had."

It would be nice to have an eternity to get life right, but we only get this one time around. If you are a follower of Jesus, then He has placed in Your heart that which is to be most valued in your life. I say it again. You must know, be able to clearly define, what you value in life. Failure to do so is to live the "unexamined life," which, according to Socrates, is a shame. ("The unexamined life is not worth living.".

Knowing what you value is just the beginning. It is not enough to know. We must pursue it. Otherwise, the distractions in life, ("the lust of the eyes, lust of the flesh & the pride of life" 1 John 2:16) will suck us away like coffee grounds by a vacuum cleaner. There are many distractions. We each have our own challenges, but some are more destructive than others. Consider the following:

"The trivial-information-overload distractions may pull our attention away from the work right in front of us, but the larger distractions in life prevent us from realizing the life our souls are calling us to live—one focused on goals of true significance and meaning. Lifestyle distractions such as homes, cars, success, occupations, entertainment, sports, relationships, and social networks keep us from achieving a deeper purpose in our lives. It is easy to notice when I stay up too late scrolling through TikTok videos, yet far more difficult to recognize when I have sacrificed my child's well-being for a new promotion at work." (Joshua Becker)

Lord, keep us from living lives that are insignificant simply because we fail to identify what You want us to value in this life and pursue it. Thank You.

293 ONE

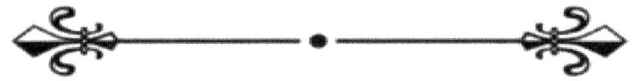

John 17:20-21 (NIV) "My prayer is not for them alone. I pray also for those who will believe in me through their message, that all of them may be one, Father, just as you are in me and I am in you. May they also be in us so that the world may believe that you have sent me.

I often hear people say—and I have said it myself—"We are works in progress." But why is that? I understand it when we are newly born followers of Christ. Yet why, after 5, 10, 20, even 30-plus years, have we still not reached the place where we can truly say Jesus' prayer has been fulfilled, where we have become as one?

Could it be that, even after many years as Christians, we are still in spiritual kindergarten? In kindergarten, not much was expected of us. Is that how we view our lives now—accepting that not much is expected? We maintain the visible outward practices—going to church, helping others, keeping a regular prayer and Bible devotion routine—but is that all there is?

But what about the advanced courses like - oh - better not go there. I was about to give some examples but God spoke to my heart and said, "the advanced courses I have for you Paul are NOT the same that I might have for another."

Oh, how true. Only God can mature us until we are like "one" with Him. We still have a responsibility to have a deep desire to know God intimately.

Before you can possibly be "one" with anyone you must know that person well. Really well. The same applies with our relationship with God. "Oneness" with God requires we earnestly seek to know

Him intimately, and become familiar with all of His ways (See Philippians 3).

"The things that happen either make us evil, or they make us more saintly, depending entirely on our relationship with God and its level of intimacy." ...."Jesus prayed nothing less for us than absolute oneness with Himself, just as He was one with the Father. Some of us are far from this oneness; yet God will not leave us alone until we are one with Him—because Jesus prayed, "that they all may be one." Excerpt From My Utmost for His Highest Oswald Chambers

Father, I am beginning to understand that much of life will be a mystery until I am one with You. Thank You for taking us on this journey and not giving up on us - even though we may be really slow learners. Thank You.

294.COMMON-SENSE (AGAIN)

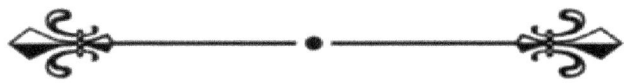

Matthew 6:25 (NIV) "Therefore I tell you, do not worry about your life, what you will eat or drink; or about your body, what you will wear. Is not life more than food, and the body more than clothes?

Matthew 14:28-29 (NIV) "Lord, if it's you," Peter replied, "tell me to come to you on the water." "Come," he said. Then Peter got down out of the boat, walked on the water and came toward Jesus.

I think most of us consider it good to have common sense and to act on it. But let us challenge that a little. Consider the passage above. Was it "common sense " for Peter to step out of the boat? I don't think so. Or how about the widow that gave all she had for an offering. Was that common sense? Consider Christians who have left home, fortune, and ease of living to serve as missionaries around the world. Does that make "common sense" to you? No, none of these are "common sense." But they are examples of the extraordinary sense of God's call in people's lives.

"Jesus summed up common sense carefulness in the life of a disciple as unbelief. If we have received the Spirit of God, He will squeeze right through our lives, as if to ask, "Now where do I come into this relationship, this vacation you have planned, or these new books you want to read?" And He always presses the point until we learn to make Him our first consideration. Whenever we put other things first, there is confusion." (Excerpt From My Utmost for His Highest Oswald Chambers)

We all rely on our "common sense" to make life decisions, but what if I told you that this might be a mistake? What if even the simplest "common sense" decision, made on our own, could lead us astray? Why? Because God desires to lead us by His Spirit. As long as we rely solely on common sense, we will never experience the great adventure of stepping out of the boat—leaving our comfort zone—to accomplish exploits for God, whether big or small.

Father, this thought makes me a little uncomfortable, and I hope it challenges my readers as well. Being led by You is rarely a common sense experience. Lead us, Lord, by Your Spirit, whether it seems to make sense or not. Thank You.

295.COMMUNITY

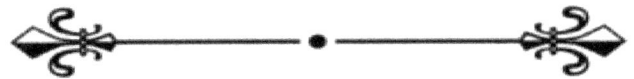

Matthew 10:2-4 (NIV) These are the names of the twelve apostles: first, Simon (who is called Peter) and his brother Andrew; James son of Zebedee, and his brother John; Philip and Bartholomew; Thomas and Matthew the tax collector; James son of Alphaeus, and Thaddaeus; Simon the Zealot and Judas Iscariot, who betrayed him.

If you are like me, you have read the above scripture and "moved on," not giving much attention to the list of names. After all, they are just names, aren't they? Recently something caught my attention.

Think about the people you usually gather with. Are they mostly like you? They often dress like you, share similar habits and goals, and tend to align in their values. They are frequently like-minded when it comes to spiritual beliefs and what they consider important. Their social, political, and spiritual views are often similar—or if they differ, those differences rarely come up in conversation. Isn't that what defines a community? People with shared interests moving toward a common goal, purpose, or destiny.

Look again at the above list. The Roman sympathizer and collaborator (Matthew) in community with the rebel determined to defeat Rome by violence (Simon the Zealot) - how well does that work? Can you just hear the discussions around the table? Matthew suggesting they increase the taxes on the people so they can take an extra share for "ministry" and to keep the Roman occupiers happy. Simon shouts him down demanding they put an end to the Roman occupation through violent upheaval. "Kill the occupiers" is his mantra.

Of course, I just made that up, but really it would be like having a Biden supporter and a Trump advocate trying to come up with a common understanding of just about anything. Not a very harmonious group.

Jesus saw it all differently. Everything is reconciled in Him and through Him. No more Jew or Gentile, no more master and slave, no more male and female, no more Biden and Trump. All as one in Christ. That is the true challenge. We must bring all our prejudices to the table and in Christ they all must go, banished from our lives.

Look again at the people you "hang with." Probably most look very similar or you find yourself agitated with the one(s) not like you. How different it might be if you were "One in Christ," one in community?

Father, it is only In Christ that we can truly be disciples of Jesus. Lead us to do what He did, to love one another. Even those not like us. Thank You.

296.PRAISE

Psalms 113:1 (NASB) Praise the LORD! Praise, O servants of the LORD, Praise the name of the LORD.

Philippians 3:10 (NIV) I want to know Christ—yes, to know the power of his resurrection and participation in his sufferings, becoming like him in his death,

Praise is an expression of approval and or admiration. Praise comes in many forms. Sometimes verbal recognition of an accomplishment, sometimes with an actual reward, or medal or social recognition. At times it is given quietly. Other times it is broadcast for all the world to know.

Why do we praise someone or something that has been accomplished? Simple, because it is praiseworthy in our eyes, and we know about it. That sounds pretty obvious to me and here is the point of this devotion. We are told over and over again in the scriptures to give praise to God.

Can we truly praise God if we do not know Him? I mean really know Him. Oh yes, I am pretty confident we know ABOUT Him. Our heads are full of knowledge of Him. But, do we KNOW Him?

As much as we might try and want to praise God, we are seriously handicapped if we only know about Him. You see, praise comes spontaneously from our hearts when we know Jesus as the Savior of our soul and the Redeemer of the world.

(Life Application Bible Commentary New Testament) PRAISE. Praise is the heartfelt response to God by those who love him. The more you get to know God and realize what he has done, the more you will respond with praise. Praise is at the heart of true worship.

Let your praise of God flow out of your realization of who he is and how much he loves you.

Jesus, my desire is to know You intimately and to become familiar with all your ways. Fill my heart with praise for You. Thank You.

297.FRIENDS

Proverbs 18:24 (NASB) A man of too many friends comes to ruin, But there is a friend who sticks closer than a brother.

John 15:14-15 (NASB) You are My friends if you do what I command you. No longer do I call you slaves, for the slave does not know what his master is doing; but I have called you friends, for all things that I have heard from My Father I have made known to you

It is a most wonderful thing to have people in our lives that we call friends. Some may be acquaintances while others are much closer. What makes the difference? Friendships usually begin with mutual interests and can grow into friendship as people spend time together.

At times, life's circumstances result in people who once were close to us becoming distant. Not because of anything we or they do. It is just the simple fact that most friendships require an investment of time. They must be nurtured or they will wither on the vine.

But it is not always so. Sometimes relationships span the depths of time and distance and the friendship stays strong and vibrant. How is this so? It comes down to how much of ourselves we reveal to one another.

When two people become vulnerable toward each other, sharing some of their deepest thoughts, a deepening friendship usually evolves over time. As we get to know our friend we get to love him or her. As we mutually share the deepest things in our hearts, we end up having shared hearts that can be like one.

My hope is that we all have at least one such friend. If we are married hopefully we see our spouse as such a person. If not, there is something you can do about it.

In the above scripture Jesus calls His disciples friends. Why? Because He shared the deepest things in His heart with them. Is this not a good example for us? Yes, I know we become vulnerable when we share our hearts with others but in so doing a friendship can emerge that transcends all your other relationships. When we open our hearts to another we create the space where two people can become like one.

Father, few have deep friendships that can span the test of time and trials. You have given us the capacity to have such relationships. Please help us, Lord, that we be the models of how this is done, in Christ. Thank You.

298.RSVP

Revelation 19:9 (NIV) Then the angel said to me, "Write this: Blessed are those who are invited to the wedding supper of the Lamb!" And he added, "These are the true words of God."

I think "R.S.V.P' ing" has gone the way of the horse and buggy. There was a time when, perhaps out of courtesy, perhaps out of obligation, most people responded to an invitation. It does not seem to happen so much anymore, at least not in the circles I participate in. I have seen pastors and other leaders practically begging folks to sign up for one event or another. Maybe people do not want to make commitments? What do you think? How are you doing in responding to invitations?

Particularly, how are you doing with responding to Jesus' invitation to live a life that is extraordinary? What do I mean by extraordinary? I mean a life fully dedicated to God, to knowing Him better and better.

Dedicated to being obedient to His commands and principles even in areas that are difficult. Dedicated to loving everyone without exception. Loving our brothers and sisters in Christ, our neighbors, our antagonist, those who disappoint us and even those who mistreat us. This takes much more than determination and willpower. It takes surrender, complete surrendered, to the lordship of Jesus Christ.

(Life Application Bible Commentary New Testament) R.S.V.P. "The traditional invitation response formula is "R.S.V.P.," which stands for a French phrase meaning "respond if you please." This response applies to the grandest invitation of all, the invitation to the wedding feast of the Lamb. God awaits our response. Our presence at the celebration is not earned nor deserved. The angel declared that those invited to the wedding feast would be "blessed" because they had accepted the invitation. They simply responded to the invitation! From the angel, through John, to the written page, the invitation goes out to us. Tell others that there is still time to respond"

Have you sent in your R.S.V.P.? Are you saying in your heart and mind, "Lord, here I am. I am your servant. Speak and I will listen and obey."

Father, here I am. I am Your servant. Speak Lord that I might hear and obey. Thank You.

299.WORKS

James 1:22-25 (NASB) But prove yourselves doers of the word, and not merely hearers who delude themselves. For if anyone is a hearer of the word and not a doer, he is like a man who looks at his natural face in a mirror; for once he has looked at himself and gone away, he has immediately forgotten what kind of person he was. But one who looks intently at the perfect law, the law of liberty, and abides by it, not having become a forgetful hearer but an effectual doer, this man will be blessed in what he does.

As followers of Jesus, we know that it is His redeeming sacrifice and His resurrection that secures our eternal destiny in God's presence for all of eternity. We know that all the good things we do will never be good enough to gain entry into heaven. We have our "ticket" so to speak, bought and paid for, waiting to be redeemed.

However, that does not mean we should sit on the side lines waiting for the pall bearers to take us away. Yes, we have a "spot" reserved for us in God's presence for all eternity. There must be heavenly locations on the hillside with a panoramic view of the mountains and the sea. Maybe there also are "spots" with not such a great view? A view of the neighbor's laundry?

The point I want to make is that how we live our lives now will matter for all eternity. There is some kind of "reward" system established by God for those whose names are written in the Lamb's Book of life.

(Life Application Bible Commentary New Testament) The idea of judgment by works is a theme throughout the Old and New Testaments..... No one will be forgotten at this final gathering—... Believers will be judged—not to see if they merit eternal life, for their names will already be in the Book of Life. This will be a judgment for rewards.

A word of caution, though. If we do "good stuff" for the purpose of getting a reward we might find our "good works" are nothing but wood, hay, and stubble. On the other hand, if the good we do is motivated by our love for and flow out of our relationship with Jesus, there will come a day - and what a day that will be - when Jesus takes us by the hand and leads us through the promise land. WOW! What a day that will be!

Father, regardless of our finances, health, abilities, relationships, age, or anything else, You have prepared good works for us to do now. Please, Lord, awaken our hearts to recognize and respond to Your calling on our lives. Thank You so much.

300.FRACTURE

Isaiah 30:26 (NASB) The light of the moon will be as the light of the sun, and the light of the sun will be seven times brighter, like the light of seven days, on the day the LORD binds up the fracture of His people and heals the bruise He has inflicted.

A "few" years ago I was training for a half marathon. One day, as I stepped out of my car, I felt a sudden, excruciating pain in my foot. I limped around for a couple of days but I soon felt good enough for a practice run. It was fine while I was running but at the end of the run it hurt like the "dickens."

I took a few more days off and tried again. Same results. After a few months of this frustrating limitation I went to see a doctor who told me I fractured a bone in my foot and the only way for it to get better was to stop abusing it for six months.

Six months! How could I possibly do that? I had plans. I wanted to run. I loved running. I wasn't very good at it, but I loved the freedom of going mile after mile alone with my thoughts.

I can be stubborn, and I decided to not listen to the doctor. Instead, I pressed on. Finally, I had to give up. My plan was not working. That was the beginning of the end of my running "career."

About 6-9 months later I was able to go on short runs without pain. The long runs to "nowhere" were no longer a part of my life. To this day I miss them.

So why do I tell this story? In many lives something happens that forces us to change course. We may think it is not a good change. We can be very wrong about that. God knows what is the very best for our lives and we need to change course.

Sometimes we are so in tune with what we are doing that it becomes difficult (impossible) to hear God's soft quiet voice. The resolution? A major interruption, a fracture, that forces us to make a change. Not necessarily a welcome change at the time. Nevertheless, a needed change. Not from our perspective but from God's.

Father, it is so easy to see disruptions, pain, loneliness, grief, and other challenges as fractures in our lives. These experiences often push us in directions we had not planned and do not desire. Yet, You are our Lord. We say this now and pray to live it fully. Help us to accept all fractures in our lives as gifts from You. Only You know what is truly good for us, and we willingly submit to Your sovereign Lordship over our lives. Thank You.

301.FRACTURE(2)

Matthew 5:9 (NASB) "Blessed are the peacemakers, for they shall be called sons of God.

Matthew 5:13-14 (NASB) You are the salt of the earth; but if the salt has become tasteless, how can it be made salty again? It is no longer good for anything, except to be thrown out and trampled under foot by men. "You are the light of the world. A city set on a hill cannot be hidden;

We live in a world that is seriously fractured from what was originally intended. It has been this way since sin entered the human condition through Adam, and it will continue until the return of Jesus. Why has Jesus' life and two thousand years of Christianity seemingly made so little difference in this world fractured by pain and suffering?

Are we losing the battle with evil? Have we yielded so much spiritual territory to our enemy that evil dominates? Consider the tragic moral decline in America. We have lost our spiritual grounding and it appears that the enemy is about to stage a coupe, with the cooperation of perhaps the majority of us. I can't even imagine that 20 years ago mothers would demonstrate for the right to kill their unborn babies and having up to 60% of Americans agree (according to recent polls). Surely, we have lost our way. Do you not agree?

Consider the book of Revelations. Most of the churches mentioned are struggling with one problem or another. Much of the world has arrayed itself against God. Is God's judgment upon the earth the only recourse? Perhaps, but then why did Jesus call for His followers to be peacemakers?

Why did Jesus tell us we are salt and light if we make such little difference in our modern world? I do not have the answers, but I do know that you and I are still expected to be God's Ambassadors wherever we go and whatever we do.

(LABC, "we continue to live in a fractured world. But Jesus commands us and enables us to be peacemakers. Every day we live on earth as temporarily misplaced citizens of God's Kingdom, we can begin to demonstrate our true citizenship by offering our splendor, glory, and honor to the Lord each day. Praise God for the peace he brings you now and pray for the fulfillment of his reign on earth.

Do not forget what Jesus promised: Matthew 16:18 (NASB) I also say to you that you are Peter, and upon this rock I will build My church; and the gates of Hades will not overpower it. In the end Jesus wins and so do those who belong to Him

Father, we are deeply fractured as a nation and as Your Church. Please restore us to our rightful place as peacemakers, salt and light. Thank You.

302.DRUDGERY

Deuteronomy 31:6 (NASB) Be strong and courageous, do not be afraid or tremble at them, for the LORD your God is the one who goes with you. He will not fail you or forsake you.

The context of today's verse seems to be a time of danger, or a time of trouble and uncertainty. "Be strong and be courageous - God will not forsake me."

But what about the everyday drudgeries of life? I mean, let's admit it, a good percentage of our lives is mostly drudgery. Not interesting, mostly boring, mostly repetitive, seemingly never ending. Every day we brush our teeth, once, twice, three times, maybe more and they still get dirty. How about laundry? Once a week, twice, maybe more and it all has to be folded and put away and then we do it again.

How about meal preparation? Three meals a day to cook, three sets of dishes to get out, washed and put away, day after day with no end. Do you make your bed every day, only to unmake it every night? Clearly, there are countless other examples. Life can feel like drudgery. Who has the courage and strength to keep going under such conditions?

Perhaps we do. We can become driven by the things that "must" be done, forgetting that God is with us even in the monotony of daily life. He has not retreated to some distant place, waiting for us to finish our chores. He is right here, with you and with me. He is always by our side, a very present help in times of trouble and even in the daily grind.

"Sometimes it is not the difficulty of life but the drudgery of it that makes me think God will forsake me. When there is no major difficulty to overcome, no vision from God, nothing wonderful or beautiful—just the everyday activities of life—do I hear God's assurance even in these? ...... the most amazing strength becomes ours, and we learn to sing, glorifying Him even in the ordinary days and ways of life." (Excerpt From My Utmost for His Highest Oswald Chambers)

Father, I admit I sometimes get caught up in the drudgery of life. Forgetting You as I go about the seemingly endless chores. I ask Your forgiveness and for Your Spirit to quicken me to Your presence even in the ordinary chores of this life. Thank You.

303.HEAVEN

Revelation 4:1 (NASB) After these things I looked, and behold, a door standing open in heaven, ….Come up here,…

We know very little about this place called heaven. Yet, somehow, we all long to go there, even with so little knowledge of it. It must be the grandest getaway imaginable, a place where everything is perfect. Perhaps a place where the skies are never cloudy, and no discouraging word is ever heard. A wonderful place—but where is it? Is it somewhere in the sky? Or perhaps it is simply "up there," far beyond our reach? We are fairly certain it is not "down here." But if it is neither here, nor up there, nor down there, then where can it possibly be?

Some would say that is all nonsense. It is a spiritual place. Well, what does that mean? It is still a place so it must be "somewhere." Are you sure you want to go to a place when you have no clue where it is? Maybe it is too cold or too hot? Maybe it is too dry and your skin will crack or too humid and your hair will be a mess? Maybe it rains a lot or maybe it never rains?

And we have the problem of, "What am I going to do when I get there?" I think most of us give little thought to that question. Are we scared to find out? I truly doubt if we will be floating on some cloud somewhere playing our violin, or maybe it is a ukulele or a guitar or drums.

We do not know much about this place, we are all very anxious to get to. The scriptures give us some clues, however. Wherever it is, we know Jesus has already been there and has prepared a place for us (John 14:2-3). We know there will be no physical limitations (yes - we can go through doors like Jesus but maybe there are no doors? (1

Corinthians 14:35-49; John 20:19). It says we will be just like Jesus (hard to get my head around that one) (1 John 3:2).

We may not be able to figure it out but we are promised new bodies (1 Corinthians 15) and being there will be wonderful (even when I do not know where "there" is (1 Corinthians 2:9). And for the environmentalists among us, it will be in perfect balance (Revelations 21:1) Oh what a place that will be.

I have packed my bags. What about You? I am ready to be in the presence of God like never before (1 Corinthians 13:12; Revelations 21:3). A place with no more crazy emotions and unsettled thoughts (Revelations 21:4). A place where death is no more (Revelations 21:4). Are you packed? Ready to go?

Lord, I am packed, ready to say "goodbye" to this crazy world. Thank You.

304.MIRROR

James 1:23-24 (NIV) Anyone who listens to the word but does not do what it says is like someone who looks at his face in a mirror and, after looking at himself, goes away and immediately forgets what he looks like.

We are coming up on the one-year anniversary (July 14th) of these one-word devotions. This was an unplanned and surprising endeavor for me. I had come across a "One word Devotional" (from Guideposts) and I thought it might be "fun" to do the same. I started using the words (and thoughts) from the Guidepost devotional but soon "ventured out on my own." It has been an interesting journey for me.

Many years ago, I read that "to think deeply about things," (Stephen Covey, author of Highly Successful Leaders) could lead to greater understanding and success in life. It sounded like wise advice, yet I seldom applied it to my own life. The concept of the "One Word" has changed that for me. I now find myself reflecting deeply on the chosen word and am often surprised by what I discover and write. I hesitate to claim that my writing is inspired, but honestly, every now and then, I cannot help but wonder and believe that the words I end up writing are guided by God's Spirit.

It truly has been an adventure for me and I know it has been for some of you, too. I want to thank all of you who encouraged me along the way. But I am troubled about one thing. It is the "mirror" effect.

By "mirror effect" I mean we are impressed by something, maybe a sermon, a good book, a remarkable movie etc. It touches us in the moment and we may resolve to make some changes because of our experience. However, that rarely happens. As life moves on, as we turn away from the "mirror and forget (see verse 24 above). This bothers me when I see it in my life, and I suspect it happens to many of you also.

Please let me encourage you to give this some serious thought (think deeply). Maybe God will inspire you to write your own "one word devotional" or in some other way make what inspires you "stick to you" until it becomes who you are.

Father, I thank You for Your inspirations. May they bring glory to You. Thank You.

305.ATONEMENT

Matthew 10:39 (NASB) He who has found his life will lose it, and he who has lost his life for My sake will find it.

Atonement means to pay back what is owed. To make compensation or payment or restitution. We know it is impossible for us to make atonement for ourselves, but I want us to stop and consider for a moment how much we owe.

What is it that we could possibly give in return? The answer is simple; we must give ourselves. (Romans 12:1 (NASB) Therefore, I urge you, brethren, by the mercies of God, to present your bodies a living and holy sacrifice, acceptable to God, which is your spiritual service of worship.)

We have a very real problem when we think our lives belong to ourselves. We think we own our lives and can basically do what we want. There is nothing we have that has not been gifted us. Even the air we breathe is a gift to us. We can never pay the price of atonement, but we must not forget that we have been atoned. Bought with a very high price and, in turn, we owe our lives to Another.

I know you are already aware of all this. Yet I can't help but wonder if we sometimes take this incredible miracle of atonement for granted. After all, we have heard it so often that perhaps it no longer fully registers in our consciousness.

I am not sure, but when I look at my own life I see I still want to live my life my way. Some say that is normal. I say that I do not want to live a normal life. I want to live a life where atonement is ever present in my consciousness and where I continually yield my life to Jesus. How about you?

How can we put this devotion into practice? We can start by keeping God's will and ways constantly before us, seeking His guidance, and asking Him to reveal the paths He has prepared. If we remain attentive, we will recognize the divine appointments God has set for us. As we walk with Him, He will use us, if we are willing.

Father, please make the atonement part of our everyday thinking as we yield our lives, all of our lives, to Your Lordship. Thank You.

306.SOCIETY (COMMUNITY)

Genesis 28:3 (NIV) May God Almighty bless you and make you fruitful and increase your numbers until you become a community of peoples.

2 Chronicles 7:14 (NASB) and My people who are called by My name humble themselves and pray and seek My face and turn from their wicked ways, then I will hear from heaven, will forgive their sin and will heal their land.

When May and I were doing marriage counseling we encountered couples whose lives were so distressed there seemed to be no hope. There was no techniques that we could suggest. Just talking to each other usually resulted in heated arguments or worse.

I came to realize that "good" techniques for marriages can work when couples still like one another. But once a person's spirit closes toward another there is no "technique" that will bring them back together.

There is no "technique," but there is a process that has consistently proven successful. The couple focused on getting closer to God rather than getting closer to each other.

Can you see what happens? When you are in a three-way relationship with God, (like a triangle), as you draw closer to God you naturally draw closer to each other.

I look at our society today and I see people that are deeply fractured for many reasons. It is probably impossible to devise any "technique" to solve our multitude of issues but is it possible to be reconciled to one another if we simply turned back to God once again?

We all know that for a marriage to be reconciled both parties must work the process. In the natural, I do not see that happening in our country. But, what if revival comes? What if there is another great awakening in America?

That is my prayer this morning. God, please awaken this great nation once again to pray, to humbly seek You, and to turn from our great wickedness. Thank You Father.

307.SOCIETY (COMMUNITY)(2)

2 Corinthians 4:16 (NASB) Therefore we do not lose heart, but though our outer man is decaying, yet our inner man is being renewed day by day.

Some 40+ years ago, May and I were best friends with another couple and we shared the dream of being part of a community of people that lived together in harmony. The four of us went on a trip to Israel and visited two Kibbutz Communities. In one community the families lived in their own homes but shared meals and work details. In the other community, men and women lived separately, and the children were essentially raised by the community rather than by individual families.

We had the opportunity to sit down and speak with individual members, and from these conversations came my first realization: "wherever we go, there we are." What I mean is that the idea of living together in harmony as a society is an ideal that sounds almost like heaven. The reality, however, is that our fallen nature comes with us. Beneath the ideal facade, the everyday conflicts people usually experience still exist. Why? Because change does not come from outward circumstances but from the work of God within the inner person.

"Changed people, reconciled with God and in process of transformation, are at the very core of the gospel message"......"A better system will not automatically ensure a better life. In fact the opposite is true: only by creating a better life can a better system be developed."......" Ultimately, as liberation theologian Domingos Barbé comments, the sickness of our world is a spiritual illness that comes from a lack of a living relationship with God. Without reestablishing that relationship, there can be no deep and lasting social change." (Walter Wink)

To this day, I still have this "ideal" place in my heart. I would have liked to experience such a community in my life. It will have to wait for heaven. In the meantime, I continue to surrender to the Lordship of Jesus so that wherever I am hopefully the Lord shows up more than I do.

Father, thank You for the many, many adventures that May and I have gone on. In this season of our lives please continue to transform us as we look with anticipation on what you will be doing tomorrow. Thank You.

PS: It was on this trip that May and I started including cheese, tomatoes, and yogurt in our breakfast routine, and we still do. Since she has outlived every member of her family at 93, perhaps there is something to it.

308.NEXT

John 13:17 (NASB) If you know these things, you are blessed if you do them.

In your spiritual life are you tied to the dock or are you on open water? Are you enjoying the calm waters of the harbor where it is safe and routine? Or are you adventuring out far into the open seas of God's perfect will?

It is nice to rest now and then, maybe even idle away an hour or two, but when we continually please our old nature we soon become sluggish in our spiritual lives. I have noticed in my life that if I have too much going on I can easily wear myself out (especially as I have gotten older). I have also noticed that when I slow down too much, I become sluggish—lazy might even be the right word. The challenge for me is finding the right balance. How about you?

I shared before that the night I finished teaching the course Experiencing God, I prayed and asked God, "What is next?" God answered, "Take care of May." At first, I thought that was easy; May does not need much taking care of, just love. But as the years have passed, I have come to better understand the challenges of caring for another person. Even when love is at the center of the relationship, it can still be difficult at times. What I am learning is that I cannot stay safe in the harbor. I must let go of many things in order to do this one next thing well.

"If you believe in Jesus, you are not to spend all your time in the calm waters just inside the harbor, always tied to the dock. You have to get out past the harbor into the great depths of God, and begin to know things for yourself. When you know you should do something and you do it, you immediately know more… It is a dangerous thing to refuse to continue learning and knowing more.""Excerpt From My Utmost for His Highest Oswald Chambers)

What is your "one next thing"? Do you dare ask God what it is? Let me suggest you answer "yes" before you even ask the question. Troubles await those who ask and do not obey.

Father, I think I would have designed a world without all these challenges but You know what is best for each of us and for Your kingdom. Help us to continually seek Your will and let us refuse to stay stuck in the "harbor" when You are wanting us to get out on the "high seas". Thank You.

309.SAINT

Ecclesiastes 9:10 (NASB) Whatever your hand finds to do, do it with all your might; for there is no activity or planning or knowledge or wisdom in Sheol where you are going.

"Lord of all pots and pans and things, make me a saint by getting meals and washing up the plates!"

(Brother Lawrence)

Brother Lawrence (1614-1691) was a "no account" monk who spent the vast majority of his life working in the monastery's kitchen. He never wrote a book. Most of what we know of him is through letters written by and to him. His "only" accomplishment in life was to nurture a relationship with God.

In some ways he is my "hero." Here is a person who followed the scriptures and simply did what was in front of Him to do for the sole purpose of drawing close to God and staying in His presence. Although he never left the kitchen he became well known because of his humility.

Too often we reach after what is not ours to reach for. I know we should "be all God wants us to be" but the key idea is what God wants us to be not what we want to be. In my experience this is often most difficult to discern. Brother Lawrence knew what was most important—he knew his purpose. He was able to focus on "this one thing" even as he went about the ordinary chores of life.

Do you ever get tired of doing chores? Most of the time, I am fine with them, but every now and then, I wish they would just disappear. Apparently, Brother Lawrence did not struggle with this. He reached a place where the "chores of life" became a means of drawing closer to the presence of God.

Do you want to make a difference in your life? I believe there is no better way than to embrace what God has placed in your path—even the everyday tasks—with the sole aim of drawing near to Him. Being in God's presence transforms us. Brother Lawrence never wrote a book, yet in an era without electronic media, he became a kind of "celebrity," even though he never left the kitchen.

Father, what an awesome and simple thought. I can spend this day and every day in Your presence even as I take care of the mundane. Give us hearts to seek Your presence as our highest good. Thank You.

310 STREAMS

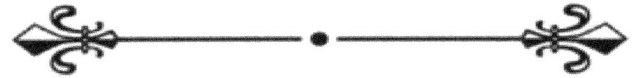

Jeremiah 17:7-8 (NASB) "Blessed is the man who trusts in the LORD And whose trust (confidence) is the LORD. "For he will be like a tree planted by the water, That extends its roots by a stream And will not fear when the heat comes; But its leaves will be green, And it will not be anxious in a year of drought nor cease to yield fruit.

Psalms 1:1-3 (NASB) How blessed is the man who does not walk in the counsel of the wicked, Nor stand in the path of sinners, Nor sit in the seat of scoffers! But his delight is in the law of the LORD, And in His law he meditates day and night. He will be like a tree firmly planted by streams of water, Which yields its fruit in its season And its leaf does not wither; And in whatever he does, he prospers

"Location, location, location" are the three most important things to remember in real estate. And perhaps they are also among the most important for us to remember as devoted followers of God.

Being planted by (near) streams of water ensures that a tree always has the nourishment it needs to grow strong and produce what it is meant to produce. When a tree is planted near the water the roots run deep. It grows to be a sturdy tree. Not easily shaken in the storms of life, giving comfort and shade when the heat comes. Even in times of great distress a tree planted by the water will yield its fruit.

In both scriptures there is a sense of staying put. The tree takes roots and goes deep. Those who delight in God's word are those who spend "day and night" in reflection and obedience to the word of God. In other words, it is more than a quick devotion in the morning or evening. More than prayer before eating. More than a cursory reading of the scriptures. It is "going deep" and allowing God's Word to transform who you are.

(Romans 12:2 (NASB) And do not be conformed to this world, but be transformed by the renewing of your mind, so that you may prove what the will of God is, that which is good and acceptable and perfect.)

Where are you "planted"? Have you settled down by the streams of living water or are you streaming the latest episode of your favorite show?

Father, please open Your Word to our understanding, so that we may live lives firmly rooted in You. Thank You.

311.STRESSFUL

2 Timothy 3:1-4 (NASB) But realize this, that in the last days difficult (stressful) times will come. For men will be lovers of self, lovers of money, boastful, arrogant, revilers, disobedient to parents, ungrateful, unholy, unloving, irreconcilable, malicious gossips, without self-control, brutal, haters of good, 4 treacherous, reckless, conceited, lovers of pleasure rather than lovers of God.

The word "difficult" in today's verse can also be translated as stressful. Who can deny that these days are stressful? Listen to tonight's news. Can you identify any of the above character traits? Try that for a week. You will hear just about all of them, some multiple times.

Is our culture not obsessed with itself? Are we not lovers of pleasure? Do we not seem to be irreconcilable (consider our politics)? Surely, we are living in a difficult (stressful) culture even though we are among the wealthiest people in the world.

Perhaps that is part of our troubles? We have so much and yet we seem to never be satisfied. The "grand pursuit" of wealth, prestige, new cars, new homes, new clothes, new dining experiences, new TV shows, new electronic gadgets new friends on social media, new experiences etc., leaves us worn out. At the end of the day where is the rest that Jesus promised?

Do you think it is possible for us to be causing some of our own stress and difficulty? There is little we can do about the times and the culture we live in, but maybe there is something we can do that will bring the stress level down a notch or two?

"If you are overwhelmed, tired and stressed, the solution is almost always less. Get rid of something, lots of somethings. Feel better by creating space for yourself." (Courtney Carver...(quoted by Joshua Becker)

Sounds too simple, doesn't it? But have you tried it? Take a look around you. Go ahead, do that right now. Do you see something you do not need or want? Ditch it. Go ahead, stop reading , get up, pick it up and put it in the trash (or donation pile) right now.

How did that feel?

Oh, you didn't do it? Well, I guess you will never know how freeing it can be to get rid of stuff you do not need. It is a bit counter-culture. That is OK, so was Jesus.

Dear Lord, Uou promised rest. Please give it to Your people. Thank You.

312.COME

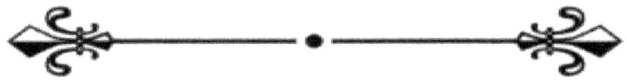

Matthew 11:28-30 (NIV) Come to me, all you who are weary and burdened, and I will give you rest. Take my yoke upon you and learn from me, for I am gentle and humble in heart, and you will find rest for your souls. For my yoke is easy and my burden is light."

I frequently heard and read that you can tell when someone has spent time with God. Have you experienced that? There is something special about being around people who are consistently spending time in God's presence. It is not so much what they do or do not do. It is just them or rather the sweet aroma that naturally occurs when a person has been in God's presence.

2 Corinthians 2:14-15 (NASB) But thanks be to God, who always leads us in triumph in Christ, and manifests through us the sweet aroma of the knowledge of Him in every place. For we are a fragrance of Christ to God among those who are being saved and among those who are perishing;

I often feel like I need to be doing more and I frequently remind myself that I am not a human "doing" but a human "being." Although the "doing" is important the "being" is essential. After all, I cannot do any good if I am not abiding in Christ.

John 15:5 (NASB) I am the vine, you are the branches; he who abides in Me and I in him, he bears much fruit, for apart from Me you can do nothing.

I am confident that God will make our lives useful and filled with remarkable peace when we learn what it means to simply "come" to Him. If this is not your daily habit, why not start to make it one today? Set aside time for God. Stop doing something that is inconsequential and instead "come" sit at the feet of Jesus.

Colossians 3:16-17 (NASB) Let the word of Christ richly dwell within you, with all wisdom teaching and admonishing one another with psalms and hymns and spiritual songs, singing with thankfulness in your hearts to God. Whatever you do in word or deed, do all in the name of the Lord Jesus, giving thanks through Him to God the Father.

"The questions that truly matter in life are remarkably few, and they are all answered by these words—"Come to Me." Our Lord's words are not, "Do this, or don't do that," but—"Come to me." (Excerpt From My Utmost for His Highest Oswald Chambers)

Father, I know we need balance but if we are to err let it be on spending "too much" time in Your presence. Thank You.

313.PRAYER

1 Thessalonians 5:17 (NASB 2020) pray without ceasing,

As some of you know, a few years ago I completed a "project" of praying through the Psalms. And a little more than 2 years ago I started praying through the New Testament.

Why do I mention this? To encourage you to do the same. Having been in this process of "praying the scriptures" for a few years, I find that when I slow down enough to pray about what I am reading it becomes much more meaningful.

Writing out your prayers may be more of a stretch than you would like to take right now? Please consider giving it a try. When you slow down to write out your prayers you will be amazed as your prayer life takes on a new dimension.

Is it time to pray? Yes, it is always time to pray:

(LABC) That the Lord hears our prayers is a common theme in the Psalms, as the following verses illustrate (quoted from NRSV):

Psalm 18:6, "In my distress I called upon the LORD; to my God I cried for help. … my cry to him reached his ears."

Psalm 28:6, "Blessed be the LORD, for he has heard the sound of my pleadings."

Psalm 34:6, "This poor soul cried, and was heard by the LORD, and was saved from every trouble."

Psalm 34:17, "When the righteous cry for help, the LORD hears, and rescues them from all their troubles."

Psalm 145:19, "He fulfills the desire of all who fear him; he also hears their cry, and saves them."

Proverbs 15:29, "The LORD is far from the wicked, but he hears the prayer of the righteous."

Please Lord, help us to draw closer by praying Your word back to You. Thank You.

314.SAINT

1 Thessalonians 3:11-13 (NASB) Now may our God and Father Himself and Jesus our Lord direct our way to you; and may the Lord cause you to increase and abound in love for one another, and for all people, just as we also do for you; so that He may establish your hearts without blame in holiness before our God and Father at the coming of our Lord Jesus with all His saints.

What makes a person a saint? Some people ascribe that title to a person who is holy or virtuous. The Catholic and Orthodox churches use it for a person who has been formally recognized or canonized by the church after death. The word is also used to describe members of the Latter-day Saints movement. But what about us? Are we saints?

I am pretty certain none of those reading this (including myself) is holy and virtuous enough to deserve that title. Since we are still alive and not members of the Mormon church the word saints still cannot apply to us. Yet I would say that indeed we are saints and, at the same time, we are still saints in the making.

It is a theme that runs throughout the Scriptures: "now and not yet." The moment I receive Jesus Christ as my Savior and acknowledge and repent of my sins, I become a saint. Not a perfect saint by any means, but a saint nonetheless. That is my position.

There is a process of refinement (sanctification) that begins at that moment and continues until the day we are face to face with our Lord (Philippians 1:6 (NASB) For I am confident of this very thing, that He who began a good work in you will perfect it until the day of Christ Jesus.)

There is a day when we will not only be saints by our position in Christ but also in our practice in Christ.

My dear friend, are you a saint by your position in Christ? And is your "sainthood" becoming more visible day by day as you "practice" who you are by your position?

"For you to say, 'Oh, I'm no saint,' is acceptable by human standards of pride, but it is unconscious blasphemy against God. You defy God to make you a saint, as if to say, "I am too weak and hopeless and outside the reach of the atonement by the Cross of Christ." Why aren't you a saint? It is either that you do not want to be a saint, or that you do not believe that God can make you into one. " (Excerpt From My Utmost for His Highest Oswald Chambers)

Lord God, thank You for sainthood. It only comes from You.

315 DEDICATE

Romans 12:1 (NIV) Therefore, I urge you, brothers and sisters, in view of God's mercy, to offer your bodies as a living sacrifice, holy and pleasing to God—this is your true and proper worship.

Today's scripture says it is only reasonable for us to dedicate ourselves to the Lord. To dedicate ourselves to the Lord means to devote time, energy, effort, talents, finances - actually everything we have. A complete setting aside of everything for this one purpose.

How are you doing? If you are like me, you are a work in progress as it seems that "life" keeps getting in the way of being totally dedicated to God. Perhaps that is why some saints retreated to the desert or the monastery in their attempts to be completely dedicated to God? It sounds good but "living off the grid" has its difficulties also.

That "fleeing to another location" might be appropriate for some followers of Jesus but that is not what the apostle Paul had in mind when he penned these verses.

You have likely heard the saying, "We are in this world, but we are not of this world." This is the proper context for this verse. It may sound appealing to some to escape the world's problems and challenges, but these very difficulties we dislike can serve as stepping stones toward a closer relationship with God.

Life can be challenging and distracting at times, yet these very challenges and distractions become the proving grounds for our devotion to Christ.

We know how easy it is to be devoted to something when life goes well. What happens to our devotion when things are not going well? Sport teams have a great fan following when they are winning, not always so much when they are losing. A devoted fan stays with the team, win or lose.

Our devotion to Christ is shown when we remain loyal, regardless of circumstances, challenges, or distractions. While these may be nuisances, they also serve to demonstrate that everything Jesus allows into our lives is acceptable to us.

"There is actually only one thing you can dedicate to God, and that is your right to yourself (Excerpt From My Utmost for His Highest Oswald Chambers)

Dear Lord, lead us to the place of complete dedication to You. Thank You.

316.RECOGNITION

Matthew 6:1 (NASB) "Beware of practicing your righteousness before men to be noticed by them; otherwise you have no reward with your Father who is in heaven.

I have discovered that sometimes my true motives are buried deep within me, often only coming to light sometime after the fact. This makes me question my own intentions. I recognize that, at the core, there is a desire within me to be acknowledged. Have you noticed this in your own life?

Sometimes we can see it clearly in others, while at other times it is carefully disguised, either intentionally or because it remains hidden even to them. What we "do" as followers of Jesus is important, but it is far less significant than the "why" behind it.

Our deeply seated motives reveal whether our works are good and will stand the test of God's judgment or will burn up like wood, hay and stubble at the judgment seat of Christ.

Why do some of us have this deep-seated desire for recognition? It might be only an outer layer of a deeper, hidden motive, the desire to be desired.

"One does not merely desire the other, but desires to be desired by the other. And it is this desire to be desired that leaves us so vulnerable to the Powers." Walter Wink -ENGAGING THE POWERS)

"God wants to show us what is hidden. God will make it visible. Being revealed in public is the reward ordained by God for hiddenness. The question is only where and from whom we receive this reward of public recognition. If they long for it to be in sight of other people, then they will have had their reward as soon as they get such publicity". (Dietrich Bonhoeffer - Discipleship)

The revealing of deeply seated motives is a work of God. As we get to know Him, He not only reveals Himself to us, He also begins to reveal ourselves to ourselves. David understood this when He prayed for God to reveal any way in him that did not please God. (Psalm 139:23-24)

Oh Father, we are simply made of dust and yet we are so wonderfully made. Lead us into the way everlasting and let there be no hidden motives that keep us from pleasing You. Thank You.

317.POWERLESS

Romans 8:38-39 (NASB) For I am convinced that neither death, nor life, nor angels, nor principalities, nor things present, nor things to come, nor powers, nor height, nor depth, nor any other created thing, will be able to separate us from the love of God, which is in Christ Jesus our Lord

Do you sometimes feel powerless? Like being clueless as to how to make a difference in our culture? Or powerless to get a relationship back on track? Or seemingly unable to get past being depressed? Or powerless to stop doing something you know you need to stop? Or failing to do what you know is good for you to do but you just cannot seem to be able to get yourself motivated?

Is it possible that whenever we feel powerless, we are deceiving ourselves? After all, the scripture says, "I can do all things through Christ who strengthens me." So how is it that I can speak such powerful words with my mouth, yet in my spirit, I feel this sense of powerlessness?

"A sense of powerlessness is always a spiritual disease deliberately induced by the Powers to keep us complicit. Any time we feel powerless, we need to step back and ask, What Principality or Power has me in its spell? No one is ever completely powerless. Even if it is only a matter of choosing the attitude with which we die, we are never fully in the control of the Powers unless we grant them that power." (Engaging the Powers - Walter Wink)

As I mentioned, we play the fool when we let our emotions lead us. Just like the feeling of being depressed can keep us from doing almost anything productive. It seems to control us, the feeling is "overwhelming". Yet it is only a feeling. It has no true power over you. We choose to give it power when we yield to its suggestions.

This applies to every negative feeling we might have. Feelings can have no power over us unless we yield ourselves to that feeling.

Now please understand I know that this is difficult, but so what? Can you as a child of God do anything in Christ? Yes! You may have difficulty moving a mountain or changing a culture but you can get yourself up and get moving.

Don't believe me? The next time you feel lonely, depressed, powerless, overwhelmed or any such thing, get up and do good for another. It is how we as Christians overcome evil. Even our own evil feelings (Romans 12:21 (NASB) Do not be overcome by evil but overcome evil with good.)

Be mindful that the same Spirit that raised Jesus from the dead is the Spirit that resides in us. We do not have to yield to our feelings no matter how strong they might be.

Romans 8:11-12 (NASB) But if the Spirit of Him who raised Jesus from the dead dwells in you, He who raised Christ Jesus from the dead will also give life to your mortal bodies through His Spirit who dwells in you.So then, brethren, we are under obligation, not to the flesh, to live according to the flesh.

Father, in the midst of discouragement let us rise up through the power of the Spirit of Christ and do good. Thank You.

318.FLEXIBILITY

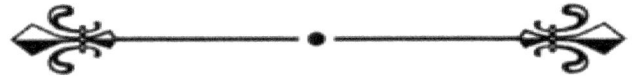

James 5:13-16 (NASB) Is anyone among you suffering? Then he must pray. Is anyone cheerful? He is to sing praises. Is anyone among you sick? Then he must call for the elders of the church and they are to pray over him, anointing him with oil in the name of the Lord; and the prayer offered in faith will restore the one who is sick, and the Lord will raise him up, and if he has committed sins, they will be forgiven him. Therefore, confess your sins to one another, and pray for one another so that you may be healed. The effective prayer of a righteous man can accomplish much.

I have never heard a sermon on the importance of being flexible. Have you? Flexibility is a valuable character trait, but it can also carry risks. It is helpful because it prevents us from being trapped in rigid patterns of behavior, always responding the same way to every situation and circumstance.

At the same time, flexibility can become dangerous when we compromise on matters that should remain non-negotiable. For example, the belief that there are many paths to God. When Jesus tells us that He is the way, there is no other path.

But maybe this is an extreme example. There is some "wiggle room" in other applications of the Christian life. Consider the above verses from James. We have some flexibility in how we pray for people who are sick.

First, we should pray for oneself. So often I have been asked to pray for others, but they have not yet prayed for themselves.

Secondly there is a time when we should call on the elders of the church, asking them to "pray over" them. I do not see this practice happening much in the modern American church. When was the last time you were sick and you asked the church leaders to come pray for you?

Thirdly, pray for one another. Pray daily, lifting each other up, whether in sickness or in health. And there comes a time when all of these can happen together.

Lord, help us to be flexible, allowing Your Spirit to lead us even in the simple act of praying. Thank You.

319 CONFESS

James 5:16 (NASB) Therefore, confess your sins to one another, and pray for one another so that you may be healed. The effective prayer of a righteous man can accomplish much.

Hebrews 10:24-25 (NASB) and let us consider how to stimulate one another to love and good deeds, not forsaking our own assembling together, as is the habit of some, but encouraging one another; and all the more as you see the day drawing near.

As I was about to send yesterday's devotion on flexibility, the word "confess" came to my mind. It is difficult to have one without the other. What I mean is that we are unlikely to confess our sins to other believers unless we have a deepening relationship with them. And it is equally unlikely that we will develop such a relationship unless we regularly assemble with them and spend time together.

May and I have been members of various small groups over most of our 50+ years together. Some we have led, others we have just participated in. In every case, over time we became fond of the people in the group and became part of their lives as they did ours.

I know many pastors use Hebrews10:24-25 to encourage people to come to church but I do not think that was what the author of Hebrews meant. After all there were no "churches" as we know them back then. There were instead clusters of small groups. Believers who came together to worship, share the word and their lives together. This is the essence of fellowship (two or more fellows on a ship).

Since Covid, we have met on Zoom. I am most thankful for the technology that enabled our small group family to survive and even thrive over these years. However, I deep miss the fellowship and the intimacy that comes from being together, face to face, with other believers.

Father, thank You for every phase of life and for the many believers who have encouraged us over the years.

320.ADAPTABLE

1 Corinthians 9:22 (NASB) To the weak I became weak, that I might win the weak; I have become all things to all men, so that I may by all means save some.

Perhaps you have heard it said, "You can't teach an old dog new tricks" It is often used to refer to an older person "stuck" in their ways. I understand the basis for the saying. As I get older, I have a growing preference to keep things as they are. I see no need to change things.

Obviously, that is just my opinion. Every time they release a new software update for my "smart" phone or computer, I get frustrated and often find myself asking, "Why couldn't they just leave things the way they were?"

On the other hand, change is a natural part of life, and those who do not adapt often find themselves "swimming against the tide." This is especially true in our culture, where everything seems to change at such a rapid pace. Yet perhaps there are times when being "unadaptable" in certain areas is not such a bad thing.

For instance, Christians in America seem to have adapted well to sexually explicit movies and shows and even commercials. We have also adapted well to materialism and getting in debt for what we want. Or how about our adaption to the right to abortions?

The early church was noted for rescuing babies. Today, according to Pew Research, over 60% of mainline Protestants believe that abortions should be legal in all or most situations. I do not know about you but for me that sounds like too much adapting to our culture.

On the other hand, there is an adaptability that is both good and appropriate for Christians. As our culture changes, it can be helpful to consider how we present Christ. For example, instead of simply urging people to "go to church," our message may be better received if we first take the time to know people and live a Christ-honoring life before them. In our fast-paced and often chaotic generation, a kind and gentle spirit may be far more effective.

The Life Application Bible Commentary, New Testament says: "With all your might and creative methods, go after people who are lost, astray from God. Be the shepherd who searches for the stranger and the straggler, to reach people living around you who don't believe."

Lord God, by Your Spirit, give us spiritual discernment in these matters. Help us to be adaptable when it is appropriate, but never to compromise Your Word. Thank You.

321.CRITICIZE

2 Corinthians 8:20 (NIV) We want to avoid any criticism of the way we administer this liberal gift.

Some years ago, I was attending a training session when the owner of the company spoke to us about not being critical of the training we were about to receive. Instead, he encouraged us to be open-minded and non-judgmental. I was surprised by his statement, as I had always thought of myself as open-minded. His brief talk made me realize just how often I am not. In fact, I found myself criticizing him in my mind even as he spoke. I can be quick to judge. Are any of you like that?

I have seen this critical tendency in me show up in many aspects of life where I think I have some experience or expertise. It can be with growing plants, teaching others, leading small groups, being a good husband etc. You name it and, left to myself ,you would think I was a built-in expert. If things are not done "my way" there is room for improvement.

Before you get too down on me, be careful. I would not want you to become critical of me in this little devotion on criticism. I may have an extreme version of this negative character trait, but I am pretty sure you have Your own traits that might need a little work. After all, are we not all "works in progress"?

The point I want to make is that just because I have a tendency to be critical, it does not mean I have to be critical. I can set my critical nature aside and be a much better learner. We can all do that if we want to. We who profess Jesus as Lord have a significant advantage. The Holy Spirit can lead us into the right attitude in every situation.

If we consider the above scripture carefully there is a dual responsibility. We should avoid being critical of others. We should also avoid doing what might cause others to be critical. Not always an easy thing but something to think about as we do life with one another.

Again, we have a significant advantage over non-believers. We have the Holy Spirit to lead and guide us, if we listen and obey.

"It is impossible to enter into fellowship with God when you are in a critical mood….Stop having a measuring stick for other people. There is always at least one more fact, which we know nothing about, in every person's situation." (Excerpt From My Utmost for His Highest Oswald Chambers)

Father, please replace my critical spirit with an attitude of love. Thank You.

322.DEVOTED

Romans 12:10 (NASB) Be devoted to one another in brotherly love; give preference to one another in honor;

In the last 50+ years, May and I have been devoted to one another. As we look at other couples, we are sometimes saddened by what we see. So many couples tolerate one another but are no longer devoted to one another despite the vows they may have made.

One of the main issues is that, over time, instead of doing life together, they live their own lives. They may still live in the same house and perhaps share in taking care of it. Maybe even occasionally do something in common. They might be friends. Yet they are not devoted to one another because they have so many other competing interests.

That is where the problem finds its source. We have a limited ability in how many things or people we can be devoted to. We might think we are devoted to our marriage, our family, our work, our entertainment, etc., but I do not think that is possible. To be devoted to someone requires an extensive effort in time and resources. Devotion towards another requires saying "no" to many otherwise attractive offers in life.

I suggest we have similar issues with our devotion to God. There are so many competing issues that we do not have time to spend with Him. Yes, we say we love God, but what is the evidence? I am reminded of the scripture Luke 10:41-42 (NASB) But the Lord answered and said to her, "Martha, Martha, you are worried and bothered about so many things; but only one thing is necessary, for Mary has chosen the good part, which shall not be taken away from her"

Are we making the right choices? What/whom are we devoted to? Are we sure? Is it the right choice?

Father, please lead us to be devoted in love to one another and especially to You. Thank You.

323.TIME

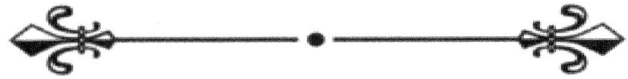

Ecclesiastes 3:1 (NASB) There is an appointed time for everything. And there is a time for every event under heaven.

I find the concept of time fascinating. We all live in a dimension governed by it, where it shapes and controls much of our existence. Despite stories like A Christmas Carol, with its ghosts from the past and future, we really have no access to either. We are confined to the present moment.

That is all we get, folks. James 4:14 (NASB): "Yet you do not know what your life will be like tomorrow. You are just a vapor that appears for a little while and then vanishes away."

God does not have this limitation. I gather that neither will we when "He takes us by the hand and leads us through the promise land." There will be no time constraints whatsoever.

Ah, but we have not arrived yet, so we must live in the present. Which means we get just one chance to do what needs to be done. Right now. Once the time is past, it is gone, we cannot make it up. I know we might argue that we can do it later. That may seem true, but the reality is that when you delay something that should have been done earlier, you end up missing the chance to do something else that matters right now. Do you see what I mean? You and I have only this moment to focus on the most important thing we need to be doing at this very instant.

The options of the "good things" we can do "right now" are virtually endless. What is the best use of your time right now? Is it reading this devotional? Or is it going for a walk? Maybe you should be doing the dishes or making the bed? Or how about that phone call you know you should make? Or maybe even coffee with a friend?

Is there someone lonely that you can comfort? There are all kinds of opportunities to spend our time doing "good stuff." But what is most important? What is it that God wants you to do with this very moment He has graciously given to you?

The answer comes from and through Your walk with God. The more you come into His presence, the more devoted you are to Him, the more You come to know Him intimately, the better choices you will make.

What do you say? What is the very best use of Your time right now? What has God prepared for you to do? Are you doing it?

Father, through Your Holy Spirit, please lead and guide us to carry out the good works You have prepared for us to do today. Thank You.

324.PEARL

Matthew 13:45-46 (NASB) Again, the kingdom of heaven is like a merchant seeking fine pearls, 46 and upon finding one pearl of great value, he went and sold all that he had and bought it.

I see a lot of professing Christians spending large chunks of time playing video games, doing crossword puzzles, reading about the latest sports events, watching the weather reports or news, etc. I find it amazing how much we can do with our electronic devices. Some are using their devices for evil (eg. pornography, gambling, etc.) but the things I mentioned above are not evil in themselves. Or are they?

It seems to me our obsession with TV has transferred to an obsession to our electronic devices. We have them ready to entertain ourselves in all kinds of ways. Is this good or is it evil?

It is not always easy to distinguish between good and evil, you know. What do you think?. What would make a seemingly innocent habit into something that is evil for you or me?

Many of us are on auto pilot. We are mostly unconscious. We do what we feel like doing. We give little thought to the usefulness or value of what we are doing. We are so habituated to some activities that they have mastered us.

Consider what Paul has to say: 1 Corinthians 6:12 (NASB) All things are lawful for me, but not all things are profitable. All things are lawful for me, but I will not be mastered by anything.

Could it be that some of our habits (like mindless scrolling through social media, playing games, watching sports, etc.) have become our master? That is ridiculous? Well, maybe. To be sure, go without it for 30 days or so, just to make sure. Go ahead, I challenge you!

But beneath it all, I think our real problem is that we don't truly know what matters most to us, so any "legitimate" activity seems sufficient. I wonder how different our lives would be if we actually understood what is truly important and pursued it wholeheartedly.

"What are you willing to die for?" (Walter Wink)

Maybe that is the question we should ask ourselves?

Father, we are so distracted. What is truly important? Lead us to live lives that are not double-minded. Thank You.

325 HOPE

Romans 5:3-5 (NASB) And not only this, but we also exult in our tribulations, knowing that tribulation brings about perseverance; and perseverance, proven character; and proven character, hope; and hope does not disappoint, because the love of God has been poured out within our hearts through the Holy Spirit who was given to us

It has been said that almost any kind of difficult circumstance can be endured if there is hope. On the other hand, when hope is missing, woe unto us.

As devoted followers of Jesus, we have a great basis for hope. A hope that this life is not the end of everything. We have the hope of eternity in the presence of God. A hope that makes our momentary sufferings seem to be little disturbances as we pursue knowing God more and more intimately.

(LABC) SIMEON'S HOPE - "Simeon was old and had much to ponder. No doubt he had disappointments in his life to worry over, much to bemoan, lots to regret. Rather than dwelling on life's rough ride, Simeon, even in old age, looked to God's future with brightness and hope. Simeon's secret was in his worship and expectation for God. Worship and praise were natural to him; they were the center of his life. Nothing is so bleak as a day without tomorrow. With God, however, every day has hope and good cheer. Neither old age nor grim circumstances should keep you from God's comfort, sufficient for your needs today. Take Simeon's example and look ahead to God's great plan for you and the world."

So let us nurture our hope in God and His redeeming work in our lives. Let us not look at our circumstances but instead look with great expectation toward that wonderful day. That day when there will be more tears, no more crying, no more sorrow, no more pain. Oh! What a most wonderful day that will be.

Father, we live in a fallen world, and are surrounded by powers and influences that want us to give up hope. Lord, let us not look at our circumstances but rather look to You. We have not yet seen, nor can we even imagine, what awaits us in Your presence. Thank You.

326.BIRTH

Titus 3:5-7 (NASB) He saved us, not on the basis of deeds which we have done in righteousness, but according to His mercy, by the washing of regeneration and renewing by the Holy Spirit, whom He poured out upon us richly through Jesus Christ our Savior, so that being justified by His grace we would be made heirs according to the hope of eternal life.

We were born physically. We have limits to what is possible. We can't fly, and few can run a mile in under 4 minutes. Some of us can lift 100 pounds but most of us struggle to lift even half that much. Who of us can go days without sleep, or without water or food?

Our physical bodies make certain demands, and we live with "built in" limitations. Most are aware of this but there are people test the limits, often to their chagrin.

What about the "new birth"? What are the limits to what God might do with and through us? Surely there is nothing impossible to God. Even our stubborn determination to live life our way will not deter Him from making us into the new creatures He desires us to be.

"The New Birth is a work of the Holy Ghost, by which man, of a sinner, is made righteous; and from being a child of damnation and wrath, is made a child of grace and salvation. This change is effected through faith, the word of God and the Sacraments; and by it, the heart, and all the powers and faculties of the soul (more particularly the understanding, will, and affections), are renewed, enlightened, and sanctified in Christ Jesus, and are fashioned after his express likeness. The new birth comprehends two chief blessings, namely, justification, and sanctification, or the renewal (. ἀνακαίνωσις a complete change for the better) of man. Tit. 3:5." (Excerpt From True Christianity Johann Arndt)

How is the renovation project in your spiritual life going? Are you fully on board, cooperating with the renewal work of the Holy Spirit? Are you yielding your will daily (every moment?) to the work of the Holy Spirit in you?

None of us are yet what we are to become. May God enable us to surrender to the molding process of the Holy Spirit so we become conformed to the image of Jesus. (Romans 8:29a (NASB) For those whom He foreknew, He also predestined to become conformed to the image of His Son

Father, thank You for making us into what You want us to be.

327.AMAZEMENT

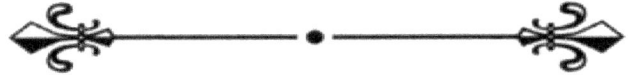

Luke 2:47 (NASB) And all who heard Him were amazed at His understanding and His answers.

Being married to May these 50+ years, I have been amazed more than a few times. One thing is her ability to receive favor even from strangers. Two instances come to mind, both during a road trip across the US. We made it a practice to stop at state capitals whenever we could and this one morning we arrived an hour or more before they opened. We had a busy travel schedule that day and when the guard saw the disappointment on May's face he said, "come with me." The next thing you know we were getting a private tour.

On the same trip we stopped at a highway rest stop near Jackson, Mississippi. The restrooms were open, but the visitor's center was closed, as it should have been as it was the wee hours of the morning. Through the window one could see this was not an ordinary visitor center. They had numerous displays regarding the local history. As we were looking through the window a guard comes up to May (notice not me) and asks if we would like to go in and look around. Sure enough we got another "private tour."

I have said many times in jest that I always go places with May because I know we will get favor as long as she is by my side. And so it has been. I am to this day amazed at how much favor she gets just by being May.

Another thing that has amazed me about May is the peace she had in her heart when three different doctors told her while I was on life support that I would never recover. I am amazed at how God gave her the favor of peace even in what might have been the most difficult time of her life.

My dear brothers and sisters in Christ, I am certain that each of you has an amazing story to share. Some may be breathtaking, while others may seem simpler, yet all are remarkable in their own way. What is it that makes our stories so truly amazing?

It is the work of God in our lives as He perfects us on this road of redemption. Is there any story more amazing than that? He has chosen us to be conformed into the image of His Son, Christ in us. YES!!! That is an amazing story.

(LABC) Sit back in amazement, just like those who heard the boy Jesus speak during that Passover season long ago, and rededicate yourself to following Jesus' example, diligently studying the Scripture to learn more about God your Father.

Father, lead us to be fully dedicated to You. Thank You for the amazing things You have done and continue to do in our lives.

328.THAT

John 17:21 (NASB) that they may all be one; even as You, Father, are in Me and I in You, that they also may be in Us, so that the world may believe that You sent Me.

Now here is a frequently used word. I do not remember what it was about this word that led me to choose it for a devotional. As I reflect on it, I realize that it is a word pointing to a person, place, or circumstance that brought something about.

In today's verse, the word appears four times. Perhaps some of you English enthusiasts might find using the same word so often a bit unusual, but I believe it communicates the message clearly.

The first "that" refers to the faithful witnesses through the ages who continue to pass on the legacy of Jesus through which we become as one with each other and with God.

The second "that" refers to the unity of the Father and the Son. They are the models for us and the ideal of how we are to view one another. No separation, unified as one.

The third "that" refers to the witness we are to the world when we are living as unified believers and followers of Jesus Christ. There is no better way for the world to know and believe than through the love and unity expressed in our daily lives.

And the fourth "that" refers to Jesus and His mission, the redemption of all mankind. Now "that" is something.

So, what does all "that" mean to you? Does it—or will it—make a difference in how you live, what your priorities are, and how you think and engage with other people, especially fellow believers? It seems to me that "that" unity is high on God's agenda in this fractured culture, and "that" would be an amazing antidote.

Father. Inspire us to unity as we devote ourselves to knowing You through Your word and the inspiration of Your Holy Spirit. Thank You.

329 GRACE

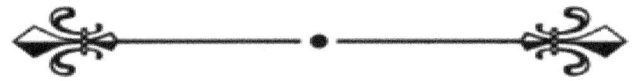

2 Corinthians 6:1-3 (NASB) And working together with Him, we also urge you not to receive the grace of God in vain— for He says, "AT THE ACCEPTABLE TIME I LISTENED TO YOU, AND ON THE DAY OF SALVATION I HELPED YOU. Behold, now is "THE ACCEPTABLE TIME," behold, now is "THE DAY OF SALVATION"— giving no cause for offense in anything, so that the ministry will not be discredited.

To receive grace is to receive favor that you have not earned. To live in grace is to behave in such a way that only the favored part of you is visible.

What do I mean? It's a little difficult to explain, but when we live in grace, the way we face life and handle challenges is different from when we are not living in grace. Living in grace allows us to reflect the light of Christ within us.

I have a mind that wanders and tries to solve all the problems of the world. This can sometimes make me anxious or worried, even to the point of sleeplessness. So, what can I do? I have learned that simply telling myself to stop the "stinking thinking" is rarely effective. Instead, I have discovered the approach that David often used in the Psalms.

Many of David's Psalms express distress of some kind or another. He lays out His difficulties before the Lord but closes with prayer and thankfulness that God will rescue Him. David does not attempt to pretend His troubles are not real or pretend that they do not concern him. He is worried. And his solution? Tell God and praise Him for who He is.

That, my friend, is how we live in grace when we feel like there is no grace. Feelings are deceptive and can lead us all over the place. When our feelings are really "stinking thinking" (woe is me, I'm in trouble, some calamity or even death is approaching, you name it) we must not give them power over us.

Grace is not only for managing our feelings. It is also for refusing to act out our "stinking thinking." When I am offended, angry, frustrated, impatient, tired, sad, etc. grace is enables me to respond with a gentle kind answer. Even to bless those who offend or seek to harm me. Without grace we are just like the world.

"One of the greatest proofs that you are drawing on the grace of God is that you can be totally humiliated before others without displaying even the slightest trace of anything but His grace." (Excerpt From My Utmost for His Highest Oswald Chambers)

Lord, lead us to live by grace in all of life. Thank You.

330 PRODUCTIVE

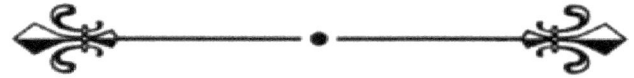

Luke 12:16-17 (NASB) And He told them a parable, saying, "The land of a rich man was very productive. And he began reasoning to himself, saying, 'What shall I do, since I have no place to store my crops

As mentioned previously (see devotion 211) I have been reading about why regenerative gardening and farming is so good for us as individuals. The most important factor is having earth (soil) that is healthy. Soil that is "virgin" or has been naturally regenerated requires little intervention in terms of fertilizers or pesticides. All the nutrients necessary for healthy growth are already present in balanced abundance. I have noticed that plants thrive best when I simply nourish the soil naturally.

Our new birth in Jesus is like planting deep roots in this regenerated soil. In Him, through His Word and the indwelling Spirit of God, we have everything we need to bear fruit for His kingdom.

1 Corinthians 1:7 (NASB) so that you are not lacking in any gift, awaiting eagerly the revelation of our Lord Jesus Christ. There is nothing we are lacking to be productive for the kingdom of God.

When a seedling is placed in good soil the chances are very high that it will produce good fruit unto its kind (i.e. apples produce apples not oranges). It does not have to try to be a good apple or orange. It is already. That is the nature God has given to it.

We, too, have been given a specific nature by God. We do not have to strive to be something we are not. We just need to let our roots go down deep into the word and presence of God. He does all the work when we are deeply rooted.

(LABC) "So how are believers to bear good fruit? God calls them to be "active" in their obedience. To be productive for God means obeying his teachings, resisting temptation, actively serving others, and sharing the faith"

Would you like to be a productive Christian bearing much good fruit? Simply surrender and obey God's teachings and principles.

Father, we know there is no need for us to strive to be productive. We just need to be in Christ. Thank You.

331 REPENT

Luke 3:10 (NASB) And the crowds questioned him, ... what shall we do?

When I was very young (6-12) I was a practicing Catholic altar boy. I sincerely wanted to be "right" with God, and I was taught to go to confession regularly, every Saturday, before receiving Communion on Sunday. I often did but as I remember it now, I saw it as an obligation, as something I "had" to do. I am not sure if I ever repented.

The dictionary tells us that repent means to feel sincere regret or remorse for one's wrongdoing. The church tells us it is a change in direction. If I am confessing the same wrongdoings time after time I surmise I have neither deep regret nor changed direction.

We must also consider why we feel remorse and why we decide to change direction. For instance, I might feel remorse not for the action itself, but for getting caught, and I might change direction out of fear of the consequences.

True repentance requires proper motivation. Why do I want to repent? Is it to save myself embarrassment, or difficulty or punishment? Or do I want to repent because I have displeased God and deep down my true desire is to please Him?

I know that many of us (including myself) have issues that we have "repented" of, perhaps many times, and yet they continue to recur in our lives. If so, our repentance in this particular area might be superficial.

On the other hand, we are all "works in progress (See Philippine 1:6). In some areas the process of falling and getting back up gets repeated multiple times until finally we are all that God wants us to be. Sanctified, finally, someday, it will be so.

The folks asked John the Baptist "what they should do" and his answer was mostly directed toward an outward change in behavior:

(LABC) "WHAT SHOULD WE DO? John's message demanded at least three specific responses:

Share what you have with those who need it.

2. Whatever your job is, do it well and with fairness.

3. Be content with what you earn.

John was calling the people to right living. What changes can you make in how you share what you have, do your work honestly, and be content?

But is repentance not more than outward change? Yes, it is a heart change as Christ takes over our lives.

Father, we bow before You and surrender ourselves to be transformed. Thank You.

332 STONE

Ezekiel 36:26-27 (NASB) Moreover, I will give you a new heart and put a new spirit within you; and I will remove the heart of stone from your flesh and give you a heart of flesh. I will put My Spirit within you and cause you to walk in My statutes, and you will be careful to observe My ordinances

I believe it was President Barack Obama who declared that the United States is no longer just a Christian nation. To him, I understand, that was good news. We were no longer bound by the teachings and principles of Christianity. We could make our own rules and act as we pleased, much like what is described in the book of Judges. As a progressive society, we believe we know better than God.

Obama was right. Not that we suddenly changed and discarded Christianity. We had embraced a "form of godliness while denying the power of God." We have been on this course of severe moral decline in America for some time.

We have come to a place where good is often seen as evil and evil as good. I wonder what happened to this country where people once knew what was right and the majority tried to live righteously (at least on the surface).

Could it be that all along, even though we acted mostly as Christians on the outside, in reality we had hearts of stone? Although we claimed to be a Christian nation, if you study our history we have been "unchristian" in many aspects for many years.

Could it be that we mostly went through the motions of being Christian but as a nation we only had a facade of being Christ followers? Could it be that we have proclaimed the rule of Christ on the outside, but our hearts are like stone?

I leave you to decide if there is any basis of truth in what I have just written, but what is the condition of your heart? Are you content to follow the rules and to act like a Christian while still having a heart of stone? Or, have you come to the place where only Christ truly matters?

Lord, You alone are in the "heart business." Please make this scripture real inour hearts. Take away our stoney hearts and transform us. Thank You.

333 FORM

2 Timothy 3:2-5 (NASB) For men will be lovers of self, lovers of money, boastful, arrogant, revilers, disobedient to parents, ungrateful, unholy, unloving, irreconcilable, malicious gossips, without self-control, brutal, haters of good, treacherous, reckless, conceited, lovers of pleasure rather than lovers of God, holding to a form of godliness, although they have denied its power; Avoid such men as these

We have discussed this verse a number of times but God brought it before me again. Perhaps He wants us to take another look?

An observation I have made many times in the lives of most (if not all) of the people I have known, is that we seem to be living at some level of unconsciousness. The formation of habits is a clear example of how we can perform complex tasks, such as driving a car, and for the most part remain completely unaware of what we are doing, yet still be competent.

Similarly, in conversation, we often focus on how to respond rather than being fully present and truly listening. Or we fall into the habit of making judgments about others, even as we claim the importance of not judging.

It has been said that unless we form these habits it would not be possible for us to live in a complex society. That may be true, or maybe not. I am sure that much of our lives are lived with only partial awareness of what we are truly doing. Perhaps that is not a problem at all, unless our unconscious behaviors end up discrediting Christ.

For example, we might know we should not gossip, yet we disguise our words as prayers, pretending to pray for others when in reality we are just spreading gossip. Or we hold to a "form of godliness" (i.e. going to church) and yet are rude or inconsiderate to others who are not like us. No conscious harm intended, just unconscious, not realizing what we are doing. Or when we pretend to listen to a loved one. Surely, we do not do that consciously. Conscious or not it is still condescending.

"The Unchristian Walk Of Many Persons In Our Day, Is A Cause Of The Rejection Of Christ And Of The True Faith......"For the Christian faith without a Christian life is a tree without fruit. True faith works by love (Gal. 5:6); and wherever it is found, there Christ dwells, with all his divine graces and virtues. Ephesians 3:17. ...."They, therefore, who usurp a Christian's name, and yet do not a Christian's work, shall be denied, in their turn, by the Savior when he shall pronounce the sentence: "I never knew you: depart from me, ye that work iniquity." Matt. 7:23." (CIR 1605) (Excerpt From True Christianity, Johann Arndt)

Father, once again I ask for You to awaken us from our slumbers. Reveal to us how You see us. Show us any ways in our lives that are discrediting the Gospel of Christ and compel us to change. Thank You.

621

334.STRICT

Matthew 5:30 (NASB) If your right hand makes you stumble, cut it off and throw it from you; for it is better for you to lose one of the parts of your body, than for your whole body to go into hell.

Matthew 5:48 (NASB) Therefore you are to be perfect, as your heavenly Father is perfect.

Most parents of my generation were known for their strictness. Thinking back, I cannot remember even one friend who boasted about "easy going" parents. Another thing I remember about my friends is they did not complain that their parents did not love and care for them.

It seems there was a sort of balance in the American culture. Most parents insisted that their children follow certain rules, such as being home for supper or completing homework before play, yet they also made time to be with their children. This was in an era and culture when mothers were typically at home.

As children are prone to do, my friends and I often chafed under our parents' strictness. Why couldn't I play first? I'll do my homework later. We did not always like the rules, but we also felt the security of knowing that our parents loved us and wanted the best for us.

If you read the above scriptures, do you sense God's strictness? God's standards are pretty high, off the charts, actually. Do you sometimes wish He would lighten up a bit? On the other hand, we know that He loves us. He cares for us. He knows what is best for us, even when we just want to "go play". Not all "good" things in life are truly good for us you know.

"There are many things that are perfectly legitimate, but if you are going to concentrate on God, you cannot do them. Your right hand is one of the best things you have, but Jesus says that if it hinders you in following His precepts, then "cut it off." The principle taught here is the strictest discipline or lesson that ever hit humankind." (Excerpt From My Utmost for His Highest Oswald Chambers)

Father, once again all I can do is bow in submission and obedience. Put it in my heart to "follow your rules" and to have a settled heart in the midst of Your love for me. Thank You.

335 METAMORPHOSIS

1 Corinthians 15:51 (NASB) Behold, I tell you a mystery; we will not all sleep, but we will all be changed,

In Hawaii there is a saying, "broke the mouth," which means something tastes really, really good and there are no better words to describe it. It fascinates me that the word Paul uses, which is translated as "mystery," comes from a term that literally means "to shut the mouth."

In other words, Paul is about to describe a mystery that is so incredible that there are no words that can accurately describe it. What is this mystery? It is God's sovereign act of transformation that takes (is taking) place in every follower of Jesus.

Perhaps you have heard, or said yourself, "I am only human." This is often used to justify a wrong action by blaming our nature rather than taking responsibility for our free will. But did you know that for those who are disciples of Jesus, this is not true?

We are not merely human. A transformation has taken place. We have become divine, for Christ lives in us, and we live in Him.

2 Peter 1:3 (NASB) seeing that His divine power has granted to us everything pertaining to life and godliness, through the true knowledge of Him who called us by His own glory and excellence.

Although our own righteousness is like filthy rags, God still lives in us, and the simplest acts of obedience bear fruit for the Kingdom of God.

"As fruit, which is not valuable in itself, surprises the spectator into a love of it, when served up in vessels of precious gold: so our prayers and acts of devotion, though of no account in themselves, are exalted in Jesus Christ, in whom, as in the beloved, we are made accepted with God. Ephesians. 1:6." (Johann Arndt)

I know we sometimes fail to live up to who we have become, but do not stay down. Let us rise from our beds of shame, self-centeredness, depression, sadness, frustration, anger, revenge, grief, etc. and embrace whom we have become in Christ.

Oh, God, please let the metamorphosis continue until we are what You intend us to be. Thank You.

336.LEADING

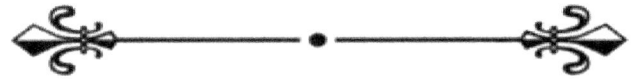

James 1:2-4 (NASB) Consider it all joy, my brethren, when you encounter various trials, knowing that the testing of your faith produces endurance. And let endurance have its perfect result, so that you may be perfect and complete, lacking in nothing.

I do not know about you but I do not like trials. They can be quite stressful. I always thought of myself as mostly calm and in control when trials come, however, recent events prove that was really a facade. Perhaps it is because I am getting older? Or because I have things to learn and experience? I am not sure but I do know that lately trials stress me out and in the midst of such times my brain seems to get a little short circuited.

On the far side of a particular difficulty, I often wonder why I felt so stressed. It was not really that awful. Yet when I am in the midst of it, I seem to lose the ability to think clearly. This is a new experience for me, and I believe God is showing me that, despite all my talk about trusting Him, I still have a ways to go when life becomes challenging.

(LABC) "THE HOLY SPIRIT'S LEADING - Some Christians feel that the Holy Spirit will lead them always "beside quiet waters" (Psalm 23:2 NIV). But that is not necessarily true. He led Jesus into the wilderness for a long and difficult time of testing, and he may also lead believers into difficult situations. When facing trials, first make sure you haven't brought them on yourself through sin or unwise choices. If you find no sin to confess or unwise behavior to change, then ask God to strengthen you for your test. Finally, faithfully follow wherever the Holy Spirit leads."

Today I write this with no troubles troubling me. I like this place. It is more comfortable for sure. However, I have a sense that God still has more opportunities in store for me to practice being at peace in Him, even when I am not okay.

Lord, I thank You that I am not facing this season alone. How wonderful to be able to pray and seek Your face, knowing that You have this, regardless of what the future holds. I pray for my brothers and sisters in Christ who are dealing with various trials. Please give them strength to endure and even to thrive. Thank You.

337.WRITE

Revelation 21:5b (NASB) ….” And He *said, “Write, for these words are faithful and true.”

“When I write I think deeply about my friends, I pray for them, I tell them my emotions and feelings. I reflect on our relationship, and I dwell with them in a very personal way” (Excerpt From The Road to Daybreak Henri J. M. Nouwen)

The above quote is from a book by a Catholic priest. It is a series of journal entries as he seeks clarity, direction and purpose in serving God. I found it a most interesting read because the author is sharing his heart, his struggles, his worries, his inadequacies, his victories and, perhaps surprisingly, the intimacy of writing.

Over the years, I have encouraged many believers to take up journaling. I believe most of David's Psalms were originally his personal journaling. I suggest this because I have personally found it to be an excellent way to navigate difficult times, celebrate victories, and pray for myself and others. I am not referring to a journal that simply records your daily activities, but rather a personal reflection journal that explores how you are truly feeling—both the good and the challenging, along with any real victories along the way.

Perhaps it is because I am an introvert at heart, but I have often found it difficult to express to others what is really happening in my heart. I sometimes get the sense that most people are not particularly interested. That could just be my perspective, and I may be mistaken, but it often seems that people are absorbed in their own lives and emotions, leaving little energy to process feelings with others.

And that is partly why I suggest journaling. It is a way to be heard and to find great clarity. The pen and paper are always ready to capture one's feelings. They are not judgmental but somehow able to bring clarity when strong emotions are confusing, upsetting or in some cases (like depression) debilitating.

My dear friend, once again let me encourage you to take up this challenge, especially if you do not have a good friend that can and will listen. But let me give you one more word of advice. Write your journal as if you were writing to God (actually you are). Be sure to keep Him in focus, because despite your troubles, He does listen. He does care and He has you no matter how you feel.

Lord God, thank You for all seasons of life. May we rejoice in you in everything we do. Thank You.

338.FRET

Psalms 37:8 (NASB) Cease from anger and forsake wrath; Do not fret; it leads only to evildoing.

"Worrying always results in sin. We tend to think that a little anxiety and worry are simply an indication of how wise we really are, yet it is actually a much better indication of just how wicked we are. Fretting rises from our determination to have our own way. Our Lord never worried and was never anxious, because His purpose was never to accomplish His own plans but to fulfill God's plans. Fretting is wickedness for a child of God." (Excerpt From My Utmost for His Highest Oswald Chambers)

Is that not an interesting quote? All our "concerns and worrying and fretting and anxiousness are just indications of how wicked we are." They are wicked because our real purpose in life is to not to live out God's plans for our lives but rather our own plans (to be doing what we want to do (the book of Judges).

Is it possible to become so settled in our spirit that we want what the Father wants for us more than what we want for ourselves? I know it is easy to profess this to be so but when we become anxious are we not giving evidence to the contrary?

In this day and age, we can fret about many things. The cost of living, the car repairs, the hospital bill, the political situation, the anger and animosity that seems to have swept across our nations, the suffering from natural and man-made disasters, wars, famines, relationships gone south - gee - there really are a lot of things that can cause us to fret and worry and to become anxious about. Perhaps you can identify with one or more of these?

But in the midst of life's storms, we have been given some extremely good advice. Philippians 4:6-7 (NASB) Be anxious for nothing, but in everything by prayer and supplication with thanksgiving let your requests be made known to God. And the peace of God, which surpasses all comprehension, will guard your hearts and your minds in Christ Jesus.

We must not hide under our pillows and pretend the world is well. It is not. We are in deep trouble. However, we have our instructions. In everything pray with thanksgiving, and let His peace consume us. Not peaceful yet? Go back to step one.

Father, in these times of great difficulty, lead us to seek You with all diligence that Your peace that is beyond understanding will be ours. Thank You.

339.RAGE

Luke 4:28 (NASB) And all the people in the synagogue were filled with rage as they heard these things;

Rage is one of those things that we Christians want to avoid at all costs. There have been a couple of times when I have been consumed by rage. Consumed is probably not an adequate word. Rage takes full control and compels one to do evil that would otherwise never be done.

Thinking back on my own experiences, I believe rage arises when someone does not get what they want. I don't mean simply wanting things for ourselves, but rather wanting our way with others. It is an uncontrollable urge for domination, a trait that probably exists, to some extent, in every human being.

Rage comes about when we attempt to dominate another and they resist. The anger builds and often so does the resistance. Within minutes all sense of respectability and gentleness yields to uncontrolled anger (rage) and often violence, as one becomes increasingly determined to dominate another and the other continues to resist being dominated.

It is important to avoid even the slightest inkling of rage in our lives. Simply prefer others more (much more) than ourselves. Simple, yes? Of course not. Yet through the Holy Spirit it can and will be accomplished if and when we yield to the Spirit of God in us.

Are you troubled by outbursts of uncontrolled anger? Please take notice, this is not an acceptable behavior for a child of God. You know that already, but the spirit of domination still has a governing influence in your life. Your only hope is full surrender and a complete turn-around.

The object(s) of your rage must be turned around to become objects of your love. Stop wanting to get your way and help them to get their way. Have a conscious understanding that they are more important and more valuable than you are. You must literally die to yourself and become a servant to the objects of your rage. I think it is futile to search for the cause of one's rage. What is needed is complete surrender to the Spirit of God.

Not easy, you say? Actually quite impossible if you continue to allow your flesh to lead you. But if you are In Christ all things are possible.

Father, rage is an almost normal occurrence in our culture but we know this is not normal for Christians. Please, dear God, lead each of us to where uncontrolled anger in our lives suffers a complete and final death. Thank You.

340.CHOOSE

Joshua 24:15 (NASB) If it is disagreeable in your sight to serve the LORD, choose for yourselves today whom you will serve: ….. but as for me and my house, we will serve the LORD.

Did you notice the word "today" in today's scripture? I have hurried past that word many times before, but today it is there, staring at me as if it were underlined and highlighted over and over. Yes, I know there was a specific moment in time when we chose Jesus as our Savior, but we must choose Him again today.

Every day we have opportunities to choose to serve the Lord. We do this when we respond with a gentle word to someone who speaks angrily, when we notice someone is hurting and move closer to comfort them, when we see a need and take action, when someone is sick and we visit and pray for them, when we yield control so we might serve others, when we set aside time to be in God's presence, when we refuse to let negative feelings steal our joy, and when we respond with kindness, gentleness, and self-control even in the most difficult circumstances. Even when the telemarketer calls again.

If you are like me, you probably come up a little short. Don't we all? We are doing life "one step at a time" as we continue on this journey consciously making the godly choices, one at a time, regardless of our feelings or how we are hurt or offended.

"Choose for yourselves this day whom you will serve." Your choice must be a deliberate determination—it is not something into which you will automatically drift.…...You have no business trying to find out where God is leading—the only thing God will explain to you is Himself. Openly declare to Him, "I will be faithful." (Excerpt From My Utmost for His Highest Oswald Chambers).

Father, in every moment lead us to choose You, to always be faithful. Thank You.

341.ZEIGARNIK
(ZEI-GAR-NIK)

James 5:12 (NASB) But above all, my brethren, do not swear, either by heaven or by earth or with any other oath; but your yes is to be yes, and your no, no, so that you may not fall under judgment..

I am pretty sure this is a strange new word for you. It was for me. The Zeigarnik Effect, named after the Russian psychologist who first noticed it, Bluma Zeigarnik, explains that the human brain tends to remember unfinished or interrupted tasks better than completed ones. (Joshua Becker)

A simple example is when you are listening to a song you like but you get interrupted. Does the song keep playing in your head? Or when you know there are things you need to do but haven't, the list keeps flowing through your mind and sometimes even disrupts your sleep?

Apparently, the mind wants to get things done, to bring them to completion. When it is done it is easily forgotten.

I keep a running grocery list. May asks me if I have put something on the list and usually I am not sure. I think I have (because that is my habit), but honestly most of the time I do not remember. Why? Because my mind discards it from active memory.

I have read and can confirm from experience that our minds can hold only a limited number of unfinished items in active memory. That number is typically around seven, though it can vary from person to person.

Regardless, our capacity to "keep things in the air" is limited. Even though the undone things may be easier to recall they also get "forgotten" when we have too many "open" items.

The point of this devotion? If we said "yes" to something, then by all means, let us do it before it falls into the never-never land of "Oh, I forgot."

Father, how easy it is for us to say "yes" but never quite get around to doing it. Help us be more mindful of keeping our word before we forget we gave it. Thank You.

342.CHEEK

Luke 6:29a (NASB) Whoever hits you on the cheek, offer him the other also;

Have you noticed that when violence is responded to by violence it creates more violence? Consider what is going on in the Middle East right now. Every act of violence results in more and more violence as attempts are made to retaliate and get vengeance. No wonder God tells us that vengeance is His to administer. Humans are incapable of vengeance without becoming what they hate. The more we respond to violence with violence the more we become like our enemies.

Jesus gave us another way, a way of complete non-violence. It is the most difficult way because it strongly goes against our innate desire to get even and make things right.

Violence can never make things right. It results in more violence. There is no such thing as redemption through violence (redemptive violence) which has been the default of mankind for a very long time.

"The only way one could naturally strike the right cheek with the right hand would be with the back of the hand. We are dealing here with insult, not a fistfight. The intention is clearly not to injure but to humiliate, to put someone in his or her place. ......Why then does he (Jesus) counsel these already humiliated people to turn the other cheek? Because this action robs the oppressor of the power to humiliate. The person who turns the other cheek is saying, in effect, "Try again. Your first blow failed to achieve its intended effect. I deny you the power to humiliate me. I am a human being just like you. Your status does not alter that fact. You cannot demean me." (Walter Wink)

As I read the headlines of the wars in the Middle East and Ukraine, I find myself on one side and not the other. Every time "my side is ahead I am pleased and dismayed when the other side seems to be getting even.

As a follower of Jesus should I not be dismayed in both cases? Does not war bring great suffering to many innocent people on both sides? Are we not as guilty as them when we do what they have done? Are we not as guilty when we cheer "our side" on?

All this shows me that I have not yet embraced the way of Jesus to abhor violence in all its forms. Yes, we must resist evil, but we must not resist by doing evil. We can only resist evil by doing good.

Romans 12:17-21 (NASB) Never pay back evil for evil to anyone. ..., be at peace with all men. 19 Never take your own revenge, beloved,..., "VENGEANCE IS MINE, I WILL REPAY," says the Lord. 20 "BUT IF YOUR ENEMY IS HUNGRY, FEED HIM, AND IF HE IS THIRSTY, GIVE HIM A DRINK; .. 21 Do not be overcome by evil, but overcome evil with good.

Father, this is difficult but it is what You have commanded. I surrender my heart and its evil thoughts and desires. Thank You for renewing us In Christ.

343.COMPASSION

Matthew 9:13 (NASB) But go and learn what this means: 'I DESIRE COMPASSION, AND NOT SACRIFICE,' for I did not come to call the righteous, but sinners.'

I've shared this story before, but God has brought it back to my memory again. It goes something like this.

On our way to Church one evening, we stopped at a nursing home to visit a little old lady who suffered severely from arthritis and whom we had grown very fond of. Despite her suffering she was always in good spirits, gracious to us and genuinely pleased to see us. But this night was different. She was in so much pain that I do not think she even knew we were there. She just kept weeping and moaning from her pain.

We did not know what to do. We felt helpless but we stayed. It seemed more important to be present with this hurting person than to continue to church. We could not help her so we just prayed, held her hand, and cried a bit with her. What else could we do?

I do not remember how it started but May and I began to softly sing some of the praise and worship songs we knew. Please understand that neither May nor I can keep a tune but we sang anyway. Soon her roommate lowered the TV and began singing along with us. Gradually, the crying softened into a whimper, then stopped completely, and, praise God, she started singing with us.

When the visit was over, we told each other, "now this was church." Even though nearly 50 years have passed since this happened, it is a remembered milestone of how the Spirit of God will show up even (especially?) when we are helpless and do not know what to do. It was one of the early lessons in our lives about following the Spirit and not to be bound by the outward appearances of worship.

(Life Application Bible Commentary New Testament) When you are in a situation where the law of God seems to collide with the love of God, do what Jesus did: obey the law of love. In other words, when in doubt, err on the side of compassion.

Lord, give us hearts of compassion. Thank You.

344.COMPASSION (2)

Colossians 3:12 (NASB) So, as those who have been chosen of God, holy and beloved, put on a heart of compassion, kindness, humility, gentleness and patience;

Compassion is concern for the sufferings and the struggles of others. It can be expressed in many forms such as physical or financial help, prayers, phone calls, letters, cards or just being present without saying a word.

Some of us are naturally more compassionate than others. For much of my life, I saw people facing difficulties as victims of their own foolishness. Because of that fundamental misunderstanding, I was far less compassionate than I could have been. I believed that those who were suffering simply needed to get their act together.

Thank God He has changed my thinking and understanding over the years. Except for the grace of God I too can be the victim of suffering just as much as the next person. Many people suffer even when they seemingly do everything right. Surely, they deserve our compassion. But even when people screw up and their troubles are their own fault they are still in need of our compassion.

Since some of us are not naturally compassionate. It takes a extra effort. A couple of things can help. First, do not judge others because of their troubles. Second, pray and ask God to give you a heart that sympathizes with others. Third, get to know people better. The deeper our relationships the easier compassion flows from our hearts. Fourth, act. Do something to help. Visit, send a card, make a phone call. Do something tangible that shows you care (even if you really do not feel like it).

Those of us not naturally gifted with this wonderful character trait can still become compassionate people. But we must make the effort. If we wait until we feel compassion before we do something we may never do anything. On the other hand, if we decide to act with compassion a new feeling will emerge, a feeling of identity and empathy with those who are suffering.

Lord Jesus, You are our model of compassion. Lead us to have compassionate hearts for all, especially our brothers and sisters in Christ. Thank You.

345.CLAMOR

Luke 9:10 (NASB) When the apostles returned, they gave an account to Him of all that they had done. Taking them with Him, He withdrew by Himself to a city called Bethsaida.

Is the world clamoring for your attention? In today's world it is almost impossible to withdraw to a quiet place unless we are intentional about it. I am an extreme introvert and when I do not withdraw on a regular basis I am easily stressed out. This is so different from the extrovert who experiences just the opposite. God has made us all unique.

But today I am not talking about the natural tendencies of introverts to withdraw or extroverts to engage with others. These are normal every day personality traits. What I am talking about is the determined and focused intention to remove oneself from the clamor of the world, so that we can find the place of God's rest and draw strength to serve Him.

(Life Application Bible Commentary New Testament) WITHDRAW TO THE WILDERNESS: Many things compete for our attention, and people often exhaust themselves trying to attend to them all. Jesus took time to withdraw to a quiet and deserted place to pray. When facing conflict or troubled times, follow Jesus' clear example. True strength comes from God, and it can only be received by spending time with Him.

We have all read countless accounts of how Jesus set Himself apart to spend time with the Father. Many preachers and teachers have reminded us, "If Jesus needed to set Himself apart, shouldn't we do the same?" Yet, few Christians I know practice this consistently. The noise of the world is persistent, and only the determined choose what is truly best.

Isaiah 40:31 (NASB) 31 Yet those who wait for the LORD Will gain new strength; They will mount up with wings like eagles, They will run and not get tired, They will walk and not become weary.

Father, I cannot do this life without time in Your presence. Please draw us to set ourselves apart to spend time with You. I pray the noisy clamor of the world will grow dimmer and dimmer in our spirt as we seek to know You with greater and greater intimacy. Thank You.

346.TRUE

John 4:23-24 (NASB) But an hour is coming, and now is, when the true worshipers will worship the Father in spirit and truth; for such people the Father seeks to be His worshipers. God is spirit, and those who worship Him must worship in spirit and truth

There are many things that that look like worship to the observer. Things like going to church, helping those in need, comforting the grieving, the lonely, and the oppressed, standing in the gap for the persecuted, reading the Scriptures, attending a small group, and so on—these are all activities every Christian should engage in. But are they truly worship, or merely a shadow of the real thing?

"From these considerations it abundantly appears, that the true worship of God is seated in the heart, and consists in the knowledge of God, and in true repentance, which mortifies the flesh; and, through grace, renews man after the divine image. In this order, man is made the holy temple of the Lord, where, through the good Spirit of God, internal worship is performed, in the exercise of faith, charity, hope, humility, patience, prayer, thanksgiving, and the praise of God. " (Excerpt From True Christianity Johann Arndt)

Worship can only happen when it comes from a repentant heart. The Pharisees in Jesus day thought they had their act together. But they had failed to hear the words of John the Baptist and repent of their sins. Because of this lack of repentance, they could not hear the words of Jesus. (Luke 7:30 (NASB) But the Pharisees and the lawyers rejected God's purpose for themselves, not having been baptized by John.)

We have the same problem when we think we are mostly OK, when we compare ourselves to others, when we have not faced how wretched we truly are and are not able worship in spirit and in truth.

Unless we confront our own sinful nature and humbly come before the Lord Jesus seeking His cleansing, true worship is not possible. Turning away in repentance from reliance on ourselves and placing complete dependence on Jesus opens the door for genuine worship to take place.

Father, we come. We bow before Your heavenly throne. Cleanse us so that we truly worship You. Thank You.

347.DISCOVER

Proverbs 2:2-5 (NASB) Make your ear attentive to wisdom, Incline your heart to understanding; For if you cry for discernment, Lift your voice for understanding; If you seek her as silver And search for her as for hidden treasures; Then you will discern the fear of the LORD and discover the knowledge of God

Is it possible to be so content in what we already know that we no longer intentionally seek wisdom? A young child is diligent about learning how his or her little world works and discovers new things everyday as they grow in wisdom and understanding. But what happens when we get older? Is the instinct to learn and grow in wisdom diminished by the routines of life?

I wonder if the discovery of new things is part of what keeps us feeling young, no matter our age. I have often noticed that when people seem to lose their interest in life—when they stop seeking new adventures, whether physical, mental, or spiritual, or cease learning new things—life begins to feel dull. It seems to be part of a slow decline, occurring when we are content to pass the time scrolling through social media, watching TV, or indulging in other passive forms of entertainment, while showing little curiosity for what is new and yet to be discovered.

How can we awaken ourselves to the search for wisdom? Today's verse from Proverbs gives us a clue. It urges us to make the pursuit of wisdom a priority in our lives. Do not be content with what we already know; instead, seek wisdom as if it were a precious metal, always alert for the hidden treasures that come with uncovering something new.

There are many ways to seek wisdom and learning. Things like dance lessons, a new hobby, traveling, learning a new skill or language. Even simple things like noticing the world around you, the beauty and intricacies of life. We are surrounded by them but often we do not notice.

However, I suggest a "more better way." Just as Jesus told Martha that Mary had chosen what was better. I suggest that seeking to intimately know God is the best pursuit of wisdom in life.

Philippians 3:10 (AMP) [For my determined purpose) is that I may know Him [that I may progressively become more deeply and intimately acquainted with Him, perceiving and recognizing and understanding the wonders of His Person more strongly and more clearly], and that I may in that same way come to know the power outflowing from His resurrection [which it exerts over believers], and that I may so share His sufferings as to be continually transformed [in spirit into His likeness even] to His death...

Father, do not let us be complacent in knowing You. Please reveal Yourself to us as we earnestly seek to know You. Thank You.

348.VIGOROUS

Philippians 3:10 (NASB) that I may know Him and the power of His resurrection and the fellowship of His sufferings, being conformed to His death;

I am often puzzled when I place two plants side by side and one thrives while the other, sometimes just a few feet away, struggles and never reaches its full potential. Both receive roughly the same amount of sunlight, water, fertilizer, and care, yet one flourishes while the other does not. I find myself asking why this happens.

I notice a similar phenomenon among professing believers. Even when exposed to essentially the same teaching, support, lifestyle, and opportunities, one person becomes a vibrant follower of Jesus while another seems to merely go through the motions. I wonder why this is.

Please let me ask you, are you a spiritually vigorous saint? Is your Christian life characterized by being hearty, strong, tough, thriving, animated, spirited, lively, active, spry, playful, dynamic, tireless, full of life, upbeat, effervescent, etc.? Or is your spiritual life characterized by boring rituals and obligations?

"The aim of a spiritually vigorous saint is "that I may know Him." Do I know Him where I am today? If not, I am failing Him. I am not here for self-realization, but to know Jesus Christ. In Christian work our initiative and motivation are too often simply the result of realizing that there is work to be done and that we must do it. Yet that is never the attitude of a spiritually vigorous saint. His aim is to achieve the realization of Jesus Christ in every set of circumstances" (Excerpt From My Utmost for His Highest Oswald Chambers)

It matters little what we do in this life but why we do what we do matters a lot. If our aim in life is to Know Him with increasing intimacy, I am confident we will bew spiritually vigorous saints.

"God has provided His salvation that we might be, individually and personally, vibrant children of God, loving God with all our hearts and worshiping Him in the beauty of holiness. (Excerpt From Tozer on Christian Leadership)

Thank You, Lord, for revealing Yourself to us as we purpose ourselves to know You. Thank You.

349.APHIEMI (GREEK"AF.EE.AY.MEE) (FORGIVENESS)

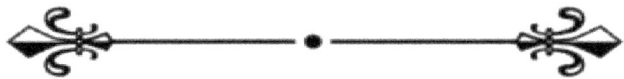

Luke 5:20 (NASB) Seeing their faith, He said, "Friend, your sins are forgiven you."

Is not forgiveness at the very core of the Gospel? We are reminded that even our own forgiveness depends on our forgiving others.

Matthew 6:14-15 (NASB) For if you forgive others for their transgressions, your heavenly Father will also forgive you. But if you do not forgive others, then your Father will not forgive your transgressions

Please do not misunderstand, we do not earn our salvation by forgiving others. However, when we hold grudges and unforgiveness, it is a sign that our own hearts are not right. When we are truly His, when we have repented and come to the end of ourselves, when we realize that we are completely unworthy to even approach the throne of God, then we will readily forgive others because we have realized how much we have been forgiven.

As human beings we often hurt and disappoint one another. Even when we want to do our very best it is not unusual to fail to meet our own expectations much less the expectations of others. That is the reality. But there is another reality of "aphiemi," which makes all things right again.

(LABC) Forgiveness means that a relationship has been renewed despite a wrong that has been done. But the act cannot be erased or changed. The notion of aphiemi, however, goes far beyond human forgiveness, for it includes the "putting away" of sin in two ways: (1) The law and justice are satisfied because Jesus paid the penalty that sin deserved; thus, sins can no longer be held against a believer. (2) The guilt caused by sin is removed and replaced with Christ's righteousness.

Lord, I sometimes doubt whether we truly understand and appreciate the power of forgiveness, especially when we are in a difficult relationship. Please, Lord, search our hearts. If there is any unforgiveness within us, reveal it so that we may forgive and make things right. Thank You.

350.ADORE

1 Chronicles 29:11-12 (NLT) Yours, O LORD, is the greatness, the power, the glory, the victory, and the majesty. Everything in the heavens and on earth is yours, O LORD, and this is your kingdom. We adore you as the one who is over all things. Wealth and honor come from you alone, for you rule over everything. Power and might are in your hand, and at your discretion people are made great and given strength.

As I read today's scripture, I had a clear sense that the author was expressing adoration for our Lord God, whom He knew very well. To adore means to love dearly, to be devoted, to cherish, to treasure, to revere, to hold in high respect, to stand in awe, etc.

"This word makes it clear that all the attention must be on Jesus and not on me. To adore is to be drawn away from my own preoccupations into the presence of Jesus. It means letting go of what I want, desire, and have planned and fully trusting Jesus and his love." (Excerpt From The Road to Daybreak, Henri J. M. Nouwen)

In our culture we seem to adore many things. We adore our homes, our cars, and our bank accounts. We adore the latest sensations in music, theater, politics and business. We adore our children and grandchildren, and sometimes our pets. But, I wonder, do we adore our God like the author of Chronicles seems to have?

I am often reminded of the Apostle Paul's desire to know God intimately (See Philippians 3). His desire was much more than a passing interest. But why? As I sit here and reflect, I wonder if adoration and knowledge are closely related.

As we adore someone or something we seek to know them more and more. As we come to know someone or something more and more, our tendency to adore increases. Are we passive in our adoration of Jesus because we only have a passing interest in KNOWING Him? Could our inner knowledge of the one true God be minuscule because we do not adore Him?

Father God, the distractions of life are endless, yet I ask that even in the midst of our daily routines, You continually reveal Yourself to us. May we grow ever more familiar with all of Your ways, and as our knowledge of You deepens, may our hearts come to adore You more and more. Thank You.

351.CHURCH

Hebrews 10:23-25 (NASB) Let us hold fast the confession of our hope without wavering, for He who promised is faithful; and let us consider how to stimulate one another to love and good deeds, not forsaking our own assembling together, as is the habit of some, but encouraging one another; and all the more as you see the day drawing near

When is a church not a church? I sense that for many Christians attending church has become a thing we do because, as Christians, we should be going to church. Are we just checking off a "to do"?

When the author of Hebrews penned this scripture, I am very sure He had a completely different concept of church than we do today. "Church" back then was mostly smaller gatherings, often meeting in people's homes. Today's large churches would have been a completely foreign concept to the author. I am sure early believers could not even imagine assemblies with hundreds and even thousands in attendance. Have we been to church when the gathering was a few people, a few dozen people, a few hundred or perhaps a few thousand? But let me ask, does size matter?

You probably answered in the negative, but if size does not matter then what does? I think today's scripture provides a few clues. We have been to church when we find ourselves inspired by fellow believers, and in turn, inspire others to love one another and perform good deeds. We have been to church when we faithfully attend gatherings with other believers, making the effort to be present even when we would rather be elsewhere. We have been to church when we encourage others and are encouraged in return. We have been to church when we come together and intentionally reflect on the return of the Lord Jesus.

"As we were together talking, laughing, singing, and praying, I experienced church in the best sense of that word: a people called together to praise God and to serve the poor." The Road to Daybreak Henri J. M. Nouwen)

Father, please help us remain faithful in coming together with one another—whether in formal church gatherings, in small groups, or even with just one or two fellow believers. Thank You.

352.SABBATH

Luke 6:9 (NASB) And Jesus said to them, "I ask you, is it lawful to do good or to do harm on the Sabbath, to save a life or to destroy it?"

Mark 2:27-28 (NASB) Jesus said to them, "The Sabbath was made for man, and not man for the Sabbath. So the Son of Man is Lord even of the Sabbath."

I have read and heard that "keeping the Sabbath" is the only Old Testament commandment that is not repeated in the New Testament. I cannot dispute that statement, however, I think it might be misleading. My contention is that every day should be lived as a sort of "sabbath day." Consider the following:

(LABC) The Sabbath, while an important day given to God's people as a day of rest and worship, was also a day for people to be merciful and kind to those in need.

I believe every day should be a day to rest in the Lord, no matter how busy or quiet our lives may be. Every day should also be a day of worship, not something we reserve for just one hour or one day a week. Instead, our worship of God should be ongoing, expressed through our work, our rest, and even through our pain and difficulties.

Every day should be a day for actively seeking people to help, either through practical help with finances, physical assistance, emotional support, etc. and/or through our prayers and active encouragement. Certainly every day should be a day where we are kind to everyone, to those in need, to believers and unbelievers and scoffers.

Every day can be a "Sabbath" day when our primary focus is upon Jesus. Otherwise, it becomes "just another day" lost among many such days.

Do you see what I mean? Every day should be a "Sabbath" day for us who are followers of the Lord Jesus Christ. As we have opportunity, let us be kind and helpful to one another,- and by all means let us set aside every day to worship God through our prayers, study of His word, and spending time in His presence.

Lord God, we are a sinful people in great need of a Savior. Help us to pause every day to recognize this reality and to live each day as a day set aside for You, a Sabbath Day every day. Thank You.

353.CALM

Luke 8:24-25 (NASB) They came to Jesus and woke Him up, saying, "Master, Master, we are perishing!" And He got up and rebuked the wind and the surging waves, and they stopped, and it became calm…And He said to them, "Where is your faith?"

In my morning prayer time yesterday, I stopped in my tracks when I came to today's scripture. Lately I have felt anything but calm. I seem to be stressing out over minor things that normally I would take in stride. Another wake up call, among many in my life, of my need to draw close to God and cling to Jesus when life is difficult.

(LABC) What should Christians do in a crisis? They should do what the disciples did: go to Jesus. He may not always "calm the storm" as he did for them, but he is in control. Christ is Lord over everything—including nature, life, finances, and all circumstances.

Are there areas of your life that you are trying to handle without Him? Learn a lesson from a bunch of frightened fishermen: submit everything to Him. He can handle it better than you can.

It is not like I am in crisis. At the moment, most things are under control, yet there is a sense of tension and stress I have not felt for quite some time. It feels almost ironic to hear myself encouraging others to trust in Jesus while I have to remind myself of the same truth.

Over the years, I have occasionally felt overwhelmed. Fellow believers have often asked me to pray for them during such times. Many well-known Christians of the past, Charles Spurgeon immediately comes to mind, experienced this same struggle. Why? Because it is a place we all must come to at some point. Our own strength is not enough. Only when I acknowledge my weakness and total dependence on God can I find the true strength to move forward.

2 Corinthians 12:9 (NASB) And He has said to me, "My grace is sufficient for you, for power is perfected in weakness." Most gladly, therefore, I will rather boast about my weaknesses, so that the power of Christ may dwell in me.

Dear Lord Jesus, lead me to cling to You. I much prefer the calm but please use this season to draw me ever closer to You. Thank You.

354.HATE

Romans 12:17 (NASB) Never pay back evil for evil to anyone. Respect what is right in the sight of all men.

"Do not return evil for evil," "Do not mirror evil," "Do not respond to evil in kind." This refusal to react in opposition is one of the most profound and difficult truths in Scripture.

"We become what we hate. The very act of hating something draws it to us. Since our hate is usually a direct response to an evil done to us, our hate almost invariably causes us to respond in the TERMS ALREADY LAID DOWN BY THE ENEMY......Unaware of what is happening, we turn into the very thing we oppose....We Become What We Hate" (Excerpt From Engaging the Powers Walter Wink)

Do you see the reality of the above quote? I hope you can. We can easily become what we hate. "No way," you say? Just consider your natural response when someone offends you, your children, or a loved one. Do you not want to "make it right" and exact revenge? How does that make you any different than the person who offended you?

Again, consider what is happening on a global scale. When one country attacks another the response is to attack back, often with ever increasing violence. What makes our violence more "right" than another? Yes, we think we are right but how can violence ever be right for a follower of Jesus? Where in scripture can you find this to be the way of Jesus?

The feeling of hate can easily arise because of an offense to ourselves or a loved one. That feeling is not sin, however, we are on the verge of sin, depending on how we respond. If we respond with hate we are no better than the one that has caused us to hate. The only appropriate response, Jesus tells us, is to love. (Matthew 5:44 (NASB) But I say to you, love your enemies and pray for those who persecute you.)

How difficult this is. Perhaps impossible unless we are led by the Spirit of God. My dear friend, whenever the feeling of hate arises in Your spirit rush immediately to Christ. Otherwise you will become what you hate.

Father, this is a hard teaching. Please lead us to always return love even when we are deeply and perhaps frequently offended. Thank You.

355.BOSS

Proverbs 6:7 (Passion Translation) The ants have no chief, no boss, no manager— no one has to tell them what to do.

In nature we have examples (like ants, schools of fish, flocks of starlings, etc.) that seem to react spontaneously in unison without any overt leader. A flock of thousands of starlings is a breathtaking sight, weaving and turning, creating intricate patterns as they fly in constantly shifting formations. How does each starling know when and how to turn without ever colliding with its neighbor? It is a remarkable display of cooperation and teamwork.

That instinctive spirit of cooperation does not appear to be common among humans. For good or for evil we seem to gravitate to a leader, the boss, if you will. How did so many German people forsake their moral integrity to follow along with Hitler and the Nazi rule of order, even to the killing of millions of innocent people? Surely, we can be like sheep without a shepherd.

In many ways our political leaders become our bosses, setting the standard for what is good and what is not. That is troubling to me as history has shown we will yield our moral truth to follow a charismatic political or religious leader.

In this life, most of us have had bosses, some better than others, for sure. We look to the boss to determine what is appropriate and what is not. My personal strategy during was to keep the boss happy so he/she would give me the freedom to do what I wanted. It worked pretty well, most of the time.

Let me ask you, who is your spiritual boss? You most likely answered "Jesus" but honestly, is He really? How do you know?

What's your evidence? Does Jesus have full and complete authority over your life? Is He Your boss in all things secular and religious?

"If our Lord insisted on our obedience, He would simply become a taskmaster and cease to have any real authority. He never insists on obedience, but when we truly see Him we will instantly obey Him. Then He is easily Lord of our life, and we live in adoration of Him from morning till night." (Excerpt From My Utmost for His Highest Oswald Chambers))

Father, the secularization of our culture encourages us to discard moral truth in favor of the latest trend. Please, Lord, open our eyes, let us slumber no more. You are truly our boss in every sense of the word. Let us act like that is so. Thank You.

356.CONVINCED

Luke 10:41-42 (NASB) But the Lord answered and said to her, "Martha, Martha, you are worried and bothered about so many things; but only one thing is necessary, for Mary has chosen the good part, which shall not be taken away from her.

I want to begin with a question. What is more important, decorating the Christmas tree or preparing your heart to celebrate the birth of the Savior of the World?

I know your answer is to prepare your heart, but are you convinced that is the true and correct answer? In my observations, for most Christians the outward celebration and pageantry of Christmas (the tree, gifts, parties, decorations etc.) seem to be much more important than preparing our hearts to celebrate the Savior's birth. If my observations are accurate, is it possible that much of our Christian walk is centered on outward appearances, perhaps to the neglect of our spiritual reality? After all, we know it is much easier to look like a follower of Jesus than to be one.

"Once I am truly convinced that preparing the heart is more important than preparing the Christmas tree, I will be a lot less frustrated at the end of the day. (Excerpt From The Road to Daybreak Henri J. M. Nouwen)

Our lives are often guided by the trivial demands of daily life, the expectations others place upon us, and the expectations we place on ourselves. Everywhere I look, it seems there is no end to the constant hustle and bustle. But what is truly, deeply important? Yes, many things may feel necessary, but what will genuinely make a lasting difference for you and for others for all eternity?

In the midst of our daily lives, it is most difficult to answer these questions off the cuff. I think we are not really convinced when Jesus tells us to seek Him first.

Matthew 6:33 (NASB) 33 But seek first His kingdom and His righteousness, and all these things will be added to you.

Don't think this is practical or would work in your life? You are probably correct because you are not convinced that God can and will do what He has said.

Dear God, please do not let us confuse outward activity with growing in intimacy with You. Thank You.

357.WALK

Isaiah 40:31 (NASB) Yet those who wait for the LORD Will gain new strength; They will mount up with wings like eagles, They will run and not get tired, They will walk and not become weary.

This has been a favorite verse for a very long time. It is so applicable to my life for a few reasons. The first being I do not like to wait. How about you? How do you do when You wait (trusting for God to show up)?

I can wait for a short season, but what happens when our season of waiting seems to have no end? I find this to be most difficult and, frankly, very frustrating. I often wish God would align with my timetable, but alas, I must remind myself He is sovereign and I am not (neither are you, by the way).

The second reason is the word "walk". Sometimes I think I should do nothing while I wait but that is not what the scripture tells us. While we wait (trusting that God will show up) we must continue to walk.

"The word walk is used in the Bible to express the character of a person—"John . . . looking at Jesus as He walked . . . said, 'Behold the Lamb of God!' " (John 1:35–36). There is nothing abstract or obscure in the Bible; everything is vivid and real. God does not say, "Be spiritual," but He says, "Walk before Me" (Genesis 17:1)." (Excerpt From My Utmost for His Highest Oswald Chambers)

In other words, when we "walk" we are to express the character of Jesus. You know, things like love, joy, peace, patience, kindness, gentleness, goodness, faithfulness and self control. I have found, and continue to find, that these characteristics tend to go into hiding when

I am frustrated, rather than waiting and trusting God to show up at the right time, in His timing.

The third reason is the meaning of the word "weary." Even though my life has been richly blessed, I still experience moments of weariness. I have learned, and am still learning, that my weariness often stems from failing to do the first two things: wait in trust and walk faithfully while waiting. I become weary when my focus shifts away from God and settles on myself or on the circumstances of my life.

Dear Father, did you know I would stumble so much? Yes, of course you did and yet You chose to love me. Please continue to teach us to wait and to walk so that we might not become weary. Thank You.

358.JEALOUSY

Romans 13:13-14 (NASB) Let us behave properly as in the day, not in carousing and drunkenness, not in sexual promiscuity and sensuality, not in strife and jealousy. 14 But put on the Lord Jesus Christ, and make no provision for the flesh in regard to its lusts

When will you have everything you desire? Do not be deceived, for the true answer is elusive. As we take part in the pursuits of our materialistic culture, it is easy to notice others who possess what we long for—a newer cell phone, a larger home, a sleeker car, finer clothes, more advanced appliances, or perhaps a more beautiful and productive garden. All of these seem to call out to us.

Or, maybe it is not "stuff" that moves you toward jealousy but things like the favor some seem to have over you. Or the charismatic personality of some people or their ability to remain calm in difficult situations.

Sometimes jealousy strikes very close to home. I remember when we had our first grandchild. I became jealous of the attention May paid to the child. Pathetic, do you not agree? Sometimes we can even be jealous of our loved ones' success, abilities, or seemingly better lives than we have had. I have seen cases where people who are grieving can become jealous over people whose loved ones are still with them.

Life affords many opportunities to be disappointed in how life has gone and/or is going. We do not have to like our circumstances. We may moan and cry over our pain and difficulties, but we may also seek better outcomes. This is a normal part of living.

Jealousy, however, is an issue when we lose sight of the fact that Jesus is the Sovereign Lord. Every circumstance in our lives has been allowed and He can and will provide all that is good for us. However, our focus must not be on our lives and our circumstances. Instead, to be truly content in life we must continually look to our Savior. It is the only way to be content with the circumstances of life that God arranges for us.

Philippians 4:11 (NASB) 11 Not that I speak from want, for I have learned to be content in whatever circumstances I am.

"It is not the man who has too little, but the man who craves more, that is poor." —Seneca

Father, may the only thing I am jealous of be for more of You. Thank You.

359.SANCTIFICATION

Colossians 1:27 (NASB) to whom God willed to make known what is the riches of the glory of this mystery among the Gentiles, which is Christ in you, the hope of glory.

My dear friends are you sanctified yet? I have been a believer for nearly 50 years and recent events revealed to me that I have a long way to go. I hope your progress is a more timely than my own. I am sometimes reminded of Paul's words in Roman 7, " Oh what a wretched man I am"

But that is OK because it is not my work to do. Rather, it is the work of Christ in me. Yes, I would like to hurry things along. And, yes, I really thought I would be further along by now. And, yes, some things were crucified in me and yet I crawl off the cross from time to time. But that is all me. I have never been very patient and that too must die and stay dead.

"The most wonderful secret of living a holy life does not lie in imitating Jesus, but in letting the perfect qualities of Jesus exhibit themselves in my human flesh. Sanctification is "Christ in you" (Colossians 1:27). It is His wonderful life that is imparted to me in sanctification—imparted by faith as a sovereign gift of God's grace. ...... Sanctification is an impartation, not an imitation. Imitation is something altogether different. The perfection of everything is in Jesus Christ, and the mystery of sanctification is that all the perfect qualities of Jesus are at my disposal. Consequently, I slowly but surely begin to live a life of inexpressible order, soundness, and holiness—"kept by the power of God" (1 Peter 1:5). (Excerpt From My Utmost for His Highest Oswald Chambers)

Every time I mess up it is a reminder of how weak I really am and how much I need Christ. That is a good thing. Otherwise I would be tempted to think there might be some good in me. My failures point me back to the cross of Jesus. It is there that I desire to stay.

I trust a day is coming when Jesus' work in me will be completed. A day when I will not only be a saint by position but also a saint by practice. I long for that day and I hope you do too.

Lord, I want to ask You to hurry but instead I ask for patience. Thank You.

360.PROJECTS

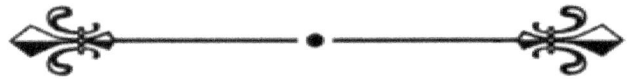

Luke 12:18-20 (NASB) Then he said, 'This is what I will do: I will tear down my barns and build larger ones, and there I will store all my grain and my goods. And I will say to my soul, "Soul, you have many goods laid up for many years to come; take your ease, eat, drink and be merry."' But God said to him, 'You fool! This very night your soul is required of you; and now who will own what you have prepared?'

Recently, I was talking to a friend of many years who was in the middle of a health crisis. I suggested it might be time to reconsider his life and what was really important. The response was, "I still have a few projects to do before I slow down."

The response reminded me of today's verse above. How like many of us so concerned about the many things going on in our lives that we put on hold what is really important. I think it is like a forgetful slumber. Although we look awake, we are in fact asleep, and we expect that by and by we will wake up and everything will be OK.

Consider the above barn builder. It seemed to him that expanding his capacity was important but he had no clue at all. Is it possible that we too are so busy with our "projects" that we are wasting time, energy, finances, skills, talents, etc. on things that, in light of eternity, are not important at all?

I have concluded that few things are truly important. And, in some cases, we will not understand what is the most important until we finish climbing the "mountain of life." It will be a sad day if we get there and we realize we have climbed the wrong mountain (Steven Covey)

I think we should have projects. They give us purpose and meaning. They give us reasons to get up in the morning and get ourselves motivated when we would prefer to stay in bed. Projects with purpose can make life meaningful.

But here is the kicker. As followers of Jesus, does it make sense for us to be engaged in projects that do not align with God's will and/or do not make a meaningful difference in the lives of others for Christ? If Jesus is truly Lord, then how can we possibly have our own projects? After all who is really the Lord of our lives?

Father, true joy in this life comes when we are about Your business and not busy with our own projects. Please make this so in our lives. Thank You.

361.PLUMP

John 7:38 (NASB) He who believes in Me, as the Scripture said, 'From his innermost being will flow rivers of living water.'"

When I came across the word "plump" in the following quote, I pictured a "fattened Christian," content and self-assured, reclining on a couch with servants attending. It was the image of a person who had truly "arrived."

"God's purpose is not simply to make us beautiful, plump grapes, but to make us grapes so that He may squeeze the sweetness out of us. Our spiritual life cannot be measured by success as the world measures it, but only by what God pours through us—and we cannot measure that at all." (Excerpt From My Utmost for His Highest Oswald Chambers)

However, as I read the phrase, "squeeze the sweetness out of us," I got a completely different picture. More like grapes in a press with a giant hand pressing out all the juice and even some of the pulp too. For sure, all of the plumpness was gone.

So, what kind of a Christian am I? Am I filled up with God's goodness, nice and fat and plump and pleased with myself? Or does the goodness of God flow out of me like living water? How about you? Are you plump and fat and satisfied with your Christian walk or do you find yourself pressed into the service of the King?

I think this is a fascinating thought and perspective. In our lives, we spend so much time and energy getting ourselves "filled," but we must ask, "so what?" It is like filling a car's gas tank only for it to sit in the garage. A full tank is meant to take us on the road. Likewise, when we are spiritually filled, it is time to go out and make a positive, meaningful difference in the lives of others. What do you think?

Oh Lord, please fill us to overflowing so that even our presence will refresh those around us, like the cool flow of a stream on a hot day. Please let Your grace flow through us to the many hurting people around us. Thank You.

362.SCORN

Luke 6:22-23 (NASB) Blessed are you when men hate you, and ostracize you, and insult you, and scorn your name as evil, for the sake of the Son of Man. Be glad in that day and leap for joy, for behold, your reward is great in heaven. For in the same way their fathers used to treat the prophets

To be scorned means others have a feeling of contempt for you. They see you as worthless and/or despicable. Their contempt for you can cause them to lash out at you even when you are attempting to do good.

For a moment, please let us put ourselves in such a place. In America most Christians are still tolerated (although scorn seems to be the prevailing direction of our culture). In some countries scorn is the normal behavior toward any who claim they are Christian. It is so prevalent in some cultures that professing Christians have little, if any, hope of advancing in their culture. They are often among the poorest of the poor and opportunities to advance are simply not available to them.

Have you put yourself in such a place? How does it feel to be scorned? How would you respond if you were scorned because of your faith in Jesus? What feelings arise in you? Is it a sense of righteousness, of wanting to stand up and defend your beliefs, or perhaps aggressively confront them and "set the record straight"?

May & I would remind Christian married couples in conflict that one of them must take the spiritually "high" road (do not return evil for evil) if they wanted to move beyond their current circumstances. What if you were being scorned?

Do you think you would take the high road? What exactly is the high road you ask? Simple. Just as the scripture above tells us, "e glad in that day and leap for joy, for behold, your reward is great in heaven. For in the same way their fathers used to treat the prophets".

Consider it all joy? (James 1:2 (NASB) Consider it all joy, my brethren, when you encounter various trials

Father this is a another "tough" one. When we are personally attacked we often want to respond in kind. Lord, give us Your perspective and consider it a joy to be scorned for You. Thank You.

363.WHATEVER

Colossians 3:16-17 (NASB) Let the word of Christ richly dwell within you, with all wisdom teaching and admonishing one another with psalms and hymns and spiritual songs, singing with thankfulness in your hearts to God. Whatever you do in word or deed, do all in the name of the Lord Jesus, giving thanks through Him to God the Father.

The word "whatever" indicates a lack of restraint or restrictions. Everything is included and nothing is left out.

"The residents of Colossae were mainly Gentile of Greek descent, with a large Jewish group living there as well. The population was predominantly Greek, but there was a significant Jewish presence in the city." (AI)

Jew or Greek, it makes no difference. As Christians we live in cultures and subcultures that may or may not be supportive of our Christian beliefs and our walk of faith. So, when we read the words "whatever you do in word or deed," the cultural setting doesn't matter. Nor does your ethnic background, family, upbringing, troubles or blessing.

Neither does it matter how you naturally think about things or what you were taught before you became a Christian. Nor does it matter how much you want to do something (or not do something). Whatever (everything) must be done in the name of the Lord Jesus. Now this is a lot. It includes everything, even your thought life.

(LABC) Everything believers say and do should be carried out in the name of the Lord Jesus, with an awareness of His constant presence, bringing honor and glory to Him in every aspect of daily life. As it is written, "So whether you eat or drink or whatever you do, do it all for the glory of God" (1 Corinthians 10:31 NIV).

Lord God, this can only be done with the leading and enabling of Your Spirit. Please put to death whatever might be in me that does not bring glory to Your name. Thank You.

364.IMPOSTER

Luke 6:27-29 (NASB) But I say to you who hear, love your enemies, do good to those who hate you, bless those who curse you, pray for those who mistreat you. Whoever hits you on the cheek, offer him the other also; and whoever takes away your coat, do not withhold your shirt from him either.

For many years, I have reflected on Jesus' command to love our enemies. I agreed with it in principle, but honestly, I cannot claim that it has been evident in my own life. Nor, to my knowledge, is it evident in the church in America. In fact, I do not believe I have ever met a Christian who has been truly faithful to this command.

I have read about Christians who demonstrated love for their enemies even to the point of death. But I do not think I have ever met one. (Ghandi also claimed never to have met one.) How about you? Is it possible that those who love their enemies are the "real McCoy" and the rest of us are imposters?

I hope not. Clearly, there is a lesson here for us. Loving an enemy requires a grace that surpasses human capacity. The ability to do so is genuine evidence that we possess the divine nature Jesus is shaping within all believers.

To love a personal enemy (not some real or fictional person or situation "out there") is one of the most difficult things to do. How does one say, "I forgive you and I love you," while you are being beaten to death or suffering great humiliation or other terrifying circumstance? Is Jesus not clear that it is our responsibility?

When I hear or read about people causing harm and stress to others my natural inclination is to want to harm them. The opposite of what I am called to do as a believer. How about you?

Can we apply this scripture to our own lives? Can we begin in our homes, and families, and neighborhoods, by demonstrating love to those who annoy us or are not like us?

"When Jesus drives something home to you through His Word, don't try to evade it. If you do, you will become a religious imposter. Examine the things you tend simply to shrug your shoulders about, and where you have refused to be obedient, and you will know why you are not growing spiritually" (Excerpt From My Utmost for His Highest Oswald Chambers")

Father, is this not the most difficult command of all? Please, Lord, enable us to love those that we do not even like. Let there be no imposters among us. Thank You.

365.URGE

Romans 12:1 (NASB) Therefore I urge you, brethren, by the mercies of God, to present your bodies a living and holy sacrifice, acceptable to God, which is your spiritual service of worship.

In this life I think most of us prefer comfort over distress. We often grow and mature in times of stress and discomfort and yet, to be honest, I prefer times of comfort to times of stress. How about you?

The Greek word for "urge" in today's scripture is παρακαλέω (pronounced "parakaleo") and is used as an invitation or to implore (beg). So, the Apostle Paul is begging us to present ourselves as living and holy sacrifices. That same Greek word can also be translated as comfort. So Paul is saying a couple of things that are really important to living out the Christian life.

First, given who we have become in Christ (see "therefore in verse 1 above), we must make every effort to live like whom we have become. Second, true worship of God comes when we do.

What exactly is a "living and holy sacrifice acceptable to God"? I do not think the following encompasses everything but it is a good start:

(LABC) "WHAT IS SACRIFICIAL LIVING? Romans 12 offers an outline for breaking the world's mold. To put these directions in motion means going against the flow of society. …. The option is not whether we will conform; rather, the choice is to whom will we conform? Will our lives follow the pattern of this world or God's pattern? The following are components of God's pattern.

Offer our bodies: deliver both the inner and outer self into God's control. Divers and gymnasts know that where their head goes, the rest of their body will eventually follow.

Be nonconformists: consciously resisting the suggestions and pressures of the world around us.

Renew our minds: constantly ask God to teach us to think as he thinks. Estimate ourselves honestly having neither false humility nor inappropriate pride in our serving relationships with others.

Utilize our gifts: identify gifts to use to help others; find a purpose, a place, and a position to serve other believers.

I urge all of us to take these words seriously. It is never too late to renew our walk with Christ and today is a much better day than tomorrow.

To all of you who have encouraged me in writing these devotions, thank you, thank you, thank you. Please keep May and I in your prayers as we continue to number our days.

Father, thank you for the abundance of life and the comfort of Your sweet presence.

May went home to be with the Lord on January 4th 2025. Just a few months after I finished writing these devotions. I am in a season of grief that I was in no way prepared for. The depth of sorrow and sadness that comes with grief were beyond my understanding. Now that I stand in this place, more than ever I am thankful for knowing the God of all comfort. If I did not know Him I would surely wither away in self-pity.

But I do know my God, and though this is a difficult season, I am confident that the Lord will enable me not only to endure but to thrive. I do not know the number of my days, yet I am thankful that God is still at work in me and will bring His good work to completion.

My hope and prayer is that what is written in this book will encourage you to pursue God with all of your heart.

I can be reached at pgoeller@icloud.com

www.ingramcontent.com/pod-product-compliance
Lightning Source LLC
Chambersburg PA
CBHW060525150626
46550CB00020B/1350